MW00987948

Making Sense Together

Making Sense Together

The Intersubjective Approach to Psychotherapy

Peter Buirski, Ph.D.
and
Pamela Haglund, Psy.D.

A Jason Aronson Book

ROWMAN & LITTLEFIELD PUBLISHERS, INC.
Lanham • Boulder • New York • Toronto • Plymouth, UK

A JASON ARONSON BOOK

ROWMAN & LITTLEFIELD PUBLISHERS, INC.

Published in the United States of America
by Rowman & Littlefield Publishers, Inc.
A wholly owned subsidiary of The Rowman & Littlefield Publishing Group, Inc.
4501 Forbes Boulevard, Suite 200, Lanham, Maryland 20706
www.rowmanlittlefield.com

Estover Road
Plymouth PL6 7PY
United Kingdom

British Library Cataloguing in Publication Information Available

Library of Congress Cataloging-in-Publication Data

Buirski, Peter.
Making sense together : the intersubjective approach to psychotherapy / by Peter Buirski & Pamela Haglund.
p. cm.
Includes bibliographical references and index.
ISBN 0-7657-0314-9
1. Intersubjectivity. 2. Psychoanalysis. 3. Psychotherapist and patient.
I. Haglund, Pamela. II. Title

RC506 .B84 2001
616.89'17—dc21 00-052204

Printed in the United States of America

™ The paper used in this publication meets the minimum requirements of American National Standard for Information Sciences—Permanence of Paper for Printed Library Materials, ANSI/NISO Z39.48-1992.

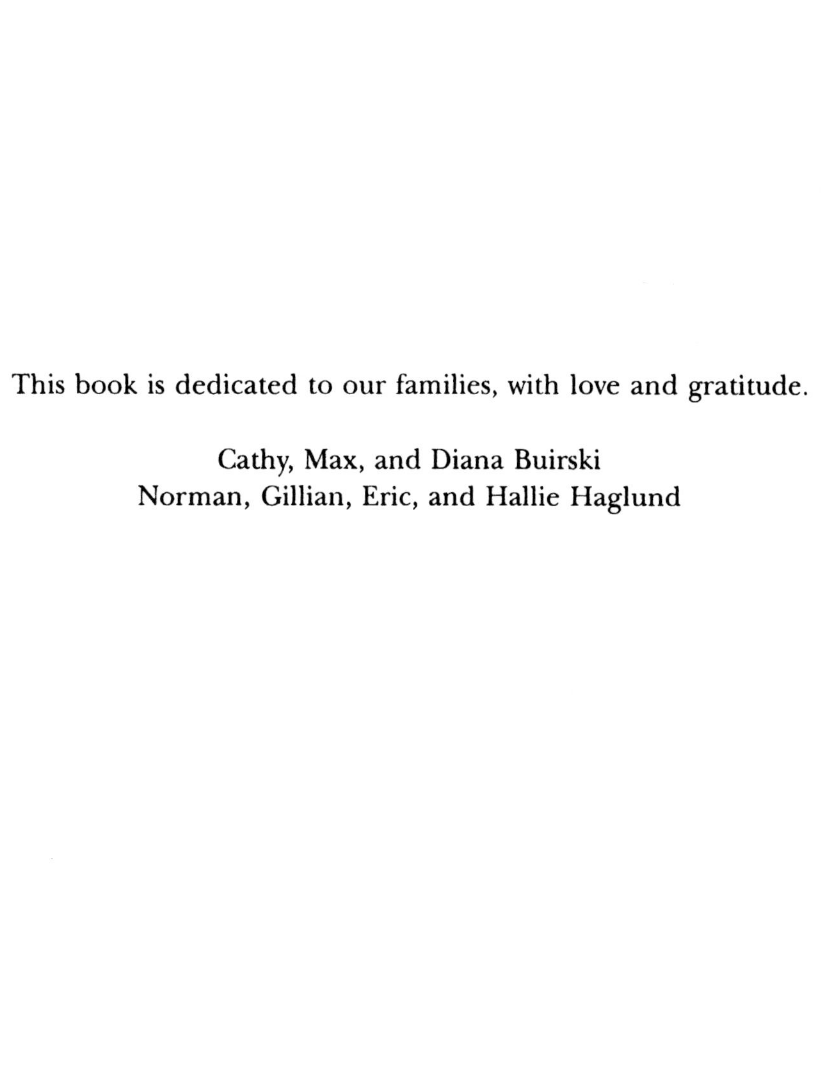

This book is dedicated to our families, with love and gratitude.

Cathy, Max, and Diana Buirski
Norman, Gillian, Eric, and Hallie Haglund

Psychoanalytic understanding is making sense *together.*

Donna Orange, *Emotional Understanding*

Contents

Foreword*

In my view, the singularly most important development in psychoanalysis (and by extension, psychotherapy) at the turn of the millennium is its ongoing liberation from the philosophical shackles that Freud inherited from Descartes. The fundamental assumptions of Freudian psychoanalysis were saturated with the Cartesian doctrine of the isolated mind. This doctrine bifurcates the subjective world into outer and inner regions, reifies the resulting separation between the two, and pictures the mind as an objective entity that takes its place among other objects, a "thinking thing" that has an inside with contents and looks out on an external world from which it is radically estranged. Cartesian philosophy, with its myth of the isolated mind, has until recently maintained a stranglehold on psychoanalytical thought.

---

*Adapted from the article "From Isolated Minds to Experiential Worlds: An Intersubjective Space Odyssey" in the *American Journal of Psychotherapy* 54:149–151, copyright © 2000. Reprinted with permission of the Association for the Advancement of Psychotherapy.

During the past two decades, a number of viewpoints have appeared that seek, in varying degrees, to emancipate psychoanalytic theory from the grip of Cartesian, isolated-mind thinking. Among such evolving efforts to create a post-Cartesian psychoanalytic theory are Kohutian self psychology, American relational theory, and the intersubjective systems theory developed by my collaborators and me. From our intersubjective perspective, clinical phenomena, such as psychopathological states, transferences, resistances, and negative therapeutic reactions are grasped, not as products of intrapsychic mechanisms originating within the interior of the patient's isolated mind, but as taking form at the interface of the interacting experimental worlds of patient and therapist. Even the very boundary between conscious and unconscious—the so-called repression barrier—is understood, both developmentally and in the therapeutic situation, not as a fixed intrapsychic structure, but as a fluidly shifting property of an ongoing intersubjective system.

In place of the Freudian unconscious—a sealed-off, underground chamber of the Cartesian isolated mind—we envision a multiply contextualized experimental world, an organized totality of lived personal experience, more or less conscious and more or less contoured according to those organizing principles formed in a lifetime of emotional and relational experience. Instead of a Cartesian container, we picture an experiential system of expectations, interpretive patterns, and meanings, especially those formed in the contexts of psychological trauma. Within such a system or world, one can feel and know certain things, often repetitively and with unshakable certainty. Whatever one is not able to feel or know falls outside the horizons of a person's experiential world, requiring no container. One is always organizing one's emotional and relational experiences so as to exclude whatever feels unacceptable, intolerable, or too dangerous in a particular intersubjective context.

In this view, psychoanalytic therapy is no longer an archaeological excavation of deeper layers of an isolated unconscious mind. Instead, it is a dialogic exploration of a patient's experiential world, conducted with an awareness of the unavertable contribution of the therapist's experiential world to the ongoing exploration. Such inquiry seeks comprehension of the principles that prereflectively organize the patient's world and that keep the patient's experiencing confined to its limiting horizons. By illuminating such principles in a dialogic context, psychoanalytic therapy aims to expand the patient's experiential horizons, thereby opening up the possibility of an enriched, more complex, and more flexible emotional life.

In essence, we are recasting psychoanalysis as a contextual psychology, which recognizes the constitutive role of relatedness in the making of all experience. Experiential worlds and intersubjective fields are seen to mutually constitute one another. Unlike Cartesian isolated minds, experiential words, as they form and evolve within a nexus of living, relational systems, are recognized as being exquisitely context sensitive and context dependent. The Cartesian bifurcation is mended, and inner and outer are seen to interweave seamlessly.

The dialogic nature of psychoanalytic inquiry is captured beautifully by the title of the present volume, *Making Sense Together*. Buirski and Haglund have done us all a great service by providing a superb introductory text presenting the basic ideas of intersubjectivity theory in clear, down-to-earth, user-friendly language that will be very accessible and extremely valuable to students and trainees in psychotherapy. The rich clinical illustrations make the intersubjective perspective come alive for the reader. *Making Sense Together* will be enormous help to therapists in their efforts to explore hitherto uncharted regions of intersubjective space.

—Robert D. Stolorow

Preface

This book is intended for students of the psychotherapeutic process and particularly those interested in the intersubjective perspective. In our own professional development we have followed many paths that have led us to the point of writing this book. We have been patients in psychotherapy and psychoanalysis, students in graduate and postgraduate training programs, and teachers of psychoanalytic theory and practice to graduate psychology students and candidates in analytic training.

We were both first exposed to psychoanalytic theory and treatment from the perspective of ego psychology. Over the years our thinking and practice have evolved. We have found that arriving at a theory of practice has been an ongoing, long-term evolutionary process. Like being a patient in psychotherapy, becoming a psychotherapist is a highly personal experience of deepening self-awareness. There are times of anxiety, dread, and self-doubt, as well as times of hope, confidence, and joy in the mutuality of the endeavor. Growth occurs slowly, incrementally, and imperceptibly, over long periods of time.

Our experience is that becoming a psychotherapist is indeed an unfolding process of lifelong learning, like becoming an adult. There is no quick, short-term strategy to reach a final, fully formed developmental stage. In raising children, each unique parent and child pair emerges from the ongoing, mutually influencing relationship, that exists within a complex context of a given cultural, historical, and socioeconomic climate. So it is with evolving as a psychotherapist. Imagine if parents and children functioned like a managed care family: "You have ten years to grow up and that's it." Unfortunately, the context in which we currently work and write places this kind of demand on therapists and patients.

Our original training was in ego psychology and we have grown into intersubjectivity theory over many years. Our theoretical evolution was influenced more by a dawning realization that our practice had changed in ways no longer consistent with our original theory. Over time, we found ourselves more focused on the quality of our relationship with our patients. More and more it seemed that what patients experienced as most helpful was not insight, but the accepting and affirming nature of the relationship that had been constructed. In fact, we realized that we could remember very few of the interpretations our analysts gave us. When we reflected on what was helpful in our own treatments, what stood out was some aspect of personal engagement with our analysts.

With intersubjectivity theory, we have found a sound theoretical approach that matches the ways we feel comfortable practicing. It makes sense to us and we hope it will make sense to the reader.

Acknowledgments

We have tried to accurately cite the writers whose work has influenced our thinking. However, thoughts and ideas often have a lineage for which there are no DNA markers. Many of "our" ideas have their roots in our relationships with patients, therapists, supervisors, teachers, and friends. So much of our thinking has been shaped by these relationships that we are not certain whom to credit for what. Therefore, we would like to thank those who have influenced our understanding in ways too nonspecific to enumerate.

Peter Buirski is grateful to Elliot Adler, Ph.D., Cathy Krown Buirski, M.S.W., Harold Cook, Ph.D., Abe Fenster, Ph.D., Max Geller, Ph.D., David Hurst, M.D., Amanda Kottler, M.A., Frank Lachmann, Ph.D., Louise McDonald, M.D., Norman Portnoy, Ph.D., Lynn Rosdal, Psy.D., Betsy Rubin, Ph.D., Robert Shapiro, Ph.D., Ruth Shapiro, Ph.D., and Stanley Teitelbaum, Ph.D.

Pamela Haglund wishes to thank Earlene Dal Pozzo, M.D., Ralph Fisch, Ph.D., Norman Haglund, J.D., Mitch Handelsman,

Ph.D., Betsy Rubin, Ph.D., Karen Rosica, Psy.D., Ann Sartori, Psy.D., Liz Shane, Psy.D., and Barbara Unger, Ph.D.

The students we have taught and supervised at the Graduate School of Professional Psychology at the University of Denver have also shaped our understanding of the psychotherapy process. Many of our clinical examples are drawn from our work together. These have been important formative relationships for us, and we would like to thank Susan Albers, Dina Elias, Robin Eskey, Amy Favero, Victoria Gould, Mary Mikhail, Mike Monroe, Anne Reckling, Martha Ryan, Rod Schmidt, Suzanne Shaker, Trish Short, Katie Snipes, Elaine Stando, and especially H. C. Brunette, who courageously participated in our supervision experiment and co-authored Chapter 9 with us.

We would like to thank those who provided indispensable assistance in bringing this project to fruition: Tracie Kruse for structuring our time, guarding the door, and ensuring us quiet time to work; John Kirk, Cara Latazorri, and Caroline Martin, who transcribed videotaped therapy sessions; and Lynn Tran and Vincent Diep at the Hong Kong Café whose hospitality and culinary nurturance enabled us to occupy a table for hours on end where much of this book was thought through.

We would especially like to thank Robert Stolorow, Ph.D., whose support and encouragement for this project has been very meaningful to us.

Finally, we are indebted to those individuals whose anonymity we need to preserve, who have shared their intimate lives with us and are coconstructors of this book.

Introduction

Intersubjectivity is a construct that is found in the thinking of a variety of psychoanalytic theorists, such as Aron, Benjamin, Mitchell, Ogden, Stern, and Stolorow, who use it to describe their vision of the relational dimension of the psychoanalytic process. However, all of these important contributors have come to intersubjectivity from their own theoretical and philosophical traditions, attribute their own unique meanings to intersubjectivity, and apply it in their own particular way. Unfortunately, space and time do not permit us to discuss the various meanings that these theorists apply to intersubjectivity. (See Teicholz 1999a, and *Psychoanalytic Dialogues* 10(2), 2000, for discussions of some of the various uses of the term *intersubjectivity.*)

Our interest has been drawn to the work of Stolorow, Atwood, Brandchaft, Orange, and other like-minded colleagues and collaborators and their particular understanding of intersubjectivity. Briefly, this view is founded on two assumptions: that our subjectivity (our moment-by-moment experience of ourselves and the world) emerges within a dynamic, fluid context of interfacing subjectivities, and that we can never completely bracket our subjectivities to observe things as they "really" exist. This book then grows out of the personal meanings that this view of intersubjectivity has for us. Our view is in no way meant to diminish the significance and importance of the contributions of other theorists. It is just that intersubjectivity, as it has been elaborated and articulated by Stolorow, Atwood, Brandchaft, and Orange, speaks to us most clearly. Therefore, when we discuss intersubjectivity throughout this book, we are referring to the particular meanings and understandings that we have derived from that body of literature. While we locate ourselves and this book within this psychoanalytic tradition, we do not presume that others in this tradition will agree with all we have said.

Intersubjectivity theory is to us a modern relational psychoanalytic theory. Like other nonstatic psychoanalytic theories, intersubjectivity theory and practice are continually under construction, being elaborated and refined over time. We hope that this book will contribute to the evolution, development, and dissemination of this intersubjective perspective.

This book discusses how our intersubjective perspective informs, shapes, and guides the psychotherapeutic process. We have developed our ideas using as little technical jargon as possible. However, each theory speaks in its own specialized language and requires its own vocabulary. Therefore, becoming fluent in the language of intersubjectivity theory requires adjusting one's ear to new terms and concepts. Sometimes familiar terms and concepts are used in new ways with new meanings. This is an unfortunate source of confusion, and, where possible, we have tried to use nontraditional words to indicate different meanings. For example, we prefer the term *articulation* to *interpretation*. Even though both refer to the therapist's verbal intervention, by articulation we intend something different from the traditional meanings ascribed to interpretation.

We begin, in Chapter 1, "Subjectivity and Intersubjectivity," with an overview of the theory of intersubjectivity. We introduce the language of intersubjectivity and describe the fundamental concepts. Theory necessarily informs practice and Chapter 1 provides the framework for later chapters on practice.

Chapter 2, "The Intersubjective Sensibility," addresses some of the fundamental assumptions we make about the nature of treatment and the organization of psychopathology. In addition to the theory of mind, this chapter describes our mindset as we approach the treatment situation.

Chapter 3, "Understanding the Patient's State of Mind: Affect Attunement and the Empathic-Introspective Stance," discusses the centrality of affect in personality formation and malformation. We describe the therapist's primary listening stance, distinguishing it from the activity of responding to affect.

Chapter 4, "The Centrality of Relationship," addresses the importance of the therapist–patient relationship and its significance within the intersubjective perspective. In this chapter we subscribe to a revised view of the traditional notion of "transference."

Chapter 5, "Practicing Intersubjectively," offers an overview of the practice of psychotherapy from the intersubjective perspective. We offer a variety of practice guidelines for beginning therapists and those new to working from this particular intersubjective perspective.

Chapter 6, "The Articulation of Subjective Experience," discusses the articulation of the patient's subjective experience. We provide a verbatim transcript edited from two sessions with explication of the therapist's interventions.

Chapter 7, "The Antidote Dimension of the Therapy Relationship," highlights a particular, common aspect of the therapeutic relationship that has not received much attention.

Chapter 8, "Expanding the Field: Intersubjectivity Theory and Supervision," offers our thoughts on the supervision process. While supervision typically focuses on either the patient or the therapist, from the intersubjective perspective the supervisor is inevitably part of the treatment context, and supervision must address the entire intersubjective field formed by the mutually influencing subjectivities of supervisor, supervisee, and patient.

Chapter 9, "The Treatment of a Patient from the Intersubjective Perspective," provides a lengthy case report of the first year of treatment of a 40-year-old man. This case report, written with H. C. Brunette, summarizes her treatment of this man, which was simultaneously supervised by both Buirski and Haglund. We provide extensive verbatim material and commentary on the treatment.

Translating theory into practice involves the very processes we explore in this book. That is, we necessarily view the evolving body of intersubjectivity theory from our own subjectivities and within our individual contexts as supervisors and practitioners. Not surprisingly, the very process of writing this book, which grew out of our collaborating and intersecting subjectivities, has influenced our understanding and practice. As we are limited by our subjectivities, we hope to encourage future thinking and discussion on the application of intersubjectivity theory to the practice of psychotherapy, and we look forward to what will emerge from this dialogue.

1

Subjectivity and Intersubjectivity

Psychoanalytic theories of mind consist of comprehensive explanations of human behavior and motivation. Such theories seek to account for normal and abnormal development at both the population and individual levels, but these abstract and global ideas can seem distant from our personal, moment-by-moment, lived experience. Intersubjectivity theory has reformulated psychological concepts of why people act, feel, and behave the way they do in terms that directly capture our internal and relational experiences. This book discusses these compelling ideas and demonstrates how these concepts apply to the practice of psychotherapy. This chapter unravels the paradox that intersubjectivity presupposes subjectivity and subjectivity presupposes intersubjectivity.

A central organizing concept of intersubjectivity theory is that our experience of ourselves is fundamental to how we operate in the world. Our subjective experience is the phenomenology of all that one might be aware of at any given moment and much of what is out of awareness, as well. Over time, the complex interweaving of individual abilities and temperament, relational configurations with caregivers during infancy and childhood, and the lucky or harsh realities of one's life circumstances converge to form patterns. These patterns of experiencing oneself and the world describe our subjective, personal reality and become structured as our organizations of experience. In treatment we hope to understand these patterns in the context of a relationship that becomes a new lived experience and the basis of new organizing patterns.

All psychoanalytic theories of personality begin with some conception of the central motivational constructs that underlie both normal and pathological human behavior. For example, Freudian theory sees human motivation as deriving from the instinctual drives of sex and aggression, while modern relational theories typically view motivation as springing from some need to create or maintain bonds to others.

Along with other modern relational theories, developments in self psychology and intersubjectivity theory point to the inadequacy of earlier psychoanalytic conceptions of motivation to explain human psychology. In work that has had a strong impact on intersubjectivity theory, Lichtenberg (1989) has observed that "motivations arise solely from *lived experience*" (p. 2). Human motivations, whether for food, sexual gratification, or attachment (Lichtenberg posits five motivational systems), serve to promote, maintain, or restore a fundamental sense of self-cohesion. "Lived experience is about how we human beings consciously and unconsciously seek to fulfill our needs and desires by searching in potential events for affects that signal for us that experiential fulfillment" (p. 2).

By affects we are referring, in everyday language, to how one feels. Affects are emotions that refer to a subjective "state of mind or condition of arousal" (McWilliams 1999, p. 103). As signals, emotions alert us to our needs and our desires and, along with our sensory perceptions and our beliefs and ideas, constitute the "stuff" of immediate experience. Emotions guide us and inform us about matters of survival, safety, and satisfaction. We now recognize the important role of affects in organizing experience, and therefore as the core of subjective experience. From this perspective, the central motivational construct for intersubjectivity theory now stresses the role of affect rather than drive.

Lichtenberg (1989) further states "The vitality of the motivational experience will depend initially on the manner in which exchanges between infants and their caregivers unfold" (p. 2). He points us to the contextual nature of our emotions. Whatever our needs and the emotions associated with them, we initially experienced them in the earliest caregiving relationships. As Stolorow and Atwood (1992) make clear, "The 'affective core of the self' (Emde 1983) derives from the person's history of intersubjective transactions, and thus the shift from drive to affect resituates the psychoanalytic theory of motivation squarely within the realm of the intersubjective" (p. 26).

We have begun this book with a focus on affectivity, and will devote part of Chapter 3 to the subject because it is both a central organizing construct in intersubjectivity theory and the fundamental organizer of subjective experience. The generation, regulation, and integration of affect occur within an intersubjective context, and we will trace the thread of affectivity as it is woven throughout intersubjectivity theory and treatment.

Psychoanalytic theories can be characterized by their distinctive domains of inquiry, treatment aims, and investigatory stances (Stolorow 1994a). This chapter examines intersubjectivity theory from the perspective of its particular domain of inquiry, treatment aims, investigatory stance, and the central role of affectivity in each of these areas.

DOMAIN OF INQUIRY

Intersubjectivity theory is an evolving body of knowledge, the central focus of which is the psychology of human subjectivity.

Unlike Freudian theory, which has its roots in the medical sciences and takes as its object of study the interaction of mental and biological processes within the mind of the individual, intersubjectivity theory concerns itself with the field created by the interplay of worlds of subjective experience and personal meanings.

Focusing as it does on the patient's patterns of construing and making sense of his personal world, intersubjectivity theory attends to subjective experience. The therapist informed by intersubjectivity theory does not necessarily listen for personality structures associated with psychosexual stages of development, for derivatives of drives or conflicts, or for unconscious motives, defenses, or resistance. Through the intersubjective lens, patients are not viewed as trying to hide or dress themselves up. Rather, their presentations are seen as dynamic solutions to the universal problems of managing affect within their individual developmental contexts. By appreciating this adaptive solution and the complex system from which it emerged, the striving for health rather than the pathology of the patient's experience is affirmed. When the therapist responds from this perspective, the patient can feel more real to himself and more trusting in his perceptions and his own experience.

Before we can explore intersubjectivity, the complex field that is created when two or more individuals with their unique subjectivities come together, we must first examine the nature of human subjectivity. Intersubjectivity theory assumes that one's experience of oneself and the world is the fundamental focus of psychoanalytic inquiry. This assertion means that the personal ways in which we have come to view and experience ourselves, both privately, within our skin, and as we move about among others, are all that can be understood through the psychoanalytic dialogue. As straightforward as this statement seems, it is the basis for a theoretical revolution in psychoanalysis. No longer are universal assumptions about developmental imperatives and crises imposed on the patient's unfolding story. Gone is the belief that the therapist holds a privileged, objectively "true" perspective on the reality and meaning of the patient's experience. Rather, the overarching psychological construct is the validity and reality of the patient's perspective, his subjective experience.

Human subjectivity becomes organized into patterns based on repeated emotional experience within the child–caregiver dyad. The creation of such patterns, irreducibly embedded in the emotional quality of formative life experience with parents and caregivers, constitutes the sense of subjective experience (Orange et al. 1997). Such patterns are the scaffold on which the coherence and continuity of experience depend. Because this structure is considered essential to psychological functioning, Stolorow and colleagues (1994) have included it in their understanding of an important source of human motivation. As they observe, "The *need to maintain the organization of experience* is a central motive in the patterning of human action" (p. 35).

Human infants require sensitive care by others who take pleasure in their health, comfort, and well-being. Ideally, a system develops in which both infant and caregiver expect that the needs of the child will be met in ways that are satisfying to both. However, whatever quality of care is given, the developing child organizes those patterns of experience into expectations for the future. Without generating expectancies, experience is random and unmanageable, and every new circumstance would require new learning. Part of human adaptation involves the ability to organize experience into meaningful patterns. These patterns, or organizations of experience, contribute to the essence of subjectivity and the sense of a cohesive self.

Intersubjectivity theory recognizes that the therapist's understanding of the patient's experience is inescapably circumscribed by the therapist's own subjectivity. Therefore, while striving to comprehend the patient's view of the world through the patient's eyes, the therapist must be tentative and nonauthoritarian regarding what she believes she understands about the patient's subjective reality. By holding this perspective of fallibility, the therapist facilitates the opportunity for expanding the subjectivities of both patient and therapist. That is, the potential for new patterns to emerge exists for both the therapist and the patient, and these new patterns may develop in the organizations of their subjective experience when their archaically formed (that is, formed during childhood) organizing principles are disconfirmed in the treatment relationship.

Making subjective experience and its construction in intersubjective contexts central to the theory of personality and treatment is what distinguishes intersubjectivity theory from other psychoanalytic theories. In traditional psychoanalytic theory, the focus of attention is on the intrapsychic life of the individual. Psychological phenomena are understood in terms of the interaction and conflict between the three mental structures—id, ego, and superego. According to Brenner (1982), one of the leading theorists of the modern Freudian tradition, "The fabric of psychic life as we know it is woven of drive derivatives, of anxiety and depressive affect, of defense, and of superego manifestations" (p. 252). He then goes on to make this global yet questionable statement: "Compromise formations arising from psychic conflict comprise virtually all of psychic life which is of emotional significance to us" (p. 252). This kind of thinking illustrates what Stolorow and Atwood (1992) refer to as "the myth of the isolated mind" (p. 7).

The myth of the isolated mind portrays the human mind as existing independent from the physical world and the world of others. For psychoanalysis, the myth of the isolated mind finds its expression in Freud's view of the mind as a "mental apparatus," a drive-discharge, tension-reducing machine. In ego psychology, the myth of the isolated mind is expressed in the value placed on the achievement of separation and autonomous mental functioning. The notion of the isolated mind not only finds expression in metapsychology but is deeply embedded in psychoanalytic technique. The traditional concepts of neutrality, abstinence, the purity of the transference field, the focus on regression, the idea that associations can be free, and the conviction that transference must be resolved before termination are examples of the way that a fundamental assumption about the isolated mind can infuse and influence psychoanalytic practice. The unexamined acceptance of isolated mind notions even underlies education and training in psychoanalysis. It was once a common practice at institutes of the American Psychoanalytic Association to assign candidates in training to their training analysts. The myth of the isolated mind can readily be seen behind this practice—the assumption that analysts are interchangeable and that any skillful analyst can serve as the opaque screen onto which patients can displace and project their inner life. In this earlier theory, the notion was that the major function of the *relationship* between patient and analyst was to establish the working alliance. *Relationship* became a technique to be employed by one isolated mind upon another.

Much of post-Freudian theorizing has been, in one form or another, an effort to counteract this isolated mind construct. Winnicott's (1965) famous dictum that there is no such thing as a baby without a mother and Sullivan's (1964) similar idea, "Personality is made manifest in interpersonal situations, and not otherwise" (p. 32), are examples of early formulations of the relational nature of the mind. The characterizations of traditional psychoanalytic treatment as "one-person" in contrast to the "two-person" view of modern relational thinking and the systems view of intersubjectivity theory have been ways that this paradigm shift has been conceptualized. Expanding on this multiperson direction in theory, Stolorow and Atwood (1992) state, "The concept of an intersubjective system brings to focus both the individual's world of inner experience and its embeddedness with other such worlds in a continual flow of reciprocal mutual influence" (p. 18).

For intersubjectivity theory, then, psychological phenomena form, not in the isolated mind of the individual, but in an intersubjective context. This intersubjective context refers to the reciprocal experiences of mutual influence between two or more subjectivities. When two or more people come together in relationship, for instance the child and the caregivers or the patient and therapist, each brings his or her own world of subjective experience to the interaction. Together, they create a field, or a dynamic system, that contributes to the subjective experience of the other. Intersubjectivity theory takes as its domain of inquiry the field created by the interplay of these subjectivities. Thus, broadly speaking, intersubjectivity theory is a dynamic systems theory.

Beebe and Lachmann (1998) address the organization of a dyad in a systems paradigm, first by examining mother–infant interactions and then generalizing these findings to the therapy situation. According to their formulation, "A theory of interaction must specify how each person is affected both by his own behavior, that is *self-regulation,* as well as by the partner's behavior, that is *interactive* (mutual) *regulation.* Each person must both monitor the partner and regulate the inner state" (p. 482). Self-regulation refers to the person's capacity to regulate or control internal states, such as affectivity, arousal, or responsiveness. Interactive or mutual regulation refers to the extent that each person influences the other, though not necessarily to the same degree (what Aron [1996] has described as mutual but not symmetrical). The significant point is that, for infants and adults, the way one self-regulates will impact the other, which will have a reciprocal impact on the experience of self. Infant research has demonstrated remarkable examples of mutual influence. In one study of electroencephalogram patterns of 10-month-old infants shown a video of a laughing or crying actress, the infants' brains were positively or negatively activated in correspondence to the affect on screen (Davidson and Fox 1982). This phenomenon of matching affective patterns holds true for adults as well: perceiving the affective state of the other produces a similar state in oneself. As Beebe and Lachmann (1998) put it, "As two partners match each other's affective patterns, each recreates in himself a psychophysiological state similar to that of the partner, thus participating in the subjective state of the other" (p. 490). This capacity for two people to match and mutually influence each other's internal affect states has important implications for the role of empathy in psychotherapeutic treatment.

In individual psychotherapy, the system encompasses the field created by the coming together of the subjective worlds of the patient and the therapist. While it is impossible to identify all components of the system, since each system is unique, some of the likely shared components include the personal worlds of subjective experience of both, the situational and cultural contexts that encompass the system, and the interacting organizations of experience. Not surprisingly, the psychoanalytic theory of the therapist, with its assumptions and inferences, is an integral part of the context and impinges on the overall system. We will develop this further at a later point.

Individual therapy can be considered a dynamic dyadic system, and a very complex one at that. The variables that might affect the system are too numerous and their interaction too complicated to thoroughly specify. Think of a pool table, where the path of the cue ball will be deflected by even minor contact with any other ball. Now imagine how such obvious variables as the age, gender, religion, race, and attractiveness of one might affect the subjective experience of the other. Given our exquisite sensitivity to the influence of others, we suggest that the powerful intersubjective field created in psychotherapy is a context in which both participants will inevitably be influenced and changed.

It is important always to bear in mind that while we stress subjective experience, such subjective experience is continually being constructed in the present out of the past experience of the individual and the current context in which she finds herself. "One's personal reality is *always* codetermined by features of the surround and the unique meanings into which these are assimilated" (Stolorow and Atwood 1992, p. 21). For instance, if the patient's experience while growing up was of an aloof, demanding, and critical father, then this particular set of experiences will contribute to shaping her view of herself and her expectations of relationships with others in the present. Furthermore, the specific ways in which the events, affects, and bodily sensations associated with these experiences of "father" came to be organized and understood in their original context will contribute to the highly specific subjective meaning of new "father-like" contexts in the present.

Note that in the preceding paragraph we referred to the patient's *experience* of the father, rather than to what the father "actually was." The reason for this semantic distinction is that, from the intersubjective perspective, the tools of psychoanalytic psychotherapy do not permit us to know another's reality in any objective sense. We cannot know how the father really was with his daughter; we can only know the daughter's subjective experience of her father as she communicates it to the therapist today. This has on occasion been misunderstood as implying that intersubjectivity theory holds that there is no objective reality (Kriegman 1998). This is certainly not the case. What intersubjectivity theory maintains is that objective reality is not knowable or accessible through utilizing the empathic-introspective stance of psychoanalytic psychotherapy (Stolorow 1998). One can learn all about the physical reality of a crème brûlée by applying the principles and experimental techniques of physics and chemistry to analyzing its composition. But another person's experience of the crème brûlée can be understood only from a report of her subjective experience of it. It was too rich, too sweet, and too thin—for her taste. Others might experience it differently. As therapists, we can never know what our patient's father was really like. After all, our patient's older brother, mother, and dog might have experienced him differently. Thus, all that is knowable in psychoanalytic psychotherapy, and therefore its principal domain of inquiry, is subjective experience—the subjective experience of the patient and that of the therapist, and the intersubjective field created at the interface of these subjectivities.

The intersubjective emphasis on subjective experience is in contrast to the traditional psychoanalytic position that the therapist, by virtue of her vantage point and her training, has a uniquely objective view of the patient's experience. Such an objectivist stance assumes that the therapist can make observations about the patient's experience that are not colored by the therapist's own unconscious organizing principles (Orange et al. 1997). For the intersubjective theorist, all human experience is embedded in relational systems. One cannot escape the emotional impact of the person of the therapist on the relationship with the patient. The therapist's own unconscious organization of experience, as well as her theory of mind, must color her perceptions of and reactions to the patient. When the patient says that the crème brûlée is too sweet, all the therapist can know is what "too sweet" means to her. Therefore, each patient–therapist pair is unique, formed within the intersubjective field created by the coming together of their two unique subjectivities. The interfacing subjectivities converge around the idea of "too sweet," although neither knows exactly what "too sweet" tastes like to the other. It follows that the course of any treatment will be unique to the specific pair engaged in the process.

TREATMENT AIMS

According to Stolorow and colleagues (1987), "The fundamental goal of psychoanalytic therapy is the unfolding, illumination, and transformation of the patient's subjective world" (p. 9). To approach this goal, the therapist who operates with an awareness of the intersubjective nature of psychological processes must provide an environment in which the patient's world of subjective experience is able to unfold. This environment includes the ambiance of the setting, the empathic-introspective listening stance of the therapist, and the relationship created between the two of them. In addition to these factors, many unforeseen elements arising from the histories and the organization of experience of each participant contribute to the context. "Analyst and patient form an indissoluble psychological system, and . . . neither can, without violence to the integrity of the analytic experience, be studied alone" (Orange et al. 1997, p. 76). During the course of treatment, the attuned therapist explores and draws attention to the impact of these subtleties on the treatment. Essentially, the patient and therapist together create the environment in which a therapeutic dialogue can occur. It is through this dialogue that the patient's story will unfold.

A second task of the intersubjective approach to therapy is to illuminate, to shed new light on, the patient's subjective experience and the personal meanings the patient has made of it. Intersubjectivity theory draws heavily on the hermeneutic tradition (Atwood and Stolorow 1984). Hermeneutics originally referred to the theory of interpretation of religious texts. It has subsequently been applied to the interpretation and understanding of human subjectivity. When we investigate human subjectivity, our focus is on personal meanings. Man is a meaning maker and humans create meaning out of their subjective experience. Meanings made of today's experience influence the meaning made of subsequent experience. Therefore, we must expand our domain of inquiry to include not just subjective experience, but the meaning each person makes of her subjective experience and the impact of that meaning on further experience.

Meaning itself is a multifaceted phenomenon, emerging from within the treatment context. Any context consists of an array of factors that the participants—in this instance, patient and therapist—separately organize to make sense of their experience. So, as with the hermeneutic tradition in the interpretation of religious texts, in psychotherapy the meaning we seek to illuminate is dependent on the context. Simultaneously, features of the context are selectively organized within our subjectivity, conforming to prereflective patterns. In a continuously interpenetrating process, meaning influences subjectivity and subjectivity selectively organizes context. Illumination is a process of focusing and understanding the elements (affective, cognitive, and relational) in the foreground at any given time.

For our patient who experienced her father as aloof, demanding, and critical, it is not enough to understand that this was her experience of him. We must also be concerned with understanding the meaning she made of her experience with him, in other words, how she structured or organized her experience of herself in relation to her father. Did she consider herself to be uninteresting or unappealing? After all, her father spent much more time playing with her brother and the dog. Might she have concluded that she was deficient or lacking? After all, her father seemed to set higher expectations for her brother. Could she have determined that she was worthless because her father tended to dismiss or devalue her efforts?

Continuing with our example of our patient and her father, we said above that "all that is knowable in psychoanalytic psychotherapy . . . is subjective experience." But one's subjective experience and the meaning made of it are not static—they are active and evolving. The past is as we experience it today. In therapy, as self-understanding grows, as the patient develops greater self-cohesion and enhanced capacity to listen to others empathically, her experience of the past will change. In a dynamic system, when one part changes, the whole system is thrown into disequilibrium and subsequently forced to accommodate to what is new. In psychotherapy, then, when the patient's organization of experience changes, her relationship to others, whether in memory or in her present, also changes. In this way, subjective experience can be transformed and new meanings can be constructed. For example, the father who was characterized as aloof, demanding, and critical at the beginning of treatment might be experienced later as a well-intentioned and concerned man whose own harsh and impoverished childhood led him to prepare his daughter for the cruel world of his experience by promoting self-reliance and self-sufficiency in her.

We used the illustration of individual psychotherapy to examine the complexity of the intersubjective field created by the interaction of patient and therapist. But the context can multiply the complexity, like placing more balls on the pool table for the cue ball to engage. Let's complicate the intersubjective field by introducing a supervisor into the therapy mix. In individual therapy done under supervision, the field would now include the impact of the supervisor on the system (Buirski and Monroe 2000). Furthermore, if the treatment were audio- or videotaped, the system would expand to include the real or imagined listeners. We can anticipate how the watchful eye or keen ear of the supervisor might impact both patient and therapist. However, the meaning that each makes of the experience of being observed might be quite different, depending on the organization of experience of each individual. For example, the patient might experience deep shame at revealing his flawed, devalued self-organization, while the therapist might fear being seen as hopelessly inept and uneducable.

In contrast to some other psychoanalytic theories that search for the presumed absolute or universal principles underlying human nature, intersubjectivity theory makes no such assumptions about the nature of human experience. We do not strive to fit a person's subjective experience into preexisting theoretical frameworks, such as id, ego, superego, depressive and schizoid positions, or stages of separation-individuation. Rather, these formulations are viewed as metaphors that may be helpful in understanding some people some of the time. Instead, intersubjectivity theory concerns itself with the way in which people form patterns or organize or structure their experience. According to Atwood and Stolorow (1984), "The basic units of analysis for our investigations of personality are *structures of experience*—the distinctive configurations of self and object that shape and organize a person's subjective world" (p. 33).

To say that experience is structured simply means that people organize and give meaning to the recurrent patterns or themes that emerge from their formative relationships with caregivers and other significant players in their lives. These patterns or themes or structures of experience are now generally referred to as organizing principles because they function as the emotional framework around which self-concept and self-esteem are built. In the example of the patient with the aloof, demanding, and critical father, she organized, or made sense of, her experience by concluding that she must be fundamentally defective and unworthy of love. It is important to bear in mind that the concept of organizing principles contains both cognitive and affective components. For the patient in the example above, her organizing principles concern both the idea that she is defective and unworthy of love and the painful affects of shame and self-loathing that are at the core of this organization of experience.

Another young woman had organized her experience around the idea that she lived under a black cloud that shrouded her life in bad luck. She was convinced that only disappointment and hurt would come to her if she reached for anything or anyone, and she was without hope for the future. After several years of treatment in which this organization of experience was identified and discussed, she met an attractive man at a local coffee shop. He expressed interest in her and they saw each other a few times and spoke occasionally on the phone. Eventually they began dating, and following their first sexual encounter, he suddenly stopped calling and did not respond to her phone messages. After many anxious days, she finally reached him by phone at his work, and he indicated that he no longer wanted to pursue the relationship. This was devastating for her. It fit perfectly, like a jigsaw puzzle piece, into her organization of experience. Hadn't she always known that nothing good would come to her, that she was destined for hurt and disappointment? Who would want someone as loathsome as she? Let us imagine another woman with a different organization of experience—someone who feels self-confident and worthy of love. No doubt she too would feel hurt and disappointment at such a cold rejection, but this second woman would not find this experience to be a perfect fit in the waiting jigsaw puzzle. It might be viewed as a painful piece of bad luck but not a puzzle piece that fits seamlessly into a lifelong picture.

In both examples, these organizing principles and the affects at their core, though formed in childhood relationship with caregivers, get carried forward into the present and serve as a filter through which all subsequent experience must pass. One of the tasks of the intersubjective approach to psychotherapy, then, is to identify and articulate both the organizing principles and the underlying affect states that structure people's unique experience of themselves and others.

This brings us to one of the major current controversies in psychoanalytic thought: Does psychopathology result from conflict or arrested development? The ego psychology perspective views neurosis as the compromise between conflicting forces or functions, operating predominantly within the unconscious mind of the individual. This intrapsychic conflict is understood to be occurring between the id, ego, and superego. The principal locus of psychopathology is found in the forces in conflict within the mind of the individual and the internal management of this conflict.

In contrast, developmental arrest theories, like self psychology, might view psychopathology as resulting from a developmental history of insufficient or inadequate parenting in which the person was deprived of vitally needed selfobject experiences, such as mirroring, idealization, and twinship, that promote the consolidation of a mental structure called "the self." From this perspective, the person is seen as suffering from developmental deficits in the structure of the self. The developmental deficit perspective focuses then on what is missing (Atwood and Stolorow 1997), and these defects in the structure of the self are understood to be the outgrowth of a deficient relationship with an external other.

While intersubjectivity theory values the importance of selfobject experiences for healthy development, "The concept of structure within intersubjectivity theory, by contrast, refers to broad patterns within which experience repeatedly takes form, prereflective organizing principles manifest as recurring themes in the flow of subjective life" (Atwood and Stolorow 1997, p. 520). From the intersubjective perspective, psychopathology is understood as resulting from neither intrapsychic conflict nor developmental arrest in the formation of a structure like the self. Rather, psychopathology is thought to result from something that is present: the complex context out of which the person's subjective experience became organized.

In addition to the unfolding and illumination of subjective experience, an important treatment aim of the intersubjective approach is the transformation of subjective experience. Transformation of archaically formed organizing principles does not mean that treatment leads to their modification. Successful treatment leads to the formation of new organizations of experience, new ways of understanding oneself, and new expectancies based on these new understandings. If new structures, new ways of organizing experience, new organizing principles, are constructed during treatment, what happens to the archaically formed ones? They neither disappear, are forgotten, nor are completely replaced by the newly formed ones. Rather, they persist in weakened form within the organization of the personality. In times of stress, in the absence of needed selfobject experience, old organizing principles may reemerge, reviving in the person old feelings of worthlessness or emptiness. The revival of these archaic affect states is referred to as either experiences of fragmentation, where prior attainments of self-cohesion begin to break down, or experiences of depletion, where vitality affects cannot be sustained. Because the old coexists with the new, it would be inaccurate to talk of cure. Successful psychotherapy leads to the formation of new structures, that is, new organizations of experience and new organizing principles.

The idea that what is accomplished in psychotherapy is the formation of new structures or new principles that organize experience is quite different from the idea that in psychotherapy people learn new ways of relating. If what happens in psychotherapy is that patients learn new ways of relating to others as an outgrowth of engaging in the transference relationship with the therapist, then psychoanalysis would be merely some variant of a social/learning theory.

From the intersubjective perspective, as a result of forming new psychological structures, new organizations of experience, people acquire new expectancies of relationship and are therefore capable of relating in new ways. They are capable of relating differently because they experience themselves and the world differently. It is not so much that they have learned new relating skills as that, feeling differently about themselves and their place in the world, they have become more open to risk and more resilient in the face of injury. Thus, from the intersubjective perspective, psychotherapeutic success involves structural change.

INVESTIGATORY STANCE

For Freudian theory, the investigatory stance concerned the analyst's adherence to a posture of neutrality and abstinence. Neutrality meant remaining opaque to the patient, offering little response to the patient. The analyst was expected to function like a projective screen onto which the patient displaced or projected his inner wishes and conflicts. This was the transference—the patient's distorted perception of the analyst in the present in terms of a significant relationship from his past. This formative relationship was thought to be a contributor to the patient's inner conflicts. By maintaining a stance of neutrality, the transference could be preserved from contamination by the actuality of the person of the analyst and, thereby, could be pointed out as a distortion residing solely in the mind of the patient. Any feelings the patient had for the analyst were thought to emanate from distortions due to displacements or projections from the inner world of the patient and had nothing to do with the actual person of the analyst. For example, if the analyst communicated to the patient her personal feelings of care and concern for him, this would contaminate the transference. Since any future feelings the patient experienced for his analyst might have been instigated by the analyst's actions, the patient's feelings could not be attributable solely to transference, to the reappearance of feelings from his childhood being displaced onto the present.

Through the use of such techniques as having the patient recline on a couch, the analyst sitting out of sight and maintaining a stance of abstinence (not gratifying the transference wishes), and meeting at least four times a week, regression (a resurgence of ways of coping and experiencing from childhood) was promoted. This fostered the formation of a transference neurosis in the present. The transference neurosis represented a revival in the present relationship with the analyst of the original childhood neurosis. By resurrecting the original childhood neurosis in the transference, the analyst was able to gain access to the patient's past. Resolving the current transference neurosis, through insight gained from the analyst's interpretations, was thought to mitigate the original childhood neurosis.

Another important component of the Freudian investigatory stance was the notion that buried memories of childhood wishes and conflicts could be uncovered, brought to light, and made conscious by putting them into words. Thus, the emphasis was placed on the analyst's making verbal interpretations, primarily of the transference, and on the accuracy and timing of these interpretations. The analyst's verbal interpretations, explanations of the underlying meaning of the patient's behavior or fantasies, promoted insight. And insight and understanding strengthened and extended the ego's dominion over the drives and the superego.

This abbreviated review of the Freudian investigatory stance enables us to highlight how the Freudian techniques of treatment follow quite logically from the underlying assumptions of Freudian theory. That is, the Freudian view was that current neuroses were the outgrowth of repressed childhood conflicts. Observing analytic neutrality and abstinence and promoting regression would resurrect those forgotten childhood conflicts in the present transference to the analyst. These pathogenic childhood conflicts could then be interpreted and made conscious. In a similar manner, the investigatory stance of the intersubjective approach to treatment grows out of its assumptions about the nature of psychological development.

Let us review some of the assumptions underlying the intersubjective approach and examine their influence on the investigatory stance. First is the assumption that human beings, by nature, organize experience and the need to maintain this organization of experience is a crucial motive in behavior. This supraordinate motivational principle profoundly affects the investigatory stance that characterizes the intersubjective approach to treatment and differentiates it from other therapeutic systems. Rather than listening for derivatives of repressed impulse, defense, or conflict, the intersubjective therapist's focus is directed toward discerning those principles, generally unconscious, and the accompanying disruptive affect states, that organize the patient's experience. In addition, the therapist strives to appreciate that much of what gets labeled as psychopathology represents attempts on the part of patients to maintain or restore their threatened sense of psychological equilibrium. Symptomatic behaviors, whether constructed out of concretizations, dissociations, or other psychological processes, are understood to serve the crucial psychological purpose of maintaining or restoring the organization of experience. They are dramatic manifestations of the patient's striving for psychological integrity, not compromise formations that attempt to garner disguised or distorted satisfactions. Therefore, an important emphasis of the intersubjective approach is the focus on the patient's striving for psychological health rather than on the patient's psychopathology, his propensity to repeat earlier maladaptive patterns. This, as we will see, has profound implications for the practice of psychotherapy. For example, a patient who tolerates an abusive relationship might be characterized as masochistic. That is, traditionally he may have been viewed as seeking out or needing to repeat hurtful experiences, perhaps because of the disguised sexual pleasure derived or out of an unconscious wish to be punished for guilt-laden desires. An alternative explanation that focuses on the patient's striving to maintain a precarious sense of self-cohesion might be that enduring the abusive experiences, rather than repeating, seeking, or desiring them, is the price the patient is willing to pay for maintaining a relationship that in other ways is experienced as self-sustaining. Possible organizations of experience underlying this patient's sense of himself in an abusive relationship might be that he does not deserve to be treated otherwise or that he will never have a different kind of relationship or that he could not survive without a partner, so he must settle for this current one.

As a corollary to the assumption that humans organize their experiences into patterns and expectancies, a further assumption of intersubjectivity theory is that human beings are motivated to seek out those relational experiences that will promote and enhance self-development. If an adult regulates and integrates discrepant affect states, maintains a consistent sense of self over time, and enjoys positive self-esteem, we speak of someone who has achieved a measure of self-cohesion. Those relational experiences that promote or enhance self-cohesion and the integration of affect are referred to as selfobject experiences (we will have more to say about selfobject experience in Chapter 4).

Central to the investigatory stance of intersubjectivity theory is the empathic-introspective mode of inquiry. Historically, Kohut first introduced his formulation of the empathic-introspective mode of inquiry in 1959. According to Kohut (1984), "The best definition of empathy . . . is that it is the capacity to think and feel oneself into the inner life of another person" (p. 82). Since then, there has been a tendency in the self-psychology literature to use the notion of empathy in two different ways. In the first case, empathy has been used to describe a way of responding with care and concern to another, as in, "John empathized with Mary." The other usage of the term *empathy* is as a listening stance adopted by the therapist. Stolorow and colleagues (1987) have proposed that reserving the term *empathy* for referring only to the listening stance could reduce the potential for confusion that results from the two different usages and meanings of the term. In intersubjectivity theory, then, empathy refers to a method for learning about the patient's subjective experience, and empathic listening refers to the therapist's attempt to understand the patient's experience, to the extent that one can ever fully grasp another's experience. Stolorow and colleagues propose that we use the concept of affect attunement to describe the therapist's responses to the patient's experience. For example, when the therapist says, "It sounds like you felt hurt when your father forgot your birthday," the therapist is communicating her understanding of the patient's affect state, and by doing so, providing the patient with the experience of feeling understood, or attuned to. Thus the therapist's affect attunement promotes the patient's integration of affect ("I did feel hurt") and is clearly a vital selfobject function. The empathic stance is the therapist's attempt to approximate the patient's inner experience and, from that perspective, respond in a way that the patient experiences as attuned.

Since the intersubjective approach focuses on the field created by the coming together of subjectivities of both patient and therapist, the "introspective" component of the empathic-introspective stance concerns the manner by which the therapist attunes to her own internal processes. The importance of the therapist's introspective focus is on gaining and maintaining an awareness of the impact the therapist's person is having on the patient. In other relational approaches to psychotherapy, the therapist prizes her awareness of her experience, her countertransference, for what it tells the therapist about the patient's motives. In the intersubjective approach, the introspective stance is valued for two reasons: first, for what it reveals of the therapist's impact on and contribution to the patient's experience, and second, for providing the therapist with an emotional or experiential analogue that will both facilitate access to what that patient is feeling and be a basis for responding in an attuned way. Consider, for example, the situation of a patient who does not show up for his session and neglects to inform the therapist in advance. Attuning to her experience of irritation and annoyance, the therapist might interpret the patient's unconscious passive-aggressive desires to hurt the therapist, or, for those therapists with a more Kleinian bent, the patient's unconscious desire to make his therapist feel the way he felt when his parents forgot to pick him up after school and left him stranded. Rather than assume that the therapist's experience derives from the patient's angry motives, the intersubjective approach would lead the therapist to examine her own experience of the previous session (introspection) and explore the patient's experience of the therapist during the previous session. Might the patient's absence have been instigated by some experience of the therapist, such as the patient feeling hurt or injured by the therapist? This is not to suggest that anger might not be a reactive piece of the patient's experience, but it allows for the focus to be directed to the intersubjective field constructed of the experiences of both patient and therapist to the previous session.

The above example highlights the importance of context for the intersubjective approach. For the Freudian system, the investigatory stance aims at uncovering the intrapsychic world of the patient. The aim of psychotherapy from the intersubjective perspective is to illuminate the contextual basis of experience, the patient's and the therapist's.

SUMMARY

This chapter has presented an overview of intersubjectivity theory and the intersubjective approach to psychotherapy. We have examined subjectivity, the constitutive role of context on the subjective experience of both patient and therapist, and the intersubjective field constructed by the coming together of two subjectivities in a particular context.

2

The Intersubjective Sensibility

Students are drawn to the profession of psychotherapy for many, often complex, personal reasons. Therapists who themselves have been patients in therapy often give two psychodynamic explanations for their desire to become psychotherapists: the unconscious wish to cure oneself through acquiring deep insight and understanding of one's own personality dynamics, and the wish to cure one's dysfunctional family members. When graduate students are queried, many report that they have had their own prior exposure to personal psychotherapy and feel grateful for the benefits they derived. Applicants to graduate schools in clinical psychology often write in their autobiographical statements that they come from dysfunctional families and have experienced the healing effects of family counseling or substance abuse treatment.

In general, then, a common motive reported by many aspiring psychotherapists is the desire to help others and themselves. This is a sincere desire and a noble objective. Nevertheless, the desire to help contributes, ironically, to a mind-set that is problematic for, or even antithetical to, practicing psychoanalytic psychotherapy effectively.

It seems paradoxical that the therapist's desire to help may not actually prove helpful. Responsible therapists hope that the therapeutic relationship will enhance personal growth and self-discovery for their patients. Embedded in that desire to help others, though, is the assumption that the therapist *does* something to the patient so that the patient is fixed or cured. "Doing to" establishes the patient as the object of the therapist's action rather than as a collaborator in a joint venture. This model of treatment grows out of a one-person psychology, where the patient is the object of study of a detached observer. In contrast, a two-person psychology views the relationship between patient and therapist as being central to treatment. According to Aron (1996), "The implication of a two-person psychology is that who the analyst is, not only how he or she works but his or her very character, makes a real difference for the analysand" (p. 50).

While the one-person view is consistent with the medical model, where the physician heals a patient, it is incompatible with the intersubjective perspective of psychotherapy. Stolorow has suggested that notions of one-person or two-person psychologies should not delimit intersubjectivity theory. According to Orange (1995), "Intersubjectivity theory sees human beings as organizers of experience, as subjects. Therefore, it views psychoanalytic treatment as the dialogic attempt of two people to understand one person's organization of emotional experience by 'making sense together' of their shared experience" (p. 8). Psychoanalytic psychotherapy, from this perspective, is not a repair job, like fixing a leaky faucet, but a growth process, like the sprouting of a flower, that occurs over time, often over long periods of time. Psychoanalytic psychotherapy as making sense together, or exploring and illuminating personal meanings, is often experienced as an accompanied voyage of self-discovery for both participants. Unlike an airplane flight, where the navigator plots a course, sets a speed, and estimates the time of arrival, psychoanalytic psychotherapy is more like a hot-air balloon ride, where two participants climb into the gondola and go where the wind takes them. Neither participant controls direction or velocity. One cannot predict at the beginning exactly where and when one will arrive. This type of voyage is truly a voyage of discovery, of self and of self in relation to another.

We believe that empathically attuned listening and understanding are necessary prerequisites if true help is to emerge from within the psychotherapy relationship. When the therapist's need to be helpful or to fix is activated, it disrupts and supplants the therapist's focus on listening and understanding. We cannot emphasize strongly enough that what lies at the heart of psychoanalytic psychotherapy and the intersubjective approach in particular is the centrality of exploring and illuminating personal meanings, or making sense together.

The clinical problem with attempts to fix is not that they violate some abstract philosophical perspective about the mutual construction of experience, but that fixing precludes making sense together. In other words, fixing may both confirm existing core organizing principles in the therapist and prevent us from furthering the unfolding and illuminating of those organizing principles in the patient. Let us clarify this through the use of a clinical example. Suppose that a male patient complains of not being able to meet women. Fixing could involve the therapist's suggesting such solutions as placing or answering personal ads. Much therapy time could be spent composing exactly the right wording and considering where such an ad should best be placed. However, the clinical issue of illuminating the personal meanings of the patient's actions or lack of action might get misplaced. What, for instance, is the meaning of his aloneness? Might he feel so fundamentally defective that seeking a partner seems like an exercise in futility? Most patients of average intelligence could come up with the idea of placing or answering personal ads themselves. Certainly one doesn't need to consult a mental health professional to get this advice. The bartender, the kindly old lady on the bus, or his parents could make this suggestion. Nor, by the way, is there anything in our mental health training that qualifies us as givers of advice. What, then, is the meaning of this man's inability to think of or put into effect some pragmatic problem-solving effort, such as placing or answering a personals ad? Might he believe that any woman who meets him would see through his outward facade and reject him? Perhaps what appears to be inaction might be a self-protective stance against the expectation of painful rejection. Before our hypothetical man can take problem-solving action, or be helped to take such action, his core organizing principle of inherent defectiveness needs to be addressed. If, during the course of psychotherapy, his organization of experience should be transformed so that he feels worthy and lovable, he probably would not need his therapist's helpful suggestions as to how to meet a prospective partner.

Let us examine what is to be gained by renouncing the temptation to fix and instead exploring personal meanings. First, let us speculate about the possible meaning of the patient's asking for help. The patient may feel that he has never had others in his life who took an interest in him and offered him guidance in self-exploration, perhaps because he is insignificant and unworthy of receiving their attention. Thus, he might seek to repair a thwarted developmental longing for parental guidance through engaging the therapist as a new and better version of his emotionally absent or distant parents. While for this hypothetical dynamic, giving advice might be experienced as providing the longed-for parenting function, we would not know this if we had not first explored the personal meaning of seeking and receiving advice. Also, through the exploration of personal meaning we would facilitate the unfolding and illumination of the unconscious organizing principle that he feels unworthy of receiving attention.

A second possible organizing principle for this patient is that he feels stupid and doubts his own judgment. Thus, he turns to the therapist whom he believes is omniscient to find the answer he feels incapable of coming to himself. While providing advice might seem to foster or support an idealizing transference (which Kohut [1971] believed to be beneficial), there are several pitfalls to such a well-meaning stance. If, for instance, no one answers his personal ad, then we may have succeeded in leading him into an injurious situation, a replication of the misattuned parenting he had grown up with. But more importantly, we would have missed an opportunity to explore the unconscious organizing principle that his own judgment is untrustworthy.

A third possibility is that if we provide advice he himself could generate, as a competent and intelligent adult, we would be treating him as if he were a child. This might serve to confirm already-existing organizing principles that he is incompetent and child-like.

What activates the need to help in a therapist who is committed to listening and understanding? It is not uncommon for patients unsophisticated about the workings of psychoanalytic psychotherapy to come to treatment with the expectation that the therapist will solve or fix their problems. Such expectations often engage the therapist's need to feel helpful or effective in ways that stimulate fixing interventions.

In general though, we have observed that the arousal of the therapist's anxiety often precipitates a shift in focus away from listening and understanding and redirects it toward trying to fix or solve problems. Common issues that arouse a therapist's anxiety are perceived evidence of increased suicidal risk, dangerous or self-destructive acting out, and outbreaks or intensification of symptoms. We are by no means suggesting that these anxiety-provoking developments be disregarded. Sometimes therapists must act quickly to make lifesaving decisions. However, often the therapist's anxiety does not relate to imminent threats to the patient's survival but to the subjective meanings that the patient's communication carries for the therapist. For example, a patient reports that she has decided to marry a man whom she started dating last month, and invites the therapist to attend the wedding at city hall the next week. The therapist has a number of choices as to how to respond. She might say something like "What's the rush?" which obviously conveys a negative judgment that the patient is acting precipitously in making such an important decision and an implicit attempt to get the patient to slow down. An alternative that is more consistent with the stance of listening and understanding might be, "Sounds like you've made a major decision. Tell me about it." While such an intervention might be more comfortable if the wedding date is set a year away, the therapist's urge to act quickly may be no less precipitous than the patient's. Sometimes we cannot forestall a patient from making what we predict to be the wrong choice. But how can we be certain that we know what is best for someone else? Can we be sure that this groom will wait around for us to make up our minds about his qualities as a potential spouse, or that someone more suitable will come along?

Consistent with the motive to fix is another dubious assumption that is often asserted in nonpsychodynamic approaches to psychotherapy. This perspective views the individual as made up of a collection of parts. Like repairing a car that won't run, the therapeutic task for these approaches is to find the broken part and fix it. Perhaps the points, the plugs, the carburetor, the alternator, or maybe the computer need to be adjusted. These treatment approaches view people the same way, as a collection of parts, each of which is treatable independent of the others. Aggressive patients are referred to anger management groups, the premature ejaculators are sent to sex therapists, the phobics to systematic desensitization, and the depressed for a medication consultation. Some patients get some or all of these treatments concurrently. At some clinics, the patient may be in individual therapy, couples therapy, family therapy, and various support groups simultaneously.

Most dynamic psychotherapies, and the intersubjective approach in particular, view the individual as a whole, not as a collection of separately modifiable parts. The individual's symptoms are understood to have formed out of the way his experience with early caregivers became organized. We view symptoms as having unique, idiosyncratic meanings for each particular patient. That, of course, is exactly what a symptom is—the manifestation of some underlying process, much of which is highly personal, and not a sign of any specific universal condition. A sign, on the other hand, is a concrete indicator of a specific disorder. Syphilis spirochetes in the blood are an incontrovertible sign of the disease syphilis, regardless of the meaning that being syphilitic has for the individual. In contrast, take the symptom of a high fever, for example. No specific condition can be diagnosed from the presence of a high fever. The patient might have cancer, an infected tooth, or sunstroke. High fever is not a sign of some specific disease; neither, on the psychological level, is depression, anxiety, or fear of strangers. They are symptoms, the meanings of which are uniquely personal for each individual.

Psychiatric diagnoses are based on descriptions of symptom clusters, not signs. The *DSM-IV* attaches labels (usually in Latin) to clusters of symptoms or behaviors. Labeling someone with dysthymic disorder tells you nothing about what has caused the affect state, only that descriptions of the patient's behavior meet eight criteria. The symptoms a person may exhibit are unique to that particular individual, and so is the meaning they have to him.

Symptoms are like dreams. Let us take as an example Freud's famous case of Serge Pankejeff, known commonly as the Wolf Man. Pankejeff is most remembered for a dream he had about wolves sitting in a tree. Any patient might dream of wolves but that doesn't mean he has Wolf Man's disease. To one patient, the wolf image might represent his father, to another his mother's vagina, and to another the threat of the therapist's ripping interpretations. In other words, having a dream about wolves provides us no clue as to etiology or the underlying psychodynamic configuration.

The intersubjective approach to psychotherapy views the individual as a whole. Symptomatic behaviors are understood to have grown out of the particular ways this person has organized and made sense of his unique life experience and the idiosyncratic meanings that such experiences have for him. Any transformation that occurs to this organization of experience will have a global, not specific, impact on the patient's manner of relating and behaving. The psychotherapeutic task is to illuminate the underlying organizing principles from which the behavior derives, not to modify the behaviors. We focus our attention on the process of unfolding and illuminating, not on hitting the targeted symptom. It is our conviction that the unfolding and illuminating of subjective experience will allow for the transformation of the principles that have come to organize that experience. Change results from making sense together. The process of making sense together is an irreducible context that includes the two subjectivities of the therapist and the patient, the unique field created by their mutual influence, and the specific understanding of the patient's subjective experience that emerges through their work. Transformation follows from the experience of new understanding gained in a relationship with an attuned therapist.

The intersubjective approach does not target a specific symptom, such as self-consciousness. Rather, as the patient's organization of experience unfolds and is illuminated and transformed in the therapy relationship, the patient develops new organizing principles that structure his experience.

> Jack is a young man who feels very uncomfortable and self-conscious in the presence of attractive women. Throughout grammar school he was teased and ridiculed by the other children for his pronounced acne and his big nose. Feeling ridiculed in school was overlaid on the experience of having been repeatedly criticized by his mother, who found fault with any initiative shown by Jack. Jack organized these experiences around the notion, "I am defective and inadequate and if people, especially girls, get to know me, they will find this out and reject me. It is safest to avoid other

> people." During the course of therapy, as Jack experienced his therapist as understanding and affirming of his ambitions and tentative exhibitionistic strivings, Jack began to develop a different sense of his abilities. These new experiences of feeling mirrored and accepted by the therapist fostered the development of a new organizing principle: "I have something to contribute and am worth taking notice of." Thus, having developed a new way to organize his experience, Jack's self-consciousness diminished and he became more comfortable in social situations.

What is important is that reductions in self-consciousness are the outgrowth of new organizations of experience, which support increased self-confidence. This new organization of experience, a new mental structure, exerts its influence over the full range of interpersonal functioning, transforming self-consciousness into self-confidence in areas other than just with attractive women.

Still another unfortunate formulation that has influenced the practice of psychotherapy is the notion of ideal or proper technique. Since Freud's day, it has been common to discuss the theory of psychoanalytic technique. However, the concept of ideal or proper technique, like the goal of helping or fixing, has had a constricting effect on the practice of psychoanalysis and psychotherapy. As Orange and colleagues (1997) see it, "The concept of technique includes the idea of rules of proper and correct procedure. The primary purpose of the rules of any technique is to induce compliance, to reduce the influence of individual subjectivity on the task at hand" (p. 23). Technique implies structure and conformity to rules. While Freud (1910a) may have felt that a body of rules was necessary to protect patients from "wild analysis," such rules incline us to the belief that they suit the needs of all patient–therapist relationships. This is a kind of "one size fits all" approach to psychotherapy. But, as we have been arguing, each therapeutic couple constructs a distinct intersubjective field and a unique process, and the notion that one size fits all cannot possibly apply. There are clearly better and worse ways to do psychotherapy, but there is no uniform technique that applies to all patients.

Stolorow (1992) suggests that there are two features that characterize a psychoanalytic psychotherapy process. First, psychoanalytic psychotherapy is concerned with subjective experience, the contexts that shape it, and the way such experience is organized. Second, the psychoanalytic psychotherapy process takes place within a relationship. The aim (or goal) of the psychotherapy process, as we indicated in Chapter 1, is the transformation of the organization of experience as it unfolds and is illuminated in the therapy relationship. Focusing on a concrete goal, such as symptom relief, detracts and distracts from the experience of the process. This is akin to Herrigel's (1971) observation in *Zen in the Art of Archery* that to become an accurate marksman one must first renounce the wish to hit the target and instead immerse oneself in the process.

It takes a unique type of person to be drawn to the pursuit of psychoanalytic psychotherapy. If the therapist needs to control, is made anxious by ambiguity or uncertainty, must know where she is going and what lies ahead, relies on tools and techniques (the tricks of the trade) in order to feel competent, and relishes being treated as an authority, then psychoanalytic psychotherapy, and the intersubjective approach in particular, is not for her.

Working intersubjectively requires commitment to a particular stance or sensibility (Orange et al. 1997). There are many aspects to this sensibility, and psychotherapists must bring this sensibility with them to the beginning of each new psychotherapy relationship. This stance views the psychotherapy relationship as a collaborative venture of making sense together. What emerges in the process is coconstructed, that is, both parties contribute to the construction, although not necessarily in equal measure. If two people are baking a cake, one might bring the liquid and the other the cake mix. The cake can be thought of as having been coconstructed in that it could not have been made without the contribution of both parties, but the contributions of each may be quite different. Using another metaphor, let the patient be represented by an ice cube and the therapist by a glass of water. When the two are brought together, the water is cooled, the ice cube is warmed, and both are changed by the experience. In both metaphorical cases, each of the two elements is separate and unique and the process of their mutual endeavor changes each of them.

Another characteristic of the intersubjective sensibility is that neither party in a psychotherapy relationship is an authority on the mind of the other. By rejecting isolated mind notions and the myth of objectively knowable truth (Orange et al. 1997), the therapist remains open and willing to explore her contribution to the patient's experience of the relationship. Working intersubjectively concerns making sense together, in contrast to the classical Freudian perspective that views the analyst as a scientist, an empirical observer of objectively verifiable phenomena. The Freudian scientist, through the stance of neutrality and abstinence, believes she will gain access to objectively verifiable facts about the patient's unconscious motives, which are then interpreted or transmitted to the patient. The intersubjective approach, which focuses on the process of making sense together, immerses therapist and patient in the fluid and amorphous realm of the patient's personal meanings.

The implications of this sensibility are that, as psychotherapists, we must take some responsibility for our contribution to the patient's experience of being in relationship with us. This has profound ramifications for the way we diagnose and treat. Diagnostic labels tend to pathologize and blame the patient. The label "borderline" is typically applied to patients who are quick to anger, become abusive to others, and alternate between viewing others as all-good or all-bad. From the intersubjective perspective, we need to examine the context within which the patient's actions coincide with descriptions of borderline behavior. If a patient who tends to idealize the therapist becomes suddenly angry and abusive, is the patient showing his true borderline colors by manifesting splitting behavior? Or has something in the therapeutic relationship activated strong negative affects in the patient? According to Stolorow and colleagues (1987), "The psychological essence of what we call 'borderline' is *not* that it is a pathological condition located solely in the patient. Rather, *it refers to phenomena arising in an intersubjective field—a field consisting of a precarious, vulnerable self in a failing, archaic selfobject bond*" (p. 116). The patient's precarious, vulnerable self-organization was structured in reaction to a chronic destructive caregiving environment, while the failing selfobject bond is an aspect of the present relationship with the misattuned therapist. The following clinical example illustrates what we mean.

> Gerri, a woman of 27, came for therapy because she had a history of chaotic, unstable relationships with friends and lovers. She developed close and intense relationships that, after a short period of time, she abruptly terminated because she became enraged with what she experienced as the other person's unreliable and inconsiderate treatment of her. During the third session, the telephone rang and the therapist answered. The conversation was kept brief and within a few seconds the therapist returned her attention to the patient. Gerri, however, became enraged with the therapist and fired off a volley of verbal abuse that perceptively attacked the core of her psychotherapist's professional self-image. "Your actions are unprofessional; you are unethical and should be reported; you shouldn't be licensed; you need more supervision and personal therapy to get you to stop acting out with your patients; this is my time and you are using it to take care of your own business and I won't pay for this session."

From her therapist's perspective, Gerri was overreacting to the degree of interruption and was responding in her characterological fashion of lashing out. This raises one of those choice points that frequently confront therapists. Whose subjectivity gets privileged in this situation? Should the therapist focus on her experience of being overreacted to and abused excessively, or should the therapist focus on Gerri's experience of having been narcissistically injured? The therapist might have resorted to the personal safety and comfort of blaming the patient for the patient's experience in therapy by pathologizing the patient and calling her names, like "narcissistic" or "borderline." She might further have sought to reassure herself by hiding behind transference interpretations involving projection or displacement ("You are treating me like your mother who was always uninterested and preoccupied when you wanted to talk to her"). However, even if such an interpretation would capture something of the patient's formative experience, it would also fail to acknowledge, in fact would disregard or deny, the therapist's contribution to the patient's angry reaction. The intersubjectively oriented therapist would choose to privilege the patient's subjectivity. Our reasoning is as follows: this is a patient whose personality structure is vulnerable and prone to fragmentation. In answering the phone, the therapist has provoked a profound narcissistic injury in the patient. (Clearly not all patients would experience the therapist's answering the phone as so profound a narcissistic wound. But Gerri, by virtue of her history of chronic and persistent misattunement by caregivers, is uniquely vulnerable to failing selfobject bonds.) Gerri had entered therapy hoping for a new relationship that would fulfill her lifelong need for attuned responsiveness from a caring other. By answering the phone, the therapist's behavior fit neatly into the patient's organization of experience that she was not worthy or important enough for someone, her mother or her therapist, to respond to her emotional needs.

The therapist's owning her error and affirming and validating Gerri's subjective experience of devastating injury sets a reparative experience into motion. During the course of treatment, Gerri's repeated experiences of attunement, affirmation, and repair will lead to increased self-confidence, the capacity to integrate disruptive affects, the regulation and modulation of intense affect states, and trust in the constancy and continuity of good objects.

Rather than having before us a borderline patient (one characterized by intense and extreme swings in interpersonal relating), we have a patient with a precarious, vulnerable personality organization and a therapist who has failed to provide the longed for selfobject functions of attuned responsiveness. A differently organized patient with a more cohesive personality structure might respond to the therapist's transference interpretation with, "I'm angry at you because you are self-centered and inconsiderate, just like my mother was." The present is not being distorted or contaminated by the past, as in the traditional view of transference. Rather, the present relationship is being assimilated into the patient's invariant organization of experience. We will elaborate on this different conception of transference in Chapter 4.

In the above clinical example, Gerri responded in what might be labeled a "borderline" way to her experience of the actions of the therapist. Putting ourselves in this patient's shoes, we can appreciate that her angry and vituperative outburst was provoked iatrogenically by the injurious actions of the therapist. This patient is not a borderline. Rather, this vulnerable, fragile patient responds with rage when disappointed and injured by someone she wished would be attuned to her. Gerri's characteristic lashing out and her rage function to manage her feelings and ideas that would otherwise disrupt her sense of psychological integrity. Her organization of experience not only includes how she expects to be disappointed and hurt by others but her habitual ways of keeping herself psychologically intact when threatened. Gerri's attack is in fact a counterattack, launched in an effort to protect her sense of personal integrity, and, as self-defeating as her actions appear to others, they represent the best she has been able to develop to this point in her life. When not injured, she is not rageful. The patient is reacting within a specific context shaped by her invariant organization of experience and her therapist's behavior.

The therapist in this example recognized that she had injured the patient (while allowing that the patient was extremely sensitive—of course! That is why she was a patient in the first place) and proceeded to express her appreciation of how answering the phone had been experienced as uncaring and hurtful. The therapist apologized for her actions and agreed not to interrupt further sessions. Gerri warily accepted the apology and reassurance. Two years later, during a session, having forgotten to forward calls to her voice-mail, the phone rang and the therapist answered reflexively. The therapist instantly remembered the earlier session, realized that she had blundered by breaking her promise, cut the call short, and began to apologize. Gerri casually brushed aside the apology, saying, "Oh, it's OK," and continued on with what she had been talking about. Later in the session, at an opportune moment, the therapist reflected back on what had happened between them. How was it that what had so infuriated Gerri two years ago was no longer salient? Gerri explained how over the last two years she had come to experience and trust that the therapist was really "with me" and such a minor interruption did not disrupt that feeling.

Has the patient become less borderline? To avoid pathologizing one-person labels, we would formulate the change in this way: Gerri has become less vulnerable and prone to fragmentation. She has come to feel increasingly understood, safe, and trusting in her relationship with her therapist. Therefore, within the changed context, she did not experience the therapist's answering the phone as injurious. Having developed a more cohesive self-structure through repeated experiences of feeling understood by her therapist, the kind of actions that had formerly signaled a failing selfobject relationship no longer were experienced as hurtful. This reflected the development of a new organizing principle: I am worthy of caring, attention and consideration.

This clinical example raises another fundamental assumption that intersubjectively oriented psychotherapists need to bear in mind as they begin a treatment. The typical intake procedure is satisfied to seek out the presenting problem that presumably brings the patient to therapy in the first place. However, we have become convinced that while patients might articulate very specific goals for therapy, such as overcoming some fear or acquiring new interpersonal skills, on a fundamental level all patients are seeking a new, reparative experience from the therapeutic relationship. That is, patients are at the deepest level seeking a selfobject relationship in which their thwarted developmental strivings can be repaired.

Lay people often disparage psychotherapy as a form of paid friendship. They argue that all a troubled person needs is a good friend (as if this is so easy for people with troubled interpersonal relationships to achieve). There is certainly merit to the idea that all people need good friends. Kohut (1984) argues persuasively that all people, including psychologically healthy people, have a lifelong need for selfobject relationships. But friendships are reciprocal in nature, whereas functioning as a selfobject is often a one-way street. Under the best circumstances, as a selfobject for the patient, the therapist should possess a cohesive self-organization in order to suspend her own personal longings while she attunes to the needs of the other. Aron (1996) has observed that mutuality but not symmetry characterizes the psychotherapy relationship. By noting the essential asymmetry of the therapeutic relationship, Aron is referring to "the important differences between patient and analyst in their roles, functions, power, and responsibilities" (p. 124). Unlike a reciprocal friendship, it would be inappropriate for the therapist to demand or expect that the patient take her needs and feelings into account, at least in the beginning phases of treatment. Eventually, as the therapeutic relationship matures and develops its own characteristic ways of noticing and opening up experience, we expect that the patient's interest in and capacity for appreciating the different subjectivity of the therapist will expand. The use of the intersubjectivity construct to refer to such mutual recognition (the patient's recognition of the selfhood of the therapist) is central to the thinking of the group of theorists that Teicholtz (1999a) calls the "moderate postmoderns," such as Ogden and Benjamin.

Frequently, it is just those individuals with difficulties in sustaining reciprocal relationships who find their way to psychotherapy. Some come with an organization of experience that leads them to anticipate that this new relationship, too, will fail. While they hope for a new, attuned relationship unlike what they have experienced in the past, they nevertheless expect to be disappointed and injured and to suffer retraumatization at the hands of this new/old object. Typically, these patients are described as resistant; that is, they are blamed for their ambivalence and their unenthusiastic embrace of the benevolent therapist. They tend to be diagnosed as having character pathology.

Some people, on the other hand, do come to the therapy relationship with a greater sense of hope. These patients generally receive more benign diagnoses of the Axis I variety (such as dysthymic disorder or anxiety disorders) because the therapist experiences them as more receptive, if not more idealizing. While symptoms of anxiety and depression are often clearly present, these less difficult patients also view the world through their characteristic organizations of experience, formed in the context of their early relationships with caregivers and operating in the present to maintain cohesion, continuity, and stability in the self-organization. For both types of patient, a therapist informed by intersubjectivity theory will come to understand the ways these patterns structure the patient's view of the world and himself. As we discussed above, specific symptoms, whether benign, endearing, or distancing, represent only part of the whole picture of a patient. We understand very little of a person by a diagnostic description alone.

But we do understand that, for all patients, operating behind the initial reaching out to the therapist is a wish, however dim, that this new relationship will offer the opportunities for care and understanding that were unreliably and inconsistently met growing up. The wish that, in this new relationship, the developmental longings that were thwarted by misattuned caregivers would now, for once, be met with attuned responsiveness. As Stolorow and colleagues (1987) put it, "Patients enter analysis with hopes for an intersubjective context in which thwarted strivings for differentiated selfhood may become liberated" (p. 65). In other words, a fundamental conviction of the intersubjective perspective is that a striving for psychological health motivates all people, and patients are no exception. Profound implications for the practice of psychotherapy follow from this conviction. The implications apply to the process of treatment as well as to how the therapist understands all that a patient brings to treatment. So, from the intersubjective perspective, even the most self-defeating and outrageous characteristics of patients are thought of as their best efforts at staying safe and solid given the entire constellation of their personal history and individual qualities.

The significance of the assumption that all of us are striving for psychological health cannot be overemphasized. If there is one pearl of wisdom for therapists to use as a guiding mantra it is this: At the core of whatever a patient reveals is the hope of being accepted and cared for. Ironically, debilitating symptoms, disruptive behavior patterns, and disappointing relationships will all ultimately make sense as part of how the patient managed to remain psychologically intact in the face of barriers to feeling loved and accepted. One patient, seen over several years for crippling anxiety in work and social settings, eventually realized that the only time he felt sure of the love of his family was when they offered help after he left a job or could not function socially. For him, their enthusiasm for his "success" when he worked or socialized meant that they only loved him if he performed well. The only caring that felt authentic to him was what he experienced from them despite his failures and limitations. On top of this wish to be loved and accepted for who he was lay fears and misunderstandings of other people and their motives that occasionally bordered on paranoia. Interpersonally, he tested the patience of lovers, friends, and his therapist by measuring their love for him by whether they stuck by him after he disappointed them.

Another important core assumption of the intersubjective perspective is that the therapist's theory of mind is an integral part of the therapist's subjectivity. Theory necessarily contributes to structuring every therapist's experience. Our theories inform our understanding of normal development and developmental psychopathology as well as of how therapy works. Typically, analytic therapies search for the pathological motives behind behaviors. People are thought to be motivated by masochistic or sadistic urges, the desire to symbolically satisfy or deny oedipal strivings, and the pursuit of other antisocial or asocial expressions of sexual and aggressive drives. The fundamental assumption is that people are in conflict over their unacceptable impulses, that pressures for expression of drives and inhibition of that expression inevitably work in opposition. Thus, derivatives of the unacceptable impulse are sought and interpretive light is shone on them. The therapist's stance is directed at uncovering what is being hidden or repressed. The patient is presumed to be concealing dreaded secrets, and the therapist is experienced as allied with the id, pressing for discharge, against the ego, which seeks delay (A. Freud 1936).

If, however, the therapist approaches human behavior from the perspective that people are striving for health, as opposed to defending against their unacceptable desires, then an entirely different quality of relationship is established. From this stance, we explore what adaptive purpose could be served by seemingly maladaptive behaviors. Mary, for example, is a patient who permits herself to be abused and humiliated by her domineering partner. The traditional stance would lead us to anticipate that some masochistic motive is being expressed in this seemingly self-destructive behavior—perhaps seeking pain for sexual pleasure or possibly instigating an experience of punishment for some unconscious sense of guilt. Viewed from the perspective of health seeking, we learn that, however hurtful this relationship is, Mary believes that it is the best relationship that she has had or hopes to have. The pain is the price she is willing to pay to preserve the needed connection she experiences in the relationship. The relationship is not maintained because it provides the opportunity for pain or self-punishment. Rather, the treatment Mary receives from her partner and her view of herself in relation to him fit with a way of organizing her self-experience that derives from her childhood. This abusive relationship fits with Mary's early solution to the problem of how to feel psychologically secure and valued in her family. She maintains her tie to her parents through attending to the needs of others at her own expense. Much of her psychotherapy will center on making sense of this current relationship in light of her historically formed organization of experience.

Going hand in hand with rejecting the myths of neutrality, objectivity, and other isolated mind notions is the need to maintain a stance of fallibilism, which Orange (1995) defines as "an attitude recognizing that what we 'know' or understand is inevitably partial and often mistaken" (p. 43). To be fallible as a therapist means to be tentative about the hypotheses we generate regarding why a patient reacts, thinks, feels or behaves in a particular way. It means taking the patient's view of the treatment seriously and it means reflecting, again and again, on our own subjectivity and its possible influence on the patient. A stance of fallibilism leads us to reject such therapeutic goals as perfecting technique or formulating exact interpretations.

Working intersubjectively is a collaborative venture of making sense together. The stance that best promotes making sense together is one of empathic-introspective inquiry. According to Orange and colleagues (1997), "Such inquiry seeks to illuminate the principles unconsciously organizing the patient's experience (empathy), the principles unconsciously organizing the analyst's experience (introspection), and the oscillating psychological field created by the interplay between the two (intersubjectivity)" (pp. 43–44). We develop our thoughts on empathy and on the empathic-introspective stance more fully in the following chapter. However, within this oscillating field there is much room for misperception and misunderstanding. For example, our subjectivity may interfere either with the capacity to listen or with our understanding of the patient's organization of experience. Remaining fallible necessitates that the therapist maintains an appreciation for the complex and highly subjective filtering of what both the patient and therapist think is going on.

Nevertheless, working from the intersubjective perspective, like other forms of dynamic psychotherapy, requires a great deal of training. A necessary complement to the acceptance of fallibility is the capacity to manage one's sense of uncertainty. Psychotherapy is a very ambiguous and confusing process. Experienced therapists often feel adrift and anxious about how and where the voyage is going. Like a kayaker paddling through strange rapids, you may not be familiar with the waters or with what lies around the bend. However, if you know how to maneuver your kayak, keep it upright, and right it if you get swamped, then your anxiety and uncertainty are more easily tolerated. Course work and supervision, as well as one's personal psychotherapy, all enhance this process. Being a psychotherapist requires lifelong learning.

Every treatment is different because with each new patient, a new and unique intersubjective field is created. Thus, while there are guidelines to follow, such as professional ethics, there are no absolute rules of the game. For example, how many sessions a week constitute a proper analysis? The question of session frequency as a measure of the psychoanalytic validity of a treatment was raised early last century and continues to be debated to the present day. Abraham Kardiner (1977) reports that Freud always saw his analytic patients six days a week. However, when Kardiner and five other foreign students arrived in Vienna hoping to be trained and analyzed by Freud, Freud had only thirty hours available, time enough for only five of them to be seen. Anna Freud reportedly figured out that if five patients are each seen for six hours, which totals to thirty patient/hours, then six patients can be seen for only five hours, which totals to the same thirty patient/hours. Therefore, if each student gave up one session a week, the one hour saved from each of five patients would allow for a sixth patient to be fit in. So the six sessions per week analysis became five sessions per week, and nowadays many analysts consider that a proper analysis can occur in four, or three, or even two weekly sessions. Some argue persuasively that a psychoanalytic process should not be defined at all by structural factors like frequency of contact (Fosshage 1997a, 1999, Stolorow 1994b).

Clearly conventions change and there is nothing sacred or scientific about the frequency of sessions. The same can be said for the duration of a session. The fifty-minute hour has, for many analysts, now shrunk to forty-five minutes. In this way therapists have countered currency inflation with session length deflation: more sessions can be fit into the day. Now, then, if we set the length of a session at forty-five minutes, is this some immutable boundary that must never be violated? As we have seen, the length of the therapy session is set, not just with the best interests of the patient in mind, but also in accord with what suits the therapist. Are we not permitted to go over a few minutes if the patient is in great distress at the end? The answer to this question, as to so many other questions concerning analytic rules, must be, "It depends."

At this point, we would like to comment on the notion of eclecticism in psychotherapeutic theory and practice. We often encounter colleagues and students who would like to take the most applicable aspects of diverse theories and techniques and mix them according to the needs of the patient. We agree with Greenberg and Mitchell (1983), who in describing the two major psychoanalytic traditions, the drive/structure model and the relational model, observe, "A fundamentally different understanding of human development directs the two models toward equally incompatible approaches to the therapeutic action of psychoanalysis" (p. 390). Each theory of mind has its own unique worldview and its own distinctive perspective on the origins of psychopathology from which it derives its principles of therapeutic action. While one can be a little bit empathic, empathy is not a technique but a sensibility. The therapeutic effectiveness of the empathic-introspective stance derives its mutative power from a commitment to the consistent, not occasional, application of this sensibility.

SUMMARY

Here are some important prescriptions for the unsettling attitude we advocate for therapists: Do not give in to your need to act helpfully. Remain flexible, fallible, and uncertain. Know that however you try to avoid influencing your patients, you inevitably influence and are influenced by them. Apart from ethical standards, there are no hard-and-fast rules to guide your work. Sometimes even the unquestioned and most universal practices have potentially detrimental consequences for treatment and ought to be handled with great sensitivity to their meanings for the patient. Finally, the patient's symptoms and behaviors, no matter how self-defeating or incomprehensible to the observer, represent his striving for health and psychological stability.

The basic orienting perspective for those practicing intersubjectively is on making sense of the patient's subjectivity within a particular context, as it is influenced by the person of the therapist. In subsequent chapters we address specific ways to enhance the therapist's capacity to understand the patient's subjectivity and how to respond, once the patient's perspective is grasped.

3

Understanding the Patient's State of Mind: Affect Attunement and the Empathic-Introspective Stance

There is an enormous amount of activity going on, at a variety of levels (individual/system, intrapsychic/interpersonal, verbal/nonverbal, conscious/unconscious, to name a few) when therapist and patient work to make sense together. We focus in this chapter on the empathic-introspective stance and affect responsiveness because they are two, perhaps *the two*, necessary processes in effective psychotherapy. These two relational processes provide the underpinnings for the all-important therapeutic relationship. Furthermore, they are the building blocks of both subjectivity, as we will see, and of intersubjectivity. This chapter elaborates on these two fundamental processes of intersubjectivity theory: a mode of responsiveness—affect attunement, and a mode of listening—the empathic-introspective stance. In practice, the distinction is labored, as patients frequently experience affirmation simply when the therapist listens with an ear to what the patient is feeling about the story he is telling.

In theory and practice, important processes converge around

the phenomenon of two people seeking to understand the internal world of meaning and affective experience of one of them. Consider, for example, such questions as how one person can share the private experience of another, how one person uses her personal experience to make a connection with another, and what transpires between the two when an understanding connection is made and communicated. Any discussion along these lines quickly becomes complex and experience-distant. It is paradoxical that when we attempt to clarify and specify the processes that promote effective treatment, we often end up obscuring what seemed self-evident.

Although we use the terms *empathic inquiry* and *empathic-introspective stance* interchangeably, the empathic-introspective stance includes the therapist's empathic inquiry both into the patient's subjective world and into her own. Affect attunement refers to the therapist's abilities to perceive correctly and respond meaningfully to various qualities of a patient's subjectivity. We specifically avoid the use of the term *empathy* as it is burdened with a long and confusing history, which we discuss below. Of the two processes, the more encompassing is that of empathic inquiry, which includes comprehending a full range of contextual elements, such as the emotional, historical, behavioral, and cognitive aspects of the patient's unfolding experience. In contrast, affect attunement straightforwardly describes what a therapist does or says in response to the patient's emotional states. To borrow a metaphor from the world of radio communication, in the empathic-introspective mode, the therapist acts as receiver of signals or transmissions from the patient (and her own internal world). The therapist fine-tunes the signal in order to hear as clearly as possible the subjective affect state the patient is communicating. In a different mode, that of attuned responsiveness (particularly to affects), the therapist functions as transmitter of a signal to the patient as receiver.

Affect attunement and empathic inquiry are two-person processes. They materialize in the therapeutic dyad, an intersubjective field formed from the subjectivities of patient and therapist. Once again, the therapist's subjectivity becomes both a source and a limiting factor for appreciating the subjectivity of our patients. To reiterate and elaborate some of our previous discussion, "subjectivity" refers to the sum of the personal internal experience of an individual, including much that is not conscious. Like the subject in a sentence, subjectivity is the totality of experience, action, emotion, and sensation, both conscious and unconscious, that an individual refers to when saying "I." Subjectivity, however, cannot be separated from that which is intersubjective because "all selfhood—including enduring patterns of personality and pathology—develops and is maintained within, and as a function of, the interplay between subjectivities. . . . The principle components of subjectivity . . . are the organizing principles. . . . These principles, often unconscious, are the emotional conclusions a person has drawn from lifelong experience of the emotional environment, especially the complex mutual connections with early caregivers" (Orange et al. 1997, pp. 6–7).

Each element of the theory is inextricably connected to the other. Subjectivity consists, in part, of organizing principles, formed out of lived emotional experiences with childhood caregivers. The context for the creation of the organizations of experience is the intersubjective field of early childhood, primarily the subjectivity of the caregivers as they learn to understand and respond to the unique temperament and personality of their child. A key factor in the quality of that early context is the capacity of the caregivers to appreciate and respond in soothing and affirming ways to the emotional life of the child. Therefore, a child's experience of being understood or not, especially when he contends with intense affects, is the intersubjective context (lived experience) out of which his subjectivity develops. There is no subjectivity without intersubjectivity. The critical features of the intersubjective field as it contributes to positive and stable subjectivity are those experiences that affirm, regulate, and integrate affect for both members of the dyad. It is always a system of mutual influence, with the subjectivity of each member of the dyad continually and inevitably shaped by the other.

AFFECT RESPONSIVENESS IN INTERSUBJECTIVITY THEORY

A therapist's sensitivity to affects is fundamental to the intersubjective approach to treatment for two reasons. First, as we have noted earlier, affectivity is considered the primary organizer of experience. The way we organize our experience and the principles we develop to make sense of that experience have emotion at their core. The templates formed around repeated or highly intense affective moments contribute to our development in various ways. As an example of the process, a vivacious single woman in her mid-30s became overwhelmed with anxiety whenever she participated in casual, flirtatious banter with men. For her, early experiences in which her father and older brother responded to her playful seductiveness with irritation and discomfort left her feeling bewildered and ashamed. As an adult, she believed that she was behaving inappropriately whenever she enjoyed the attention of men and responded to it. She made sense of the early affect of shame by constructing a view of herself as "silly and bad." She fit subsequent exciting interactions into these organizing ideas about herself and was left with feelings of self-loathing.

Second, affect identification, regulation, and integration are fundamental to promoting in our patients a stable, cohesive, and continuous self-experience. To extend the previous example, this patient recognized her responses of shame and bewilderment and subsequently developed an appreciation of their original intersubjective context. That is, she accepted her childhood wishes to be seen as pretty and special and recognized the discomfort of her father and brother with her playfulness—key contextual features of her early lived experience. Over time, as she understood herself and felt herself understood, her intense anxiety subsided. These transformations of affect are essential to the creation of new organizations of experience, an important goal of treatment from an intersubjective perspective. Clearly, the therapist's developing capacity for affect attunement is critical to becoming an effective clinician.

Humans are distinguished from other species in part by their capacity for abstract thought. This stunning intellectual capacity often overshadows the vitally important emotional underpinnings of our evolutionary adaptation and our psychological life. Any attempt to discuss effective treatment practices must address the phenomenon of affect. As Nancy McWilliams (1999) straightforwardly asserts, "For therapists, attention to affect has never been a choice. Patients fill our offices with their feelings" (p. 105). When emotions cannot readily be observed, therapists note, wonder, and explore their apparent absence. The therapist's personal emotional experience of working with a particular patient, in general, and at particular moments in treatment, provides essential clinical information. More than any other single factor, affective understanding grounds and guides effective treatment.

Our emphasis on affect attunement in the practice of psychotherapy places us at the center of cross-currents of contemporary psychological theory and research. Interest and debate associated with the role of affective experience in treatment extends beyond psychodynamic practice. Neuropsychologists (Grigsby and Stevens 2000, Schore 1994), cognitive theorists (Ekman 1984), process/experiential therapists (Gendlin 1996, Greenberg et al. 1993), trauma theorists (Krystal 1988), and infant researchers (Emde 1983, Tronick 1989), among many others, recognize the pivotal role played by emotions in personality development. From our theoretical perspective, affects serve as the substrate of organizations of experience. Therefore, recognizing, exploring, and integrating affects become fundamental to creating new organizations of experience.

If patients become emotional in the consulting room or appear numb to their emotions, we as therapists are contributing to their experience. "Affectivity is something that from birth onward is regulated or misregulated, within an ongoing intersubjective field" (Stolorow et al. 1999, p. 382). Inevitably, then, affective experience will be an important component of the intersubjective field created in the context of psychotherapy. In treatment, affect, or a significant lack of it, points the way to personal meaning and reveals in-the-moment processes within the intersubjective context—what is happening between therapist and patient. Therapists working from the perspective of intersubjectivity theory line up with generations of psychotherapists of many persuasions who have considered affect the "gold" of a treatment hour (Lichtenberg et al. 1992), invaluable in identifying and understanding a patient's deeper experiences of both their formative early life and the immediate therapeutic relationship.

In the evolution of psychoanalytic ideas, and for intersubjectivity theory in particular, affects have replaced drives as the central motivational construct. As we integrate findings from infant research, neuropsychology, and ethology, we find convergence around the centrality of affect for making sense of personal experience. Much has been written about emotion, and theories of emotion include evolutionary, psychophysiological, neurological, and psychodynamic constructs, each deriving from a particular scientific tradition (Plutchik 1980). However, an extensive exploration of these theories is beyond the scope of this book. For our purpose—to enhance the capacity of therapists to notice and respond to their patients' affect—we offer a brief overview of generally agreed upon ideas.

Tomkins (1962, 1963), Plutchik (1962, 1980), and Izard (1971, 1977) identified several primary inborn affects of infants. Roughly, these can be grouped as either positive or negative. According to

Izard's (1971) typology, they are interest-excitement, excitement-joy, surprise-startle, fear-terror, distress-anguish, anger-rage, contempt, disgust, and shame-humiliation. Tomkins (1962) proposed the emotional categories of interest, surprise, joy, anguish, fear, disgust, and rage. So, from two basic emotional states, distress and contentment, the fundamental affects appear spontaneously in newborns. As development proceeds, the subtlety and variety of responses increase, giving nuance and texture to our emotional life.

The hard-wired, observable emotions identified by Tomkins and others appear to be responses to either internal or environmental stimuli. When physically uncomfortable, as in the cases of hunger, pain, or exhaustion, distress-anguish, fear, or a related negative affect may register. When the infant whimpers or screams, an attentive adult moves into action to relieve the discomfort. Alternatively, the social smile, contented gurgling, and expressions of absorbed interest of infants stimulate siblings, parents, and the casual observer spontaneously to engage with them. Clearly, affective signals are vital for an infant's survival and optimal development. In addition, they guide the efforts of caregivers to soothe or stimulate the child. In the process, when all goes well, caregivers and baby create ways of relating in which each of them feels effective and cared for.

Lichtenberg (1989) and Lichtenberg and colleagues (1992, 1996) link the biology of affects with psychological motivation; they posit five interconnected motivational systems, each with characteristic affects that function across the life span: (1) the need for psychic regulation of physiological requirements, (2) the need for attachment-affiliation, (3) the need for exploration and assertion, (4) the need to react aversively through antagonism or withdrawal, and (5) the need for sensual enjoyment and sexual excitement.

> During infancy, each system contributes to self-regulation in mutually regulatory interactions with caregivers. . . . The

> "self" develops as an independent center for initiating, organizing, and integrating motivation. The sense of self arises from experiencing that initiating, organizing, and integrating. Experiencing has an active (agent) and passive (receptor) mode. . . . The vitality of the motivational experience will depend initially on the manner in which affect-laden exchanges unfold between infants and their caregivers. . . . Lived experience is about how we human beings consciously and unconsciously seek to fulfill our needs and desires by searching in potential events for affects that signal for us that experiential fulfillment. [Lichtenberg 1989, pp. 1–2]

Lived experience, affects, needs, and motivation operate interdependently. So, for example, Lichtenberg and colleagues (1996) suggest that affective experiences associated with the attachment-affiliation motivational system include "affection, trust, love, contentment, generosity, pride, respect, courage, optimism, and moral goodness. . . . To the sugar of these feelings, the spice of moments of anger, doubt, envy, jealousy, fear, shame, and guilt intensify an attachment experience" (p. 128). Patterns emerge from lived experiences that color attachments throughout life. In a similar way, individuals form characteristic combinations of affects that influence how they go about meeting their needs in all areas. The feelings associated with activities such as assertion, ambition, or sensual pleasure derive from early lived experience and they recur repeatedly in many contexts. By attending to affects, we are alert to what needs patients may be revealing and to their characteristic ways of organizing around these needs.

Affects, then, arise in the body either to signal and/or to amplify internal experience or in response to external circumstances. They alert us to what is happening and guide us to satisfaction of our needs. From the beginning, they are powerful constituents of our subjective and relational lives. Emde (1988a,b) has described a very similar scheme based on what he considers the biological preparedness of the affective core of self. He concludes that subjective affective experience, expressed and regulated in the caregiving context has "adaptive function in facilitating self-development—that is, in sustaining and enlarging working models of the three dynamic aspects of the self system: (a) the experience of self, (b) the experience of the other (e.g., attachment figure), and (c) the experience of self with other or 'we'" (1988a, p. 37). These aspects of what he refers to as the self system are inextricably joined. Our organizations of experience (in Emde's vocabulary, our working models of ourselves) form at the interface of affect expression in the caregiving surround. In other work, Emde and Sorce (1983) cite the emotional availability of the caregiver as a primary factor in the levels of pleasure, calm, and curiosity of infants. Orange (1995) makes the case that similar emotional availability is an intersubjective quality in the treatment of adults. She characterizes such availability as a readiness to attune and respond to the patient's emotional expressions in an atmosphere of safety.

Infant studies and theories of affect provide for clinicians a topographical map of how to understand the emotional expressions of our patients—not a street map with each boulevard, lane, and landmark designated; not a trail map, with one well-trod path clearly marked. The preceding ideas on affect reflect not a universal developmental perspective with milestones unfolding in sequence, but rather a contextual, dynamic view of development. They are offered here to provide therapists with some sense of how emotional expression relates to the intersubjective world of the patient. Just as the relational world of the young child gives rise to emotions and shapes their appearance and fate, a therapeutic relationship offers the possibility for recontextualizing needs for attachment and assertion, for example. The dimension of affective expression in the context of a different lived experience in treatment allows for the transformation of core organizing principles. Is the patient offering us a glimpse of an accomplishment with pride and appropriate exhibitionism at the core? Or do we sense fear in the lack of anything to say? We don't know the meaning of our patients' emotions without exploring them together. However, we set the stage for the work of making sense of the affect by being available to notice it and by our conviction that it is important. For us, it is the thread we follow to find what is personally meaningful to our patient.

As Emde (1988a) states, "Because our affective core touches upon these aspects of experience which are most important to us as individuals, because it organizes both meaning and motivation, it also allows us to get in touch with the uniqueness of our own (and others) experience. . . . It is the emotional availability of the caregiver in infancy which seems to be the most central growth-promoting feature of the early rearing experience" (p. 32). We recognize that what originates in infancy within the caregiving surround does not correspond literally to the therapeutic dyad. Patients are not infants and therapists are not parents. However, our ability as therapists to recognize and even to share the affective experiences of patients is profoundly important to growth and change in treatment.

Stolorow and Stolorow (1987) focus in depth on the nature and quality of responsiveness to patient's affective states in treatment. Regarding a developing sense of self, the authors point to the relationship between the integration into self-experience of "affect states involving pride, expansiveness, efficacy, and pleasurable excitement [and] the consolidation of self-esteem and self-confident ambition" (p. 68). In contrast, "early experiences of oneness with idealized sources of strength, security, and calm, . . . indicate the central role of soothing, comforting responses from caregivers in the integration of affect states involving anxiety, vulnerability, and distress" (p. 68). They link what is needed from the caregiver with the specific positive or negative affective state of the infant. To develop ambition and positive self-regard, caregivers must accept and affirm a child's early efforts to learn, to do, and to show. To support the capacity to tolerate and modulate affect, caregivers soothe children when they are upset. By a short and direct leap, we infer that a therapist's capacity to identify correctly a patient's affective expression bears directly on the nature of her response. The accuracy with which the therapist understands the emotional experiences of her patient and her own emotional availability in affirming or soothing them contribute much to the patient's improvement. (And, significantly impact the therapist, as well.)

Infant and caregiver and patient and therapist form dynamic dyads operating as self- and interactive regulation systems (Beebe and Lachmann 1998). What is being regulated is affect arousal for each member of the dyad. The implications for understanding treatment processes are enormous, and we deal with them extensively in subsequent chapters. However, in our present discussion we note that, as a system, whatever feelings or behaviors an individual expresses is a function of the operation of the system, not the exclusive domain of either individual. As mentioned above, Emde (1988a) identifies three aspects of the self system: the experience of self, the experience of other, and the experience of self-with-other. We extend his schema to the dyad. That is, wherever in the self system a person's (subject's) attention is focused (whether on self, other, or self-with-other), what is felt and experienced is inextricably related to the dyadic system. Any feature of one member of the pair can be understood fully only in terms of how each is simultaneously experiencing self-arousal and emotional regulation within the dyadic context.

Beebe and Lachmann (1996) identify affect as central to each of their "three principles of salience in the organization of the patient-analyst interaction" (p. 7). The principles are metaphors derived from infant research that the authors consider applicable to adult treatment. They are (1) ongoing regulation, (2) disruption and repair, and (3) heightened affective moments. The authors consider heightened affective moments to be

> jointly constructed by both participants. An expectation of how the interaction will go is transformed for both analyst and

> patient. Simultaneously, the patient's state is dramatically transformed. These moments can be integrative, *thereby* altering the transference. The therapeutic action of heightened affective moments is mediated through state transformations that potentially usher in opportunities for expanded self-regulatory range and altered patterns of mutual regulation. [p. 7]

In the language of intersubjectivity theory, since experience is organized around affect, experiences of affect in treatment provide opportunities for new organizations to form, as well as for growth in the areas of self-regulation and sharing of affect states.

We wish to extend the discussion of shared affective moments beyond mutual influence and mutual regulation. In terms of our discussion of affective expression within an interpersonal world, we understand intersubjective influence and regulation to be operating at birth. Later, at the age of 7 to 9 months, infants develop a capacity to recognize shared affective experience (Stern 1985). When an infant expresses emotion and that expression is mirrored or matched by a caregiver, the infant can notice that the other is experiencing the same subjective state. Stern gives the following example:

> A ten-month-old girl finally gets a piece in a jigsaw puzzle. She looks toward her mother, throws her head up in the air, and with a forceful arm flap raises herself partly off the ground in a flurry of exuberance. The mother says "YES, thatta girl." The "YES" is intoned with much stress. It has an explosive rise that echoes the girl's fling of gesture and posture. [p. 141]

Stern describes this state as interaffectivity, an intersubjective experience that includes recognition of shared experience. So, not only is mutual influence continually operating in the service of regulating the arousal and behavior of each member of the dyad, but also sometimes the two subjectivities share a common emotional experience (interaffectivity). This can happen when either of the pair notices some demonstration of emotion and does something that the first one recognizes as a match. These are clearly powerful moments. Infant researchers will have more to tell us about the meaning of these preverbal experiences. Such shared moments probably represent the point at which empathic inquiry has informed the response of the onlooker. In a complementary way, the one whose affect inspired the response feels noticed and understood. The combined result is a shared experience that certainly contributes to formation of a bond between the two.

A final instance of how affect contributes to a core organization of experience in early childhood is that of attachment. As an infant matures and becomes mobile, an attachment to a particular caregiver ensures his proximity to someone who will anticipate his needs, recognize his distress, and protect or soothe him. At other times, the attentive caregiver may facilitate exploration or provide appropriate stimulation. When the child is excited, curious or feeling bold, the attachment bond serves to keep him safe and allows learning and exploration to unfold without the inhibiting effects of anxiety, fear, or pain. At the same time, joy, excitement, and shared pleasure enhance learning and development. Clearly, the flux of affect states becomes a kind of rhythm on which the melody of maturation unfolds. In other words, affects are part of an infant's subjective experience from the start of life and are the seeds around which patterns of organization form. They also provide the glue of attachment, in particular, and relationships, in general.

Given the centrality of affects in self- and relational experience it comes as no surprise that problems with affect can become psychological problems. If affective states are repeatedly experienced as extreme and not well modulated by the environment, we believe that infants develop self-protective adaptations in order to achieve a sense of physiological equilibrium. For example, the infant may look away and withdraw from interacting, may escalate crying to a red-faced bawl, or may find his thumb to suck. The affect and whatever somatic signals accompany its onset, the behavioral adaptation to contain the affect, and, eventually, the meaning the episode comes to have for a child are all of a piece. Although explicit memories of specific very early experiences are not available to the adult who enters treatment, we are certain that intense (or inhibited) affects will be revealed in the treatment as central to each organization of experience and to understanding the worldview of our patients.

An alternative psychological problem to the one discussed above, modulating and containing affect, is the situation in which the patient's affective experience appears empty, depleted, or undifferentiated. In some, the early, inborn emotions we described above seem to go underground. Those experiences of the developing child where strong affects must be disavowed or dissociated in order to maintain needed ties to caregivers are especially pathogenic. As adults, they appear to have little zest for life or not much feeling about anything or anyone. In these cases, the therapist will notice the absence of affect or difficulty in discriminating among affects or even the relationship between bodily sensations and affect states. We have more to say on the ways a therapist works with a patient to vitalize and differentiate affective experience in our subsequent discussion of selfobject functions provided by therapists. At this point we simply point out the importance of recognizing the nature of a patient's affective expression as a significant element of the patient's experience.

We list briefly, however, the ways that a therapist may respond to affective expression by a patient. First, she may recognize affect where the patient does not. The patient may not recognize that what he is feeling *is* a feeling or may not have words for the experience. By identifying and naming affects and helping the patient differentiate them, she is facilitating self-delineation. Second, a therapist may need to match or affirm proud or expansive affects in order to solidify a capacity for joy and pleasure in the sense of self. Third, by noticing, tolerating, containing, and modulating negative affects such as fear, sadness, or anger, the therapist can facilitate their integration into the sense of self. These efforts support increased cohesion and consolidation of self-experience. Clearly, articulation, regulation, and integration of affective experience in our patients enhance their subjective world. As we have tried to describe, in the process the therapist both contributes to and is changed by the work.

We wish to highlight the difference between noticing affect and sharing an affective experience: the former is a clinical practice to be developed and refined with time and experience; the latter is an ideal that will sometimes materialize out of careful, disciplined attention to the subjectivity of our patients and at other times will come spontaneously.

THE EMPATHIC-INTROSPECTIVE STANCE AND INTERSUBJECTIVITY THEORY

Empathy is an often-used term but a poorly understood concept. Like other powerful human capacities, empathy is something we recognize but find difficult to explain. Theorists agree that "it" is probably an essential element of any successful treatment, and intersubjectivity theorists, when referring to the empathic-introspective investigatory stance, consider empathic listening to be a bridge to the subjectivity of the patient. As such, the affectively attuned responses of the therapist based on her empathic understanding make possible a special kind of subjective experience for the patient, one that includes feeling known and understood, and one that provides the basis for a new organization of experience.

In Chapter 1, we described the distinction made by Kohut (1959) and discussed by Stolorow (1994a) regarding empathy as an observational stance in contrast to an emotional bond. In an attempt to reduce confusion, Stolorow suggests that empathy and other related terms refer to the particularly psychoanalytic method of gathering information on the subjectivity of the patient. For the connection between two people, the particular bond created through feeling understood, he offers the term "affective responsiveness" (p. 44). In this chapter we focus on the therapist's attempts to enter the inner experience of the patient, that form of empathy referring to the mode of psychoanalytic investigation. We also identify the affective processes in the patient and the listening strategies of the therapist. In a subsequent chapter we develop more fully the idea of relationship in the context of intersubjectivity theory, and, thereby, address the other, more universal, understanding of empathy as a "powerful emotional bond between people" (Kohut 1982, p. 397).

Empathic inquiry refers to the therapist's attempts to understand the internal world of the patient. While the traditional self-psychological stance was for the therapist to put herself into the patient's experience, understanding the patient from the patient's point of view, intersubjectivity theory recognizes that whatever the therapist sees in the patient's experience is colored by her own lens. Therefore, while our work is patient-focused, we can never fully know the patient's experience except as it is filtered through the subjectivity of the therapist.

Listening to the patient, understanding the context of the patient's life experience, and reflecting that understanding to the patient constitute the essential aspects of empathic inquiry. As simple as it sounds, recognizing the perspective of the patient poses the biggest challenge to clinical work, in our opinion. Beyond this, to work intersubjectively means grasping the "inner pattern" of the patient's life (Atwood and Stolorow 1993, p. 28) while maintaining our sense of our own subjectivity. "Grasping" another's subjectivity is what is meant by empathic understanding.

Understanding formed out of empathic inquiry concerns what is near to the experience of the patient. Psychoanalytic theories include many complex concepts having to do with intrapsychic processes, particularly unconscious dynamics. As guiding principles for therapeutic technique, they can position the therapist far from the patient's immediate experience. However, attuned affective responsiveness is measured by the way it connects to what rings true to the patient. To be experienced as attuned, a therapist's response must feel right to the patient. So, ultimately, attuned responsiveness is what the patient experiences as attuned. We do not mean, however, that attuned responsiveness only connects with what the patient is aware of or has previously recognized. We mean simply that responses arising from the therapist's grasp of the patient's personal reality resonate emotionally and intellectually for the patient. The responses do not seem far-fetched, critical, or untrue. Rather, even if the articulation communicated by the therapist has never consciously occurred to the patient before, it seems genuinely to make sense.

An important corollary to empathic understanding and attuned responsiveness is that our theory of intersubjectivity does not dictate to us what the content or meaning of the patient's experience is. Consequently, we assume nothing specific about why a patient acts in certain ways. Our theory only informs us, as we discussed in Chapter 1, that (1) humans are prewired to influence each other, (2) humans continually and inevitably organize their experience around frequently repeated patterns of interaction and associated affect states, (3) the vitality and solidity of one's subjective sense of self significantly determine one's level of functioning in virtually every area of life, and (4) the experiences of making sense together of one's core organizing principles and of feeling understood provide the possibility for new organizations of experience. Based on those assumptions, we attempt to engage the patient's experience and to articulate our understanding of that experience to the patient.

We enter into a therapeutic dialogue oriented by three aspects of intersubjectivity theory: our assumptions, our attitudes, and our subjective experience. Our assumptions concern notions of mutual influence and the nature of human beings to organize experience. Our attitudes include the conviction that the patient strives for health, that no predetermined meaning can be imposed on the patient's experience, and that we try to understand rather than fix the patient. Regarding our subjective experience, we have said that our capacity to enter into the worlds of our patients is limited by our own subjectivities. However, that very subjectivity is one significant source for understanding the other person. "Introspection" in the empathic-introspective stance refers to two processes: looking within ourselves for analogues or clues to what our patients are experiencing and attending to our contribution to the intersubjective field (Stolorow 1994b). We do this tentatively, fully aware that what we notice within are *our* affect, *our* associations, and *our* meaning formed at this moment in this particular intersubjective context. Thus, introspection allows us into the private worlds of our patients and ourselves.

To illustrate the nature of understanding developed from the empathic-introspective stance we offer a brief example. It is important to note that the patient's experience was not fully conscious for her, that the therapist's attempts at supporting and normalizing the patient's experience were not "warm" (what is popularly thought of as empathy), and, finally, that following up on the patient's emotions provided the key to understanding the patient's experience.

> A woman in her early 40s, the stay-at-home mother of three school-aged children, talked intermittently in treatment about the parenting style of a close friend and her husband. She focused extensively on her friend's husband and his limitations as a father, his inability to understand his sons' behavior, and his blundering attempts to be a parent. The patient was unaware of the source of her fascination with this couple, particularly with the husband's rigid and harsh manner with his sons. The therapist's initial responses explored the connection between her friends' parenting and the patient's own experience as the child of similarly unresponsive caregiving. These interventions were based on a

> view of the patient's childhood relationship with her parents, whose style was not abusive, but distracted, uninterested, and rigidly moralistic. Despite the positive and supportive nature of the therapist's responses, the patient remained troubled and unsatisfied by them. The therapist's initial view that the meaning of the patient's fascination with her friends' parenting style had to do with her being the child of comparable parents did not match with the patient's subjectivity. Only when the therapist "got" that the patient feared her own inability to understand her children and her impulses to respond harshly and rigidly with them did the patient feel that both she and the therapist understood why she was so interested in her friends' parenting behaviors.

The therapist's nonjudgmental acknowledgment of the patient's fears became the basis for further work, including the patient's emotional reconnection to her isolated and barren relationship with her own parents. The therapist's ultimate understanding of the patient's sense of herself as a blundering and insensitive parent opened the treatment in a way that had been blocked previously.

To further elaborate the elusive concept of the empathic-introspective stance, we note a few cases of what empathic understanding is *not*. In general, from our supervisory work with students first embarking on the practice of psychotherapy, we notice their mistaken belief that empathy corresponds with any positive response to the patient. Students frequently preface their case presentations with a remark such as, "I really tried to empathize with what the patient was talking about," and then proceed to describe agreeing with the patient, dismissing the patient's worries, endorsing the patient's behavior, or a host of other affirming actions. These interventions suggest the confusion we noted earlier between what is popularly considered to be empathy and its technical meaning for psychotherapists working intersubjectively. To further clarify some of this confusion, we address a few of the specific misconceptions about empathy that we encounter with supervisees.

The most common error is the confusion of sympathy with empathy. Sympathy represents the concordance of experience between two people—the feeling state in one is similar to that of the other. If I sympathize with another, I hurt for him based on how *I* would feel in that circumstance. Faced with similar events, our reactions coincide. However, responses derived from a stance of empathic listening are specifically based on a vicarious experience by one person of the emotional experience of another and of its meaning for that second person. We do not focus on what we would feel in a similar context but on how we sense the patient feels. The distinction is critical, as the cornerstone of psychotherapy from the intersubjective perspective, once again, privileges the subjective experience of the patient.

The crucial difference between empathy and sympathy is that empathy refers to a way of listening to the patient's experience, and sympathy is a response from the therapist based on similarity of experience between patient and therapist. So, for example, hearing that a patient spent the weekend isolated in his study, working to meet a grant deadline, a therapist might respond, "You're furious at losing an entire weekend to work!" Such a response, based on the limited information given, is as likely to derive from how the therapist might feel in a similar situation as from the patient's actual experience. While we do advocate that the therapist articulate her tentatively held understanding of the patient's affective experience, this must be done with an awareness of and appreciation for the fallibility of the therapist's understanding. The point is not what the therapist thinks and feels but what the patient thinks and feels, and therapists, in order to facilitate exploration of the subjectivity of the patient, must be alert to the difference.

A second mistaken effort that derives from the notion of empathy as a way of responding results from a therapist's intervening with a personal endorsement of the patient's behavior.

While the patient may find such interventions gratifying or validating (or, ironically, gratuitous, hollow or demeaning) they are the value-laden opinions of the therapist and not the therapist's understanding of the patient and its meaning for the patient. So, responding with "Good for you!" or "I'm proud of you!" or "That's awful!" is not an understanding grounded in the empathic-introspective stance. Such interventions are *not* outside the range of appropriate interventions, but they do not necessarily represent responses based on accurate reading of the patient's subjectivity. When appropriate, such interventions represent the therapist's attempt to interrupt the patient's self-pathologizing and to support the patient's striving for health. The essence an empathic-introspective stance is not, as is so often believed, for the therapist to be accepting, nonjudgmental, or kind, however therapeutic such responses may be. Empathy refers to a way of understanding the patient's experience, not the therapist's response to that experience.

Responses formed out of empathic inquiry do not minimize or reframe the experience of the patient. Interventions designed to make a patient feel better by telling him that what he fears or believes is "catastrophizing" or "black and white thinking" are not necessarily attuned, even if they are descriptive. For example, one patient with intense anxiety in interpersonal situations consistently interpreted the occasional hurried brusqueness of her co-workers as signs of their (anticipated) rejection of her. No amount of reasoning or reality testing altered the patient's conviction that she had finally been cast out by her peers. Only through repeated exploration of numerous instances of this experience did the patient and therapist come to make sense together of the patient's view of herself as a burdensome annoyance with whom others inevitably get fed up. Because this organization of experience pervaded her subjectivity, a more realistic appraisal of the meaning of her co-worker's intentions had no impact on the patient's level of anxiety. Only when the therapist understood well enough how, as a child, the patient had repeatedly felt that her overburdened and perfectionistic mother was frustrated with her age-appropriate needs and limitations, could the patient become less anxious in anticipation of going to work.

While subjectivity and objective reality are not mutually exclusive, the realm of experience available for observation and reflection in psychotherapy is that of personal meaning for a patient. The givens of life—our gender, basic level of intelligence, early educational opportunities, ethnic heritage, or family configuration, to name a few—clearly have a reality that cannot be reduced to the subjective. However, the personal meaning created around such givens is highly subjective and is grist for the psychotherapy mill. Focusing on how things really are is a wild goose chase for therapists and can leave patients feeling challenged, scolded, and misunderstood. Noting objective circumstances and the way they come to play in the treatment is highly important in therapeutic work when the patient wonders about them or when introduced with an ear to what the meaning is for the patient. From our perspective, when the therapist finds herself focusing on the realities of the patient's life, some anxiety about helping or feeling competent or being evaluated may have become activated in the therapist.

> An attractive Chinese woman in her 30s experienced almost delusional levels of fear over social relationships at work. Over many years of treatment and in scores of work and social situations, the patient described interactions in which she was sure that a casual look or statement meant that the other person was judging her as stupid, weird, or, worst of all, a pervert. The therapist believed that the patient's observations amounted to projections of her own intolerable subjective judgments of herself. Whenever the therapist lapsed into trying to clarify what had objectively transpired in an interaction, the treatment inevitably veered toward misunderstanding and disruption. The patient felt that the therapist

> did not believe her and, ultimately, could not accept her as she was. When the therapist examined her own subjectivity regarding this recurrent scenario, she found that accepting as subjectively valid the patient's paranoia felt to her as if she were colluding with the patient in a distortion of reality. The therapist valued highly her own capacity for reason and objectivity as a source of positive self-esteem. Only when the patient poignantly observed that the therapist appeared unwilling to accept the perversion within the patient did the overlapping and interplay of interacting subjectivities clarify for the therapist. The therapist wished to bypass or override the patient's experience of feeling like a pervert by focusing attention on how she misconstrued what people were seeing and thinking about her. By failing to see the world as the patient saw it, the therapist paradoxically contributed to the patient's feelings that her most private self-experience was offensive to everyone.

The following vignette concerns the treatment of a woman very much out of touch with her emotional core. Kim presented a challenge for her therapist because she showed determination and energy in attacking many problems that befell her. Kim's attitude initially left the therapist bewildered about why she was not able to create a life that included the intimacy and satisfaction she claimed to want. The therapist watched and listened closely to the patient's descriptions of her frustrations with co-workers and unsatisfying telephone conversations with family members. Over time, a picture of Kim's early family life, including the quality of the atmosphere at home, took shape in the therapist's mind. Repeatedly, the therapist looked within herself for emotional reactions to potential meanings of day-to-day events that Kim talked about in her sessions. Gradually, the therapist sensed the feelings of insignificance and inferiority at the heart of Kim's organization of experience. An organizing principle of Kim's subjectivity was that she not display her emotions in order to preserve needed ties to others.

> The patient, who seemed both too young and too old for her 36 years, tried to find a starting point for the session and began retelling a conversation with a friend from a few days earlier. It was a story of the patient's friend whose daughter, at age 25, gave birth to a baby, prematurely, after a risky, complicated pregnancy. The baby died after one week. Both grandmother and mother made heroic efforts to comfort their daughters, with special concern that they not feel alone. At first the patient choked back her tears but gave up and let them flow freely. When the tears were spent, she looked at her therapist, as if to ask what it all meant. So they began to explore this powerful experience. Initially, she had no idea why she would be so moved by the story of maternal love and protectiveness. Her sadness and tears didn't connect with any conscious memories or wishes or any sense of herself as identifying with one of the characters.
>
> Sitting across from her, the choice of story and her tears made sense to the therapist. Her own brusque, competent mother believed that the way to launch her children in life was to make them tough, cynical survivors, and she responded to complaints of stomachaches and sore throats with, "It doesn't hurt. You'll be fine once you get to school." And, in fact, the strategy of this patient's Korean mother, who was determined that her children be successful Americans, accomplished just that. But the price was high, and two years ago, with a dawning awareness that her frenetic work pace and active social schedule camouflaged a life without deep intimacy or the prospect of a family, the patient entered treatment. That she cried openly was very different from her initial matter-of-fact, no nonsense, business-like attitude. As the therapist articulated her understanding of her story, the patient wept softly. She felt sad for herself at age 5, going off

to school for the first time, unable to speak English, and knowing no one, sobbing while her mother walked resolutely away.

This vignette highlights a number of significant therapeutic tasks. For this patient, experiencing emotion and understanding its connection to both her early life and her current dissatisfactions has taken enormous effort. She is not a victim of physical or sexual abuse, and in most areas of her life she functions very well. However, her difficulties with emotions are at the core of her problems with intimacy.

SUMMARY

Therapy that is practiced from the stance of intersubjectivity theory weaves together an empathic listening stance and affect responsiveness to promote affect recognition, affect regulation, and affect integration in the patient. The more accepting we are of our own affects, the easier it is to engage with another in an emotionally intimate relationship.

4

The Centrality of Relationship

The history of psychoanalytic thought from Freud to the present has been characterized by the evolution of ideas and theories, their modification and revision, over time. Freud's first theory of psychopathology and treatment stressed the central role of childhood sexual trauma in the formation of neuroses. Most of Freud's first patients were young women with symptoms of hysteria (from the Greek for wandering uterus), which, in the late 1800s, was thought to be an exclusively female disorder. Through the use of hypnosis, Freud uncovered in these adult women repressed memories of childhood incestuous seductions by their fathers. He concluded that neurosis was instigated by some real-life traumatic encounter with another person, usually a close family member or friend. In modern terms, Freud was treating posttraumatic stress disorders.

What transformed this trauma theory of neurosis into an intrapsychic theory was Freud's growing conviction that what he had assumed were literal memories of real experience were actually memories of childhood fantasies or wishes. Now, instead of accepting that his patients' recollections of incestuous childhood sexual encounters were memories of real events, Freud proposed that his patients were remembering (oedipal) fantasies that they had as children. When this history is viewed in the context of today's debate over false memories, it is striking how these issues are still being discussed 100 years after Freud originally introduced them.

Freud's reformulation marked the beginning of the intrapsychic perspective, where the primary focus of psychoanalytic exploration is on the conflict between wishes and defenses within an individual isolated mind. Interaction with or relationship to another was considered to be inconsequential to the formation of psychopathology in the individual. Thus, instead of finding the source of psychopathology in disturbed relationships or interactions with external others, psychopathology was understood as growing out of the conflict between wishes and defenses within an individual isolated mind.

The intrapsychic focus in psychoanalysis continues to wield considerable influence today. However, starting in the 1950s, with the development in England of the British object relations theories of Fairbairn and Winnicott, new voices were attempting to assimilate back into psychoanalytic thinking the role of relationship with others. In America, Harry Stack Sullivan's emphasis on the interpersonal roots of mental disorders was challenging the centrality of the intrapsychic perspective. Sullivan stressed the centrality of interpersonal relations in forming and treating psychopathology. An important step in the evolution and increased acceptance of interpersonal thinking occurred in 1988 with the publication of Stephen Mitchell's *Relational Concepts in Psychoanalysis.* This book sought to integrate British object relations theory, interpersonal theory, and self psychology under the rubric of an inclusive relational theory.

Once theories of psychopathology shifted to include relational experiences, theories of technique and practice changed comparably. Many contemporary psychoanalysts now acknowledge the importance of the relationship between patient and analyst as necessary for beneficial therapeutic outcomes. However, specifically which aspects of the therapeutic relationship contribute to good treatment outcomes remain vague and unspecified.

Heinz Kohut (1959, 1966), a former president of the American Psychoanalytic Association, initiated a crucial development in theory. Kohut (1971) originally sought to expand the psychoanalytic understanding and treatment of narcissistic disorders. At the same time, he tried to remain true to his ego psychology roots by retaining its intrapsychic focus and instinctual drive theory. Patients with narcissistic psychopathology were formerly thought to be unresponsive to ego psychoanalytic treatment because they failed to develop the necessary transference neurosis (revival in the transference of the conflict from which neurotic symptoms derive). Kohut recognized that, while these patients did not form the traditional type of transference neurosis, they did develop what he described as narcissistic transferences. Kohut identified three characteristic transference configurations that narcissistic patients develop with their analysts: mirroring, in which the patient longs for the acknowledging and affirming gaze of an admired other; idealizing, in which the patient longs to connect himself to an idealized other and bask in the glow of her protective and admired qualities; and twinship, in which the patient feels a sense of oneness with a like-minded other. These three types of transference have become known as selfobject transferences because they describe three types of relationship that patients form with their therapists in efforts to satisfy previously unfulfilled selfobject longings. For Kohut, the selfobject transferences reflected the strivings of adults for the kinds of experiences a child needs to have with caregivers in order for healthy narcissism to develop. Healthy narcissism is characterized by realistic ambitions, a sense of agency and a belief that one is lovable. It is important to emphasize that for Kohut and subsequent generations of self psychologists, healthy development, the development of a vital and cohesive self, requires relationships with early caregivers in which a child's selfobject longings are met with attuned responsiveness. It follows, then, that self disorders result from persistent misattunement to the child's selfobject needs.

While Kohut tried to integrate these ideas into an ego psychology framework, his emphasis on the importance of the external other for the mirroring, idealizing, and twinship selfobject transference experiences put the commitment to the intrapsychic perspective under pressure. The intrapsychic perspective views the other in the transference as a screen onto which patients displace or project their inner conflicts. Thus, the intrapsychic focus of analysis is on what goes on within the structures of the isolated mind of the patient. The actuality of the other is extraneous to the treatment process.

As we have seen, for Kohut's understanding of the selfobject transferences the experience of the other as a participant in relationship with the patient was vitally important. Kohut (1977, 1984), therefore, found himself moving away from the intrapsychic origins of psychopathology and back toward Freud's earlier notions of psychopathology resulting from a failed relationship.

To describe the nature of the relationship with the other in the selfobject transferences, Kohut introduced the concept of the self-selfobject relationship. The construct of the selfobject was developed to explain how another person (an object) might lend certain of her psychological capacities to the subject who was deficient in these functions. For the developing child, the selfobject functions provided by the caregivers enable the child to develop a cohesive self-organization. Children and adults whose selfobject experiences were inadequate were thought to suffer from deficits in their self-organization. Kohut (1984) defined the selfobject as "that dimension of our experience of another person that relates to this person's functions in shoring up the self" (pp. 49–50). He therefore spoke of the selfobject as an object who was experienced as providing those needed psychological functions that promote cohesion in the developing or deficient self.

While Kohut was originally concerned with understanding and treating narcissistic personality disorders, he gradually came to appreciate that *all* people, the troubled and the untroubled, need the sustaining function of selfobject relationships throughout life to help maintain a vital and cohesive self-organization. According to Kohut (1984), "Self psychology holds that self-selfobject relationships form the essence of psychological life from birth to death, that a move from dependence (symbiosis) to independence (autonomy) in the psychological sphere is no more possible, let alone desirable, than a corresponding move from a life dependent on oxygen to a life independent of it in the biological spheres" (p. 47). From this perspective, inadequate selfobject experiences with caregivers during early development are at the root of all psychogenic disorders. Accordingly, all these patients can be understood as suffering from varying degrees of disorder to their self-organization.

The function of selfobject experience has been expanded and clarified since Kohut's original work. Since affects, as discussed in Chapters 1 and 3, are central organizers of self-experience, it follows that for intersubjectivity theory, "selfobject functions pertain fundamentally to the integration of *affect* into the organization of self-experience, and that the need for selfobject ties pertains most centrally to the need for attuned responsiveness to affect states in all stages of the life cycle" (Stolorow et al. 1987, p. 66).

Here we have at least a partial answer to the question of what aspects of the relationship between patient and therapist promote healthy transformations. The selfobject function of "attuned responsiveness to affect states" is that aspect of the relationship with the other that promotes the cohesion, continuity, and positive coloration of self-experience. This allows for an expansion of the construct of selfobject functioning beyond mirroring, idealizing, and twinship that Kohut proposed. Now, all those experiences with the other, whether verbal or nonverbal, that promote the integration of affect into the organization of self-experience are considered selfobject experiences.

Selfobject experience is a relational phenomenon. Concerned caregivers respond to what they believe are the needs of children; friends and partners do likewise for their loved ones; and therapists integrate their theoretical assumptions with their empathic gleanings in attempts to impart understanding to patients. Therapists strive to understand the world from the patient's perspective by listening for affect, recognizing unconscious organizing activity, and searching for personal analogues to the patient's presentation. This action of the therapist may or may not provide selfobject experience for the patient because the personal meaning to the patient is what determines the nature of the experience. A therapist attempts to provide attuned responsiveness, and the patient organizes his experience of those efforts. Whether healthy transformations grow out of the treatment is a property of the dynamic system of the dyad—the relationship.

It should be clear that since selfobject experiences by definition are those experiences that promote the integration of affect and consolidation of self-cohesion, there could be no bad selfobject experience. There are, of course, bad objects and destructive relationships with these bad objects; that is, relationships that foster fragmentation and disintegration, retraumatization and rigid defensiveness. However, these would not be considered bad selfobject relationships. Selfobject relationships are, in their essence, growth promoting. They foster transformations of self-experience; that is, increased capacity for affect integration and self-cohesion. In Chapter 6, we refer to experiences that are organizing but are not transforming; that is they strengthen defensive organizations. These experiences should not be confused with selfobject experiences.

One of the fundamental assumptions of self psychology and intersubjectivity theory is that striving for health motivates much of human behavior, even what appear to be maladaptive behaviors. Striving for health can be seen in people's attempts to engage in new relationships that will provide what was developmentally missing but needed, that is, new selfobject relationships. It is to our patients' credit that they have not retreated into depressed or psychotic isolation but have persisted in seeking out needed selfobject experiences by risking a new relationship with the therapist, whom they hope will become the needed and wished for new object.

Striving for health can also be seen in people's attempts to avoid retraumatization. Let us take as an example the notion of the negative therapeutic reaction. Freud (1923) observed that some patients, when offered "correct" interpretations, got worse instead of better. This has been variously explained as the patient's wish to frustrate the analyst, as an expression of the patient's underlying masochism, or as a manifestation of an unconscious sense of guilt. However, if we examine the patient's "negative" reaction from the perspective of seeking health, we turn our attention to the perceived dangers the patient experienced or anticipated to be coming from the "correct" interpretation. One possible source of danger might be the therapist's misattunement to the patient. If the therapist believes she has made an accurate or correct interpretation but the patient gets worse or responds negatively, might it be that the therapist, who apparently steadfastly believes she is correct in spite of the patient's response, is actually quite wrong for the patient? The attitude betrayed in the label "negative therapeutic reaction" implies that the therapist is the sole judge of correctness and knows better than the patient what is good for him. It is presumed that the analyst's interpretation is correct and that the patient is to blame for his resistance to benefiting from the analyst's truth. This is, in itself, a major misattunement in that it fails to recognize the subjective correctness of the patient's response. The patient's worsening condition might not be a manifestation of resistance to the therapist's correctness. Rather, it might indicate that the patient is suffering from iatrogenic injury resulting from the therapist's failure to attune to the meanings the interpretation has for the patient. We would certainly hope that the therapist's subjectivity and the therapeutic context include a theory that allows for the latter hypothesis to be explored seriously.

Some colleagues dismissively assume that being experienced as a selfobject means that we are being indiscriminately, dishonestly, and disingenuously warm, caring, nurturing, or attentive to our patients. In fact, what we try to do is relate in ways that are experienced by our patients as providing needed selfobject experiences. That is, we relate with our patients in ways that promote the recognition, articulation, and integration of discrepant affect states. In doing so, we attend to features that contributed to this patient's particular organization of experience—those experiences that have undermined the development of self-cohesion. This includes providing the opportunity for a new reparative (selfobject) relationship, as well as opportunities to develop new self-understanding through the identification, articulation, and interpretation of unconscious organizing principles (see Chapter 5).

On a most general level, facilitating a potential new, reparative selfobject relationship involves maintaining a stance of attuned responsiveness to the patient's affect states. In other words, we want to foster the experience of having one's affects accepted and understood. Accepting affects does not necessarily mean approving or endorsing them, although it might. For example, if patients express hate for people of different ethnic, racial, or religious backgrounds, we can accept their feelings, tolerate their verbal expression, and explore the roots of the feelings without approving or endorsing the feelings (Ryan and Buirski, in press). On the other hand, if a patient describes a boyfriend who belittles, berates, and verbally abuses her, the therapist might comment, "He treats you badly" or "He treats you like you are stupid."

Reflecting back to our discussion in Chapter 1, we cannot know, from our patient's experience, how her boyfriend experiences his treatment of her, or how another woman might experience this treatment. We only know how this woman experiences him and we must address her experience. While objective reality is beyond either of our knowing, we do validate her subjective reality, which she desperately wishes for us to understand. It might be argued that the therapist should say, "You *feel like* he treats you badly," thereby hedging on explicitly validating the patient's view of reality. But it does not take long for patients, especially those who are getting better, to discern the analyst's reservations and, consequently, to experience such interventions as implying doubts about the validity of the patient's experience. It is important to remember that while we have doubts about anyone's capacity to know the reality of another, we can nevertheless affirm the patient's subjective experience.

Some might fear that by affirming the patient's subjective reality we reinforce the patient's defended or distorted view of the world—that we are undermining instead of supporting the patient's reality testing. If reality testing refers to giving advice, providing education, training social skills, or offering the therapist's perspective in place of the patient's, we question whether such activity fosters good interpersonal judgment or the developmentally important ability to recognize the subjectivity of the other. Frequently, the patient's early caregivers failed him in just this way—they disconfirmed and invalidated his affective experience and tried to substitute their own. Thus, by providing reality testing the therapist risks retraumatizing the patient by repeating early experiences of invalidation. We believe that people develop the capacity for affect attunement to another's experience by having had the consistent experience of another being attuned to their own affective experience. If parents or caregivers deprive children of these experiences in childhood, then later reparative opportunities with attuned others or with a therapist can enhance the capacity for affect attunement. Let us examine a clinical example.

Marjory, a woman in her mid-forties, presented with a personality organization typically described as narcissistic personality disorder. Marjory had a powerful, dictatorial father whom she experienced as invariably critical and disapproving of her. Marjory's mother, while affectionate, was intimidated by the father and never risked intervening in support of Marjory. Marjory had little capacity for self-examination and insight, and she showed little interest in understanding the subjectivity of others. During a long stretch at the beginning of therapy, Marjory complained of loneliness, but she found fault with and dismissed every person with whom she came in contact. She mistrusted their motives, felt that they were less cultured than she, read hostility into every interaction, and displayed a defensive grandiosity that always disqualified others for not being good enough for her.

Marjory's therapist, rather than addressing her grandiosity and rejecting behavior, maintained a stance of attunement to her subjective experience. Instead of questioning her disqualification of others, the therapist attuned to her underlying feeling of having been disappointed by others. The following are examples of the therapist's interventions: "Your father never appreciated you." "It's hard to find someone as well read as you." "The women at work seem so superficial compared to you." "Joe [her first date in years] only talked about himself and seemed unaware of you." After many months of listening to her therapist validate her subjectivity, Marjory's organization of experience began to change. Having experienced her therapist's attunement to her subjective world, she began to be more self-reflective and aware of the subjectivity of others. While she still offered disparaging observations of people in her life, these were now accompanied by statements like, "I wonder if I am being too critical." Her perception of her father also showed new understanding. She observed, "I wonder if he has to throw his weight around because he doesn't really feel good about himself."

Here is another example from an early therapy session with a woman in her late twenties where the focus of the therapist's interventions was on maintaining attuned responsiveness to the patient's affect states. The patient, Jill, had been talking to her therapist about friends whom she had not heard from in the months since she relocated. Jill feared that these friends had discarded her, and she reflected on what she might have done to cause them to be upset with her. She then associated to a current situation.

Patient: I've never told you how last week, how, you know, like everyone's forgotten about me, and that I'm just not used to that. It's not like I'm used to being the center of attention either, but it's just that I'm used to having people around.

Therapist: Right now you feel like there isn't anyone around for you. You feel like you're all alone . . .

Patient: (Nodding and beginning to cry).

Therapist: . . . and even the people that are here, who you're really wanting that support from, aren't giving it to you.

Patient: (Nodding, crying, reaches for tissues). So, um . . . (shakes her head) and I feel kind of stupid bringing it up to her, you know, and I'm just like well . . .

Therapist: Tell me about feeling stupid bringing it up to her.

Patient: Well, I just kind of feel like she should realize . . . but maybe . . . you know when she moved here she came with her best friend . . . (begins crying harder and shrugs her shoulders).

Here, it might be tempting for the therapist to provide reality testing by addressing the unrealistic expectation that her friend "should realize" how Jill felt—that her friend should read her mind. However, to do so would introduce the therapist's agenda and make it more important than the patient's. If our highest priority as therapists is to attune to the patient's experience, then we would put aside our need to provide reality testing in order to be responsive to the patient's affect state. This is one of those choice points in treatment where justifications could be given for selecting either path, but we advocate staying with the patient's subjective experience in non–life-threatening situations.

Therapist: So, you're feeling disappointed that she's not more sensitive to you since she's been through this herself, that you feel like you shouldn't have to spell it out for her.

Patient: (Crying and nodding) Uh-huh.

Therapist: You want her to be more attentive to what you're feeling.

Patient: Uh-huh, yeah, and sometimes I think she's kind of just wrapped up in her own world, I mean, you know she . . . she's married, and has her married friends . . . (starts to cry harder).

Therapist: And you feel unimportant.

Patient: Yes, and I mean also um, her husband was going to go camping this weekend . . . I can't believe I'm crying about this . . . I thought we were going to spend the weekend together but she told me that she was going away for the weekend to spend time with this other woman . . . and all I could think was . . . (crying) I have to spend another weekend alone.

Therapist: And that's really hard because she's forgetting about you or discounting the plans that you had made, just the two of you.

In this example, the therapist focused on the patient's subjective experience. The therapist was trying to communicate her attunement to and her understanding of the patient by articulating, putting into words, the patient's subjective experience. There were suggestions in this vignette of possible organizing principles that may shape this patient's experience: she feels unworthy and undeserving of the attention of others; she is fundamentally unlovable; she will always be alone. If this session had occurred later in treatment, or if the patient's upset had been less pressing, the therapist might have identified, articulated, and explored the workings of these organizing principles as they emerged. But what we want to communicate with this example is that the therapist's responsiveness to the patient's affect state is a new experience for the patient. Jill felt understood and known by her therapist. Repeated experiences over time of feeling understood by her therapist would promote greater self-understanding, integration of affect, and an enhanced sense of self-cohesion and self-esteem.

If this incident had occurred later in treatment, Jill might have come in feeling angry with her friend for forgetting or discounting their arrangements. But Jill does not yet possess a consistent sense of self-worth and self-confidence that would support feeling justifiably angry or indignant—instead, she feels worthless and deserving of being discounted. We doubt that true and enduring self-worth will develop from being told that these are irrational beliefs and that she should think differently, or by offering palliative, reassuring remarks about how much she is really worth. Transformations in self-worth emerge within a selfobject relationship where the other endeavors consistently to attune to the subject's affect states. In this way the therapist allows the patient a possible new experience of feeling understood, and simultaneously promotes self-understanding through the articulation of the principles that have organized her experience.

Of the variety of selfobject experiences that have been recognized, one form in particular warrants special attention. This concerns what Stolorow and Atwood (1992) have identified as the self-delineating selfobject transference. There are many patients whose fundamental experience of themselves has been so undermined and invalidated that they no longer have any trust or confidence in their personal view of the world. They do not know how they feel or how they "should" feel. Often they preface an expression of feeling with statements such as "I must be crazy" or "You will think this is crazy." A major selfobject function of the therapeutic relationship is to offset this profound experience of invalidation by identifying, articulating, and affirming affective states that have been disowned. In many cases, the patient has disowned or disavowed certain affect states that have threatened to disrupt needed relationships. For example, if the patient's mother has been unable to accept her daughter's anger and has threatened abandonment or withdrawal of love, the daughter might need to disavow her anger in order to maintain her needed tie to her mother. Chronic disavowal or denial of affect states can culminate in an individual's losing touch with her sense of vitality, initiative, agency, and self-cohesion. The therapist's identification and articulation of the patient's disavowed affect states affirms their subjective reality and promotes their integration into consciousness. This is often experienced as a self-delineating selfobject function; that is, the therapist's noticing and naming the patient's immediate state enhances the patient's sense of being whole, real, and alive. Such self-delineating selfobject functions, experienced in the therapeutic relationship, "serve to articulate and consolidate the patient's subjective reality, crystallizing the patient's experience, lifting it to higher levels of organization, and strengthening the patient's confidence in its validity" (Stolorow and Atwood 1992, p. 35).

One of the factors that confound dialogue among the various psychoanalytic theories has been the tendency for representatives of diverse theories to use the same term to signify very different clinical phenomena. Such has been the case with the term *transference*. Freud (1915b) used the term to describe how powerful affects, like love or hate, that were originally experienced in relation to significant figures during childhood, can be revived and reexperienced in relation to the analyst during adult treatment.

Since the Freudian analyst maintained a stance of neutrality and abstinence toward the patient, the patient, by design, was thought to be shielded from knowledge of the person of the analyst. If the analyst was a neutral stimulus, then the source of strong affects must reside solely within the isolated mind of the patient. These strong feelings of love or hate for the analyst were understood to be manifestations of the patient's distortions and misperceptions of current reality in terms of the past; thus, they constituted a transference neurosis. According to the theory, a patient displaced these feelings of love and hate from the original objects of childhood onto the analyst in the present. Being able to develop a transference neurosis was considered a precondition for effective psychoanalytic treatment because, through the establishment of the transference neurosis, the past was resurrected and brought alive in the present. Successful treatment meant the resolution of the transference neurosis and, thereby, the original infantile (oedipal) neurosis. The notion that transference represents a displacement of powerful affects from significant objects in the past onto the analyst in the present has, according to Stolorow and Lachmann (1984/1985), "perpetuated the view that the patient's experience of the analytic relationship is solely a product of the patient's past and psychopathology and has not been determined by the activity (or nonactivity) of the analyst" (p. 24). Intersubjectivity theory, as we shall see, offers a very different conception of the nature of transference in the therapeutic relationship. Therefore, it is legitimate to question whether, for intersubjectivity theory, the term *transference* should be retained.

From the perspective of intersubjectivity theory, "Transference in its essence refers neither to regression, displacement, projection, nor distortion, but rather to the assimilation of the analytic relationship into the thematic structures of the patient's personal subjective world. Thus conceived, transference is an expression of the universal psychological striving to organize experience and create meanings" (Stolorow et al. 1987, pp. 45–46). The idea here is that transference does not grow out of some biologically rooted need to repeat the past (Freud's repetition compulsion), but reflects the patient's attempt to make sense of the relationship with the therapist in the present in terms of the principles that have organized the patient's experience in the past. Thus, transference is not solely an intrapsychic process generated within the mind of the patient. Rather, both patient and therapist contribute to the context in which the patient comes to feel what he feels. The patient tries to make sense of these feelings in terms of the themes that have previously organized his psychological life. If, for example, a patient experiences loving feelings for his therapist, we would not presume that these feelings derive from his unconscious love for an object from childhood being displaced onto the therapist. Nor would we understand his love merely as an irrational distortion of the present relationship in terms of the past. It is important to recognize that the patient would not have fallen in love in a vacuum. He will have spent many hours alone in a room with an attuned, accepting, noncritical person who is devoted to listening and helping him make sense of his feelings. This experience of attuned responsiveness to his affect states may be what he has always longed for but failed to experience with the significant objects of childhood.

For intersubjectivity theory, then, transference concerns the way experience is organized and meaning is created. Intersubjectivity theory recognizes that there is a selfobject or developmental dimension to all therapeutic experience. The selfobject dimension of the treatment describes the patient's experience of a needed and desired new relationship with the therapist that fulfills selfobject longings that were unmet or inconsistently met during development. Through establishing a relationship that provides selfobject functions for the patient, the selfobject dimension of the relationship represents more than a technical development that sets the stage for curative interpretations. Rather, the selfobject dimension of the treatment relationship itself, once created, promotes psychological growth and transformation. Like Winnicott's (1965) "holding environment," the selfobject dimension of the treatment relationship provides the patient with a powerful relational experience of attuned responsiveness. Once established, the selfobject dimension of the treatment relationship can occupy the foreground or background of the patient's subjective experience. Therefore, a central concern of treatment from the intersubjective perspective is that ruptures to the selfobject bond between patient and therapist be repaired so that the transforming aspects of the therapeutic relationship can be reinstated.

Let us examine an aspect of the treatment relationship from the intersubjective perspective where the present relationship with the therapist is assimilated into the ongoing organization of the patient's experience. In this example, the selfobject dimension is operating as background when a potential rupture occurs.

> Martin, a young man approaching 30 years of age, has been in treatment for two years with a male therapist. Despite his good looks and his high-paying job, Martin has been unable to establish a long-term relationship with a woman. Martin's organizing principles include beliefs that he is inadequate, inferior, and doomed to fail in comparison to other men. Strong feelings of shame accompany these ideas. A few months previously, Martin bought a new Porsche that he pointedly pronounced as a two-syllable word—por-sha.
>
> On those occasions when his therapist made reference to the car, he automatically used the single syllable pronunciation that he was familiar with (porsh), and Martin would

correct him. One session, the therapist again mispronounced the name, caught himself, smiled, and correctly pronounced the two-syllable word. Martin replied, "Touché." This response surprised the therapist because it seemed that Martin felt wounded, clearly a potential rupture to the selfobject dimension. The therapist asked, "Did you feel I was mocking you when I corrected my pronunciation?" Martin said, "Yeah, I thought you were making fun of me." The therapist replied, "I didn't mean to sound that way. I was thinking, 'How often do I have to be corrected before I get it right.' I thought I was making fun of myself." Martin replied, "I missed that. I guess I just assume I'm being put down."

As therapists, we need to be cautious about what we know of our own unconscious motives. By definition, if something in us is unconscious, then it is not easily or directly knowable to us. The therapist might unconsciously have been expressing his envy of the expensive sports car, or perhaps the therapist, who was Jewish, had negative feelings about the patient's owning a German car. Just because the therapist was not conscious of feeling hostile or competitive does not mean he should disregard the possible unconscious motives behind his intervention. With this in mind, the therapist observed, "I can see how I came across sounding that way. You said you just assumed you were being put down. It sounds like you are very alert to being treated this way. Have you had the experience of being put down or mocked before?"

This observation unleashed a flood of associations. Martin began to describe how he was the object of incessant ridicule during elementary and middle school. He had a big nose, thick glasses, difficulty reading, and he was subjected to scorn and derision by the cool kids. While the therapist had some sense of Martin's organization of experience, Martin had never, during the two previous years of treatment, been able to reveal the details of these experiences or the deep sense of shame that accompanied them. With tears in his eyes, Martin spoke of his empathy for the Columbine High School killers. He knew how those kids must have felt. He hated the jocks, too.

In this vignette, two aspects of the treatment relationship stand out. First, the selfobject dimension is operating as background. The patient feels trusting and safe in the relationship with the therapist until he is suddenly injured. However, because of the trusting nature of the relationship, the rupture was easily repaired and the patient retained ready access to his associations. In fact, as we discuss extensively throughout the book, the experience of being attuned to frequently has the effect of unleashing a flow of associations. When people feel understood, they have no shortage of things to share.

Second, at the moment of rupture (retraumatization), we can see how the therapist becomes incorporated into the patient's ongoing organization of experience. Allowing that the therapist might have felt, and unconsciously conveyed, envy or resentment, Martin nevertheless experienced this as fitting seamlessly within his ongoing organization of experience. Because of his long and painful history of feeling the sword of ridicule, he readily accepted that yet another point had been scored against him: "Touché."

A differently constituted patient might not have made an issue of pronunciation in the first place, or he might have accepted the therapist's self-correction at face value, or he might have parried with a cutting retort: "You'll pronounce it correctly when you own one." But these alternatives were not available to Martin. He could only react with hurt to the therapist's thrust because of the invariant way his experience had been organized.

A second dimension of the transference is referred to as the repetitive dimension, where the patient fears that the relationship with the therapist will repeat painful or traumatic experiences from the past. When the repetitive dimension of the transference is in the foreground, the patient attempts to engage the therapist in a relationship that will forestall injury or retraumatization. An example of this occurred with Betty:

> The oldest of five children, Betty's experience was organized around the belief that the only way to maintain a vital tie to her powerful but remote father was to anticipate his moods and act in a manner that pleased or placated him. Betty became exquisitely sensitive to her father's affect states and was quick to subordinate her needs in order to avoid displeasing and thereby provoking him. She developed a false self presentation (Winnicott 1965) characterized by cheerfulness and self-sufficiency.
>
> In the treatment relationship, this dynamic configuration found expression in Betty's attunement to her therapist's needs and moods. She seemed constantly to be concerned that the therapist would become angry with her if she appeared needy or dependent. She might begin a session with the seemingly innocuous pleasantry, "How are you?" which really meant, "Am I a burden to you and will you reject me today?" When she became upset, she apologized for acting like a baby, and was quick to make demeaning remarks about herself, as if to beat her therapist to the punch. Betty was continually vigilant and intuitive in her observations. She would observe, "You seem tired today," which often accurately captured the therapist's self-state, and she was ready to leave the session if her presence was too taxing.
>
> In this relational configuration, which emerged during the first few weeks of treatment, the repetitive dimension was clearly apparent. Betty's penchant for attending to the needs of others while asking nothing for herself led her to accept any articulation the therapist might offer as evidence of his brilliance and her stupidity. When the therapist said, "You seem to feel that you're a burden to me," Betty replied, "Yes, you have the patience of a saint." Brandchaft (1994) has

> described such behavior as pathological accommodation. Through bolstering her therapist's self-esteem and placing his needs above hers, Betty sought to avoid the threat of retraumatization that would come from incurring her therapist's displeasure. Such a stance precluded her experiencing a transformation of her organization of experience and was certainly not in her therapeutic interest. Nevertheless, the tie to the therapist was vitally needed, and she sacrificed her opportunity for emotional growth in order to avoid risking rejection.

Whether concerning positive or negative affects, the intersubjective approach addresses the organizations of experience that configure the relationship between patient and therapist. Let us examine an interaction from the treatment of Gerald:

> During the therapist's August vacation in the first year of treatment, Gerald expressed the wish for some phone contact. His therapist agreed to a weekly phone session. During the second week, Gerald's mother died unexpectedly. He felt emotionally overwhelmed and alone and from the mortuary left a phone message asking his therapist to call. His therapist called and reached Gerald at his home that evening. They had an emergency phone session. An hour after the phone session, Gerald left another message asking if he could have the therapist's vacation phone number so he could reach her directly if he felt overcome with grief during the night. The therapist received the message and returned Gerald's call. She told Gerald that she was not available for night calls but would talk to him the next day during their weekly scheduled phone session. That night Gerald left an angry message saying that the therapist was just like all the other women in his life who were unresponsive to him and he never wanted to talk to the therapist again. The following day, the therapist left Gerald a voice message saying that she understood how

> disappointed and angry he was but that she would like to talk to him and would await his call at the scheduled time. Gerald did call. He angrily told the therapist that he felt the therapist was rejecting him because his needs were too great, that the therapist must be angry with him for trying her patience, and that she must want Gerald to grow up and stop being so dependent.

Here we see a complex interpersonal encounter in which the patient has assimilated the therapist into his invariant organization of experience, that is, that he is too needy for any woman, that expressing his needs drives women away, and that no woman will ever give him the depth of love and attention he craves. There are clearly a variety of interventions available to the therapist, each informed by different theories. One possibility was for the therapist to interpret Gerald's wish for the mother of childhood to be responsive to his every need. Another option might have been for the therapist to interpret Gerald's wish to ward off separation anxiety by maintaining a constant connection to the therapist. Alternatively, the therapist might address Gerald's need to control the therapist, or interpret his wish to ruin the therapist's vacation because of his anger and jealousy. Still another option might be to interpret Gerald's wish to get into bed with the therapist between her and her husband. Yet another option might be to share her feeling of irritation with Gerald's repeated intrusions into her vacation. In the end, she chose to explain that from her perspective, what was important was that Gerald feels whatever he was feeling and be however he needed to be. He was not too needy, demanding, controlling, or angry for the therapist. The therapist wanted to work with him, and she would establish whatever boundaries or limits she needed for herself. She would tell Gerald what worked for her and it was not Gerald's problem to figure out what those were and accommodate to them. It was difficult for Gerald to integrate that his therapist was not trying to shape, modify, or control his behavior.

But this interaction became a focal point for ongoing work on these themes.

To repeat, the term *transference* derives from and is integrally related to the theoretical and technical assumptions of traditional psychoanalytic theory. Much of the traditional psychoanalytic theory of technique is an outgrowth of the traditional understanding of transference. Therefore, any change in the way transference is conceived will have profound implications for practice.

Let us reflect on some of the well-known aspects of psychoanalytic technique that derive their rationale from the traditional conceptions of transference and contrast them with the intersubjective perspective. Freud distinguished between those patients who were capable of developing a transference neurosis and those who suffered from narcissistic neuroses. Traditional psychoanalysts viewed the patient's capacity to develop a transference neurosis as crucial to the consideration of suitability for psychoanalysis. Those patients who suffer from the narcissistic neuroses were presumed to be unanalyzable. This is essentially a determination based on diagnostic criteria pertaining to the patient alone. From the intersubjective perspective, suitability for treatment is not a function of the patient's diagnosis, but is a property of the patient–analyst system. As Stolorow (1994a) puts it, of central concern to the determination of suitability for treatment is "the goodness of fit between what the patient most needs to have understood and what the analyst is capable of understanding. . . . I believe that, in principle, anyone with an intact nervous system is analyzable by *someone*" (pp. 152–153).

The traditional designations of positive (sexual) and negative (aggressive) transferences cease to be useful ways of conceptualizing underlying states. While it is obvious that some patients will experience positive, negative, sexual, and aggressive feelings toward their therapist, we do not assume, for instance, that a negative transference must be uncovered and analyzed before a treatment would be considered successful. When patients do experience feeling toward the therapist, these are explored in terms of the organization of experience of both patient and therapist, and of the present context within which the relationship occurs.

Traditional psychoanalysts employed the couch and the stances of neutrality and abstinence in order to promote regression. Regression was thought to facilitate the reemergence of childhood neurotic conflicts in the present treatment relationship. Since treatment from the intersubjective perspective does not strive to revive in the therapeutic relationship the patient's unconscious conflicts over unacceptable sexual or aggressive longings, we dispense with those techniques whose purpose is to promote regression and facilitate the formation of the transference neurosis.

Another aspect of the traditional psychoanalytic theory of technique that stems from the concept of transference is that the patient's positive or negative feelings toward the therapist must be resolved before a thorough termination experience can occur. As we have discussed previously, we reject the view that the patient's feelings for the therapist are neurotic distortions that form out of displacements and projections of the patient's inner world. From the intersubjective perspective, both patient and therapist experience termination as a suspension of face-to-face meeting. It is acknowledged that the relationship continues even though regular meetings do not. The model is one of separation, not death.

From the intersubjective perspective, no discussion of the intersubjective field can focus on the contributions of one (the patient's transference) without examining the coconstructive role of the other (the therapist's countertransference.) There has been much discussion in the psychoanalytic literature as to whether countertransference represents an obstacle or hindrance to the psychotherapy process or whether it is an important source of data about the patient, or both. However, framing the discussion this way perpetuates isolated mind notions. By viewing the intersubjective field as a dynamic system, the quality of the therapeutic relationship must be shaped by the unconscious organizing activity of both participants. If we broadly define transference and countertransference as manifestations of unconscious organizing activity, then, according to Orange and colleagues (1997), "It becomes apparent that the transference is codetermined both by contributions from the analyst and the structures of meaning into which these are assimilated by the patient. Transference, in other words, is always evoked by some quality or activity of the analyst that lends itself to being interpreted by the patient according to some developmentally preformed organizing principle" (p. 40). Taken together then, transference and countertransference "form an intersubjective system of reciprocal mutual influence" (Stolorow et al. 1987, p. 42). Transference and countertransference become qualities of the relationship formed by each unique therapeutic pair.

At this point in our discussion of the centrality of relationship we wish to address the profound importance of relationship itself to all that transpires in any particular treatment. Thus far, we have focused on aspects of the therapeutic dyad such as selfobject needs, selfobject transferences, and the intersubjective understanding of the interdependence of transference and countertransference—the cotransference. However, the whole of a therapeutic process, whether conducted from the theory of intersubjectivity or from any other theoretical perspective, is a relational context (a relationship) far greater than the sum of interpretations, functional analyses, homework assignments, gambits, assessments, attuned or misattuned responses, to name a small fraction of what therapists might describe as going on in the room. In Chapter 3 we noted that subjectivity is inevitably intersubjectively constituted. That is, our subjective sense develops, is maintained, and always refers to a relational context. So there is a certain irony in recognizing that the fundamental construct of this theory—the inescapable organizing influence of one's subjectivity—is itself formed through interplay with other subjectivities.

In our earlier discussion of sustained empathic inquiry and affect attunement, we referred to Kohut's efforts to clarify the concept of empathy by differentiating between the psychoanalytic investigatory stance, on the one hand, and a bond developed when the patient felt understood by the therapist, on the other. Once again, what at first seemed to be a logical sequence (the affective bond grew out of the correct understanding by the therapist of the patient's subjectivity) now appears to be more accurately pictured as a complex, ongoing, mutually interacting process. The patient seeks treatment hoping to escape the tyranny of the past, to be understood, and to experience himself in new and more satisfying ways. The therapist enters the treatment with her own ways of understanding, including her personal history, her self-understanding, her theoretical constructs, and her anticipation of what may happen in therapeutic relationships. These are a few of the elements that pull for organizational priority in the new relationship.

SUMMARY

Central to the psychotherapy process is a unique relationship created by each patient–therapist pair. The examination, illumination, and articulation of the dynamics of this relationship contribute to a transformational experience for both participants.

5

Practicing Intersubjectively

This chapter is intended primarily for beginning psychotherapists, although experienced therapists will find some of the ideas to be useful in their teaching and supervision. As we will discuss in Chapter 8 on conducting supervision from the intersubjective perspective, there are many important parallels between the supervision and psychotherapy processes. Learning the practice of psychotherapy is a complex, intensive developmental process that, like being a patient in psychotherapy, takes place over a long period of time. Unlike chess, where there are a finite number of allowable moves and the openings and endgames have been well documented, in psychotherapy there are an infinite and unpredictable range of possible beginnings, middles, and ends. No book can detail how treatment will unfold for a particular patient–therapist pair. However, what we can do is offer some practice guidelines for furthering and deepening the process of psychotherapy.

In the prior chapters we discussed intersubjectivity theory, the intersubjective sensibility, and the centrality of affect and relationship. These concepts form the foundation that supports informed practice. We believe that any approach to treating unhappy or troubled people must address itself to the root causes of the problem for which treatment is sought. In our experience, the vast majority of people who seek the services of psychotherapists have had, in their developmental histories, experiences of acute or chronic traumatic failures in attuned relating from caregivers. Such developmental failures are implicated in the broad range of psychogenically based psychopathology that our patients suffer from. In response to these compromised developmental relationships in childhood, our patients frequently came to organize their experience around convictions that they were the cause of the misattuned responses they received from these caregivers. They developed the invariant organizing principles that they were unlovable, undeserving, or unworthy of the attuned understanding they desired. Underlying these invariant organizing principles were the painful affects of shame and self-loathing that have been sequestered from conscious awareness. These organizing principles and accompanying affects play themselves out in maladaptive ways in the present. Because these affect states were both intolerably painful and experienced as disruptive or threatening to needed ties to important caregivers, they have been disavowed or dissociated.

The intersubjective approach to psychotherapy addresses itself to these maladaptive formative conditions in two main ways. First, through making sense together, the patient's invariant organizing principles are identified and articulated and the patient comes to understand himself and his formative history in a new light. Understanding of self in relation to others promotes the formation of new organizations of experience, and promotes affect tolerance, regulation, integration, and self-cohesion.

Second, the psychotherapy relationship offers the patient a new relational experience with the therapist (Shane et al. 1997), with whom the patient comes to feel deeply accepted and understood. Such new experience also contributes to the formation of new organizations of experience and affect integration and regulation. For example, if the patient comes to therapy with the conviction that he is worthless and unacceptable, and feels shame and self-loathing at revealing himself to another, then the ensuing relationship with an affirming and accepting therapist will serve to contradict his essential convictions. In the face of this new experience, the patient will have to form some new ways to organize or make sense of these changed feelings and perceptions. Such a modified organization might be, "Here is someone who is not repelled by me. Perhaps I am not so repulsive."

Lichtenberg and colleagues (1996) identify ten guidelines for clinical practice. To their excellent discussion, we would now like to offer some further guidelines for practicing psychotherapy intersubjectively.

Intersubjectivity theory, as we have discussed earlier, focuses on the field created by the coming together of the subjective worlds of patient and therapist. Each patient–therapist pair creates its own unique intersubjective field through the interplay of the patient's and therapist's distinctive individual organizations of experience.

Since intersubjectivity theory prizes the unique subjectivity of the participants and the distinctive field they create, it precludes the idea that there is a correct body of psychotherapeutic technique that could be universally applied to all patients or all intersubjective fields. Technique suggests conformity to uniform rules and procedures. Furthermore, technique also implies that there is a common psychotherapy process that will unfold for all pairs and that we can know in advance how this process should or would unfold.

So if there are no uniform rules of the game, how can the practice of psychotherapy be taught? How do we go about learning to make sense together? This turns out to be a much easier question to ask than to answer. Let us take our cue from the Zen archer and look to the process instead of the target. Making sense is an outgrowth of the special conversation, the dialogue, that the therapist and patient engage in together. Dialogue involves attuned listening and responding. This chapter examines the process of attuned listening and responding in an effort to develop practice guidelines, not rules of technique, that will promote a distinctive psychotherapeutic dialogue.

Since the psychotherapy process unfolds through dialogue, a primary concern of both participants must be to keep the dialogue going. To the imperfect list of metaphors used to describe the psychotherapy process, such as trekking guide or dance partners, where one leads and the other follows, we would like to offer a sports metaphor: the racquet game often seen played on the beach, sometimes known as Kadima. The object of the game is for both participants to keep the ball in the air as long as possible, in other words, to keep the dialogue going. It is an interesting feature of the game that both participants need not be at the same skill level to enjoy playing together. For the therapist's part, she comes to the Kadima dialogue informed by the intersubjective attitude or sensibility. To keep the dialogue ball in the air, one must be exquisitely attuned to the strengths and weaknesses of the other and focus on hitting to the strengths of the other. If our playing partner is completely unskilled or not strong enough to wield the racquet, we try to hit the ball so it bounces on the partner's racquet. For the game to last and for the participants to enjoy playing together, it must be a truly collaborative endeavor. And interestingly enough, as the skills of the participants increase, they tend to find ways of raising the difficulty level, by hitting the ball harder or adjusting the distance between them. Since the point of the game is to keep the ball in the air, the game tends to end if one participant feels the other is not attuned to his skill level, or is trying to show him up, triumph over him, or humiliate him.

Leaving this metaphor and returning to the psychotherapeutic dialogue, we strive to grasp, as best we can, the patient's affective experience. At the same time, we recognize that our understanding of the experience of the other is never pure or true, but is always shaped, influenced, or contaminated by our own subjectivity. The therapist's self-awareness is key in that it alerts the therapist to her inevitable impact on the patient's subjective experience. Since intersubjectivity presupposes no universal core dynamic, we try to listen with curiosity and an open mind to what the patient reveals, unencumbered by theoretical expectations. Each person, and his story, is unique, and the experience and meaning of the therapeutic work will unfold as a construction at the intersection of the two distinct subjectivities.

Attuned listening means attunement to the patient's affect states. As Stolorow has indicated, we do not so much put ourselves in the other's shoes as we try to find analogues in our own store of affective experience that resonate with the affective experience of the patient. When we think we have understood the patient's affective experience, we articulate our understanding, we put our understanding of the patient's affective experience into words that the patient may confirm, deny, modify, or embellish. Take for example, the patient who says, "I called the girl my mother wants to fix me up with and left a voice message for her but she hasn't called back yet." Based on our knowledge of the patient and our sense of his immediate affect state, we might say, "You felt hurt." This is not a question, but rather a statement of our own fallible but best guess. If we have got his feeling right, he will indicate feeling understood and proceed to say more about his experience. When we get the patient's affective state right, the patient has no end of things to say. It loosens a flow of associations that is truncated by the experience of misattunement. Therefore, free association is promoted by the experience of attuned responsiveness, not by silence. If we are slightly off base, the patient has the opportunity to modify our observation: "Not hurt, just disappointed." If we are way off base, the patient might correct us: "No, actually I felt relieved." In this example, the therapist sensed that the patient felt hurt. Rather than ask the traditional question, "How did that make you feel?" we believe that if you have a sense of how the patient felt you should articulate it and thereby communicate to the patient that you understand his experience.

Embedded in this brief example are a number of important guidelines for furthering the therapeutic process. The first one is that the way psychotherapists inquire is opposite to that of lawyers. Lawyers are taught never to ask a question they don't know the answer to. In this way, they avoid unexpected and unwanted testimony from coming forward and prejudicing their case. The psychotherapeutic process, on the other hand, is generally well served by therapists not asking a question to which they *do* know the answer.

Take, for example, the following *New Yorker* cartoon.*

"And what do you think will happen if you do get on the couch?"

What we find so funny about the cartoon is the formulaic, actually ludicrous, question of the analyst. It is transparently obvious that this dog has been punished for lying on the furniture. Surely if the canine analyst knew anything about this particular canine patient she would have observed, "You are afraid you will be punished for getting on the couch." Such an

*Cartoon © 6/10/1996 The New Yorker Collection, Charles Barsotti, from cartoonbank.com ℅ Mira. All rights reserved.

articulation would convey that the analyst understands the patient's subjective experience. This would have the therapeutic benefit of making the patient feel understood and safe to reveal more of his experience.

We want to make clear that we are not advocating that therapists avoid asking questions, only that we avoid asking questions such as, "How did that make you feel?" when we have some sense of how the patient felt. The problem with the therapist's asking questions to which she knows the answer is that such questions convey to the patient that the therapist does not understand him. Part of the difficulty is that some historical guidelines for therapeutic practice have become so ingrained in the public awareness that students come to training with preformed but antiquated ideas. For instance, it is a common belief that it is more therapeutic for the patient to verbalize the insight or come to the understanding himself rather than to have the therapist articulate it for him. This bit of psychotherapy lore derives from traditional psychotherapy approaches that view achieving insight as the therapeutic goal. However, we are not focusing on excavating the buried unconscious but putting one's understanding of the patient's subjective experience into words. Patients, like regular folk, may fail to express how they feel out of ambivalence, shame, embarrassment, fear of ridicule, the expectation of being misunderstood, or the paucity of language skills needed to express their subjective feeling states. By articulating the patient's subjective state, the therapist conveys an experience of both acceptance and understanding. As we have indicated earlier, an important aspect of any accurate articulation is that in addition to new cognitive understanding, it conveys the selfobject function of being understood. Asking obvious questions conveys misattunement. Furthermore, for patients who have had little experience with another person's being attuned to their affect states, putting a richly nuanced word to their affective experience may enhance their ability to express their feelings through language. In this way, therapists can teach the vocabulary of affective experience to their patients.

Another problem with asking questions is that it confuses the psychotherapeutic process with research. Research is all about collecting data. Most beginning therapists feel uncertain of what to say and also fear saying something hurtful. In such situations, asking formulaic questions or collecting tangential data may seem like a benign alternative. It serves to disguise the therapist's uncertainties from herself and the patient.

While we do want to know about the patient's life experience, especially his relationship with caregivers and siblings, often the information is useful only when it comes up in a specific context. Therefore, we find that it is not especially helpful to take a detailed history at the beginning of therapy. The facts or the vital data gain their therapeutic relevance from the context in which they emerge. For example, if the patient says, "My father used to work so much that I never saw him," we would not ask, "What kind of work did he do?" This kind of question reflects tangential data collecting and is not process promoting. What is salient for the patient at this moment has to do with his feelings about his father's absence, not whether his father was off mining coal or negotiating world peace. In some other context, the nature of the father's work might be extremely relevant, but most likely to the extent that it bears on some affective experience, that is, the patient felt ashamed or proud of his father. We keep the dialogic ball in the air by attuning to the patient's affective experience, not by collecting data.

Students of psychotherapy themselves often lack the vocabulary of affective experience. They have difficulty articulating the patient's experience because they don't have ready access to the words that most closely fit the experience. Therefore, it is important to be conversant with the exquisite affective nuance of words such as *horrified, shocked, appalled, aghast, sickened, disgusted, revolted, dismayed,* and so on. Too often, students like their patients, hide behind words such as *frustrated, bored,* and *uncomfortable* that disguise rather than elucidate affective experience.

Besides asking formulaic questions or collecting tangential data as attempts to ward off anxiety and uncertainty, beginning psychotherapists who are unfamiliar with the practice of articulating affective experience can sound quite inarticulate as they search for the right words to convey their impressions. This often leads to rambling, confusing interventions as the therapist struggles to buy time while becoming clear herself about what she is trying to say. This invariably improves with experience and supervision, but one guiding suggestion we have found helpful is that beginning therapists should try to keep their verbalizations to what can be said in one breath. In other words, be succinct. Verbalizations such as "Tell me more," "Sounds like you felt insulted," and "You felt unimportant" are, in effect, hitting the ball to the patient's strength.

Let us examine the following clinical vignette:

> Ryan, a 30-year-old man, begins his session complaining that his girlfriend has broken off with him because he has had several angry outbursts. While he recognizes the disproportion of his anger and the fear it generates in his girlfriend, he is mystified by her failure to value his genuine, unconditional love for her.

At moments like these therapists might hear a multiplicity of themes worthy of articulation. The therapist must then choose from a wide range of possible interventions. Some therapists might focus on how threatened and vulnerable the girlfriend must have felt and believe they should address Ryan's inability to attune to her experience. Other therapists might focus on Ryan's excessive anger and feel the need to help him develop skills for containing and appropriately expressing his anger. These are both pertinent observations about Ryan's relational style and might become the focus of the psychotherapy dialogue at some point. However, the first response privileges the girlfriend's experience—how Ryan's anger must feel to her. The second privileges the therapist's experience as the observing other—how an outside observer might feel about Ryan's anger. What is it that should guide the therapist? From our perspective, we believe that the focus of the therapist's articulations needs to be attunement to our patient's subjective experience. This guideline would then be, "Remember who is your patient." Ryan is our patient and we must remain attuned to him. While we might sympathize with his girlfriend's fear of Ryan's anger, it is for her therapist to explore the meaning of the relationship to her.

We want to communicate to Ryan our understanding of his hurt at being rejected and the meaning he makes of this eventuality. The therapist might put Ryan's experience into words by saying something like, "You are left with the feeling that your love doesn't matter to her." Trying to articulate for the patient what is most salient in his experience locates the therapist as an understanding presence, seeing the relationship and the crisis from the patient's point of view. Once such an articulation accurately captures Ryan's affective experience, he will feel understood and freer to examine in greater depth other facets of the complex relational context, such as his anger. When addressing Ryan's anger, we want to focus on his affective experience, that is, what precipitated his anger and not the impact his anger had on his girlfriend. We find that articulating the patient's subjective experience, as opposed to highlighting the impact of his behavior on the other, allows self-protective defensiveness to recede and other, less easily revealed feelings and thoughts to come to the fore.

This introduces us to another important guideline for keeping the therapeutic dialogue going: avoid interventions that injure the patient. We suspect that the roots of Ryan's fragile personality organization lie in repeated formative experiences of misattunement and invalidation. To make his psychopathology, like his inability to integrate his angry affects, the object of our attention would be to replicate his experience of being criticized and condemned. We would avoid saying, "Your anger frightened her," for two reasons: first, such an articulation focuses on the girlfriend's subjective experience, not his own; second, such a statement is likely to be experienced as blaming and shaming. Instead, we would suggest saying something like, "You got so angry because you felt so hurt," which addresses his subjective experience. From our perspective, the salient psychodynamic issue is not that Ryan gets too angry, but that he feels too vulnerable to injury.

We appreciate that at some point it will be important for Ryan to understand the impact of his anger on others. We do not dispute that Ryan lacks this awareness and that psychotherapy will have fallen short should he never develop an appreciation of and sensitivity to the experience of the other. However, we view this as an outcome of the process of therapy and not a target we must try to hit. We believe that Ryan's anger is an outgrowth of his sense of vulnerability and his susceptibility to narcissistic injury. Therefore, through our focus on attunement to his subjective affect states and articulating his organization of experience, we expect that he will gradually develop greater self-cohesion and affect tolerance, integration, and regulation. He will become more resilient, less easily injured, less affectively reactive, and, accordingly, less prone to angry outbursts.

If the therapist were to address Ryan's inappropriate anger by interpreting it or its impact on others, she would risk repeating earlier traumatic relationships by inflicting narcissistic injury that could precipitate the kind of reactions in patients who then get labeled as "borderline." This practice seems to us another form of blaming the victim because the insensitivity or disregard of their early caregivers has injured these patients in childhood. Ryan might get angry with the therapist, become verbally abusive, and perhaps even threaten to terminate therapy. To this the therapist could respond with an interpretation that Ryan is treating the therapist just like he treated his girlfriend. However, the therapist will need to take responsibility for the fact that she has inflicted on Ryan the same kind of narcissistic injury that his girlfriend did. Now, if Ryan gets verbally abusive to the therapist, this is likely to narcissistically injure the therapist, making the therapist angry with Ryan. Fortunately, the therapist can restore her equilibrium by accusing Ryan of putting his anger into her via projective identification. So who is putting what into whom? This is the kind of scenario, perhaps in the extreme, that we aim to avoid by adopting a relational stance that prioritizes attunement to the patient's subjectivity rather than blaming, pathologizing, or otherwise injuring the patient.

We appreciate that the point could be raised that Ryan needs to have his poor reality testing confronted. The desire to provide reality testing is common, especially in beginning therapists who worry that they are being negligent or irresponsible by failing to protect their patients from their self-defeating activities. If we were working from a cognitive-behavioral framework, we might institute some sort of anger management program for Ryan. However, as therapists working intersubjectively, we are more concerned with making sense of Ryan's anger and the context in which it is formed, rather than in curtailing it; that is, focusing on the process, not the target. We believe that the therapeutic stance that will diminish Ryan's inappropriate outbursts of anger involves focusing on promoting self-cohesion and affect integration.

Finally, another guideline that can be discerned from this example is that we let the patient set the agenda for the session. We do not assign homework and check that it has been done. We want the patient to feel free to explore his subjective experience, to speak his mind about the issues most salient to him. Invariant organizing principles are forever shaping the patient's immediate experiences, and there is no risk that some important dynamic will be overlooked for long. A corollary to the principle that the patient should set the agenda is the guideline of not changing the subject; that is, the therapist should not change the subject to one more interesting or more salient to her. For instance, if the patient says, "I called my son last night," the therapist should avoid such interventions as "What made you do that?" This question addresses the therapist's curiosity, without leaving the opportunity for the patient to express his concerns. Perhaps the patient would go on to say, "My wife got so angry. She hates it when I give my attention to my son. She acts like I'm taking something away from her." Clearly, why the patient called his son is not the important dynamic issue—unless he did it to irritate his wife. However, this too will become apparent when his need to discuss his feelings about his relationship with his wife becomes his priority. Rather, to the patient's remark that he called his son last night, we encourage a response that allows for the unfolding of the personal meaning of that activity. There is no one right response, but many might provide an encouraging prompt to explore in more breadth and depth what made that call important enough to speak about. Some of the possibilities include being silent for a time, a simple "Uh-huh," or "Tell me more about it."

In addition to our attunement to the patient's affective experience, we are also trying to grasp the underlying themes or organizing principles that shape his experience. Listening is guided by the idea that, whatever the current episode the patient is describing, it likely contains some expression of the patient's invariant organization of experience. Sometimes an organizing principle will announce itself with trumpet flourishes: "No man that I want will ever want me!" The organizing principle behind this might be that the patient feels fundamentally defective and unworthy of the love of a desirable man.

Sometimes an organizing principle appears unheralded, hiding behind a trivial remark or a superfluous comment. For example, the patient makes the following remark: "Remember how last week I was talking about how mean my boss can be . . ." The patient seems to be concerned with the boss's aggression. However, for no apparent reason, the patient brings this into the transference, the relationship with the therapist. Note the unnecessary word "remember." This might be a meaningless throwaway word, or perhaps it touches on something meaningful for the patient. Why would the patient phrase things this way? Has this patient's experience become organized around the notion that people don't remember? Might the patient be saying, "Nobody really listens to me," or "I am not important enough to be worth listening to"? This would then be a manifestation of the transference, of the extent to which the therapist has become assimilated into the patient's organization of experience as yet another person who does not listen. So we might venture the following tentative articulation: "When you say 'remember,' I wonder if you think that I don't remember?"

This articulation represents an exception to the guideline that the therapist should not impose her agenda on the patient. Investigation of the appearance of an organizing principle emerging in the transference temporarily takes precedence over the patient's need to discuss his feelings about his boss. Of course, it is possible, even likely, that the discussion of the boss would turn out to center around the very same organizing principle ("I'm not important enough to be remembered or taken into account"). However, the therapeutic effectiveness of articulating the personal meaning of experience is enhanced when it occurs in the here and now, especially in relation to the therapist. While valuable understanding of the patient's invariant organization of experience can be gained from focusing on important relationships in the patient's life, the power is magnified when the focus is on the transference. This practice is consistent with the traditional notion that the central focus of analytic work is on the analysis of the transference. To reframe this from the intersubjective perspective, we offer the guideline that the optimum focus should be on how the therapist is assimilated into the patient's invariant organization of experience.

This introduces yet another guideline for furthering the process. The archaic principles that have come to organize our experience are like the musical themes that flow through a symphony. While each life has many themes that wind through it, all these themes are not salient at any given time. One aspect of the process of psychotherapy, what in fact characterizes the process, is the way that organizing themes emerge, become an important focus of the treatment, and then begin to recede, allowing other themes to rise to prominence. What gives a sense of coherence and order to a psychotherapy process is the emergence and persistence of these themes over time. When an organizing theme has been sounded and is identified by therapist and patient, it becomes more easily recognizable as it reappears in new forms. The way a musical theme can be heard first in the woodwinds, and then in the strings, organizing principles may be heard first in descriptions of the patient's relationship to his boss and later in the transference to the therapist. The theme gets developed, deepens in complexity, and then drifts away as another theme is announced.

Let us return to the patient above and to the theme that no one remembers him. If the organizing principle of not being remembered has been identified previously and seems to be in the forefront of this phase of treatment, then identifying this latent, underlying theme in the transference would take precedence over any specific content. While the specific life events the patient selects to relate may shift from one person in his life to another, the theme of not being remembered will likely be running through them all. It is important that we listen for the salient theme, track its embeddedness across the various events and relationships the patient describes, and shine a light on it: "Your boss doesn't remember the good job you did," "Your father forgot your birthday," "Your mother sent you the same card this year as she did last," "Your therapist needs to be reminded of something you told her last week." These interventions are all articulations of the same underlying organization of experience. The clinical case presented in Chapter 6 provides a good example of the way an organizing theme is identified and then tracked over the two sessions described.

In addition to identifying and articulating both the patient's affective experience and the principles that organize his experience, another important psychotherapeutic practice involves elucidating the personal meanings made of subjective experience. While the accurate articulation of affective experience confirms the therapist as an understanding and attuned other, we will also further the transformative process by exploring and articulating the personal meanings the patient makes of his affective experience. Referring back to the example of the patient who was not being remembered, we want to explore the meaning the patient has made of his experience that he is not remembered. Or, put another way, what does not being remembered mean to him? If we try to make sense with the patient of the personal meaning to him of not being remembered, it might be uncovered that he has the unconscious conviction that nobody remembers him because he must be inherently empty, worthless, or otherwise undeserving of being remembered. This touches on the deepest and most painful level of subjective experience that is generally sequestered outside of awareness.

The transformative moments in treatment when the full impact of a patient's hidden, personal meaning emerges are impossible to orchestrate. Certainly, being with another human being at such times transcends technique or even practice. Probably little can be taught about how to respond or intervene in these moments. Being with another person at such intense and intimate times calls upon the full psychological resources of the therapist. Her own stability and tolerance for her own and other's affective intensity are important. Having had the experiences of being vulnerable and coming to new understanding in the presence of a trusted other is one possible way of enhancing one's capacity for sharing them with patients. We encourage students and practitioners of psychotherapy to explore and expand their subjectivities in their own psychotherapy experiences.

In contrast to those intense moments just discussed, at other points during the course of every treatment the flow seems to dry up, the material becomes vague and elusive, the patient seems distracted, the therapist feels bored and restless, or the patient seems to be avoidant and defensive. At these times, the patient is often described as being resistant. Traditionally this has meant that the patient is motivated to obstruct the therapist's efforts to uncover his unacceptable unconscious motives. From the intersubjective perspective, resistance is a manifestation of the repetitive dimension of the transference. That is, these instances of disengagement in treatment are attempts by the patient to avoid retraumatization by the therapist. With this frame of reference in mind, a therapist might turn the light of introspection on herself and wonder what aspects of the context, including their interfacing subjectivities, have contributed to the emergence of the patient's need to protect himself.

Beginning therapists often have difficulty negotiating such phases in the treatment. At these times, we have found that it is often helpful to reflect on or observe some aspect of the unfolding process and not become mired in the specific content. For example, the patient discusses spending the night with her boyfriend but glosses over an implied sexual interaction. The therapist's curiosity might be aroused by the patient's avoidance of explicit references to sexual activity in her report of the evening. Among the therapist's options might be to directly ask about the unspoken sex, saying something like, "Did you have sex?" However, we believe that this approach is problematic for two reasons. First, this is an intervention that grows out of the therapist's unsatisfied curiosity. Here the therapist would be changing the subject to her area of her interest by directly confronting the patient's discomfort and overriding the patient's reluctance to be explicit about her sexual encounter. Second, this intervention reflects preoccupation with the content, as if what is therapeutically important are the details of the sexual encounter and not the patient's reticence in discussing sex.

.We favor a different approach. While the patient's avoidance of explicitly discussing her sexual activity is interesting, we prefer to explore the patient's reticence about discussing sexual activity explicitly, rather than focusing on the content, the details of sex. So we would recommend articulating her reticence by saying, "It seems to make you uncomfortable to talk about sex." This type of intervention addresses some process event (her discomfort with discussing sex activities) rather than focusing on the specific content (the details of her sexual encounter).

In this vein of framing articulations in terms of the process rather than the specific content, the following are typical examples: "You seem to feel uncomfortable talking about sex." "You try to avoid saying something negative about your parents." "It's hard to talk about your feelings about me." These articulations do not address the specific content of the patient's behavior, but more reflect on the patient's discomfort with revealing certain feelings about her experience. Thus, our practice guideline is to examine the patient's motives for avoiding explicit content before addressing the content specifically.

We occasionally encounter patients whose affective experience has been treated as so dangerous and disruptive to the maintenance of their connection to vital others that it has been disavowed or dissociated. Sometimes, these individuals are very self-critical, pathologizing themselves for their feelings. For example, a divorced woman in her early thirties is reflecting on her current relationship with a much younger man. She berates herself for being needy and clingy. She says, "I can't stop being a pest. No wonder he is sick of me. I'm such a baby." With such individuals, it is important to remember that, in one form or another, the patient is striving for health, that is, seeking out a developmental experience that has been needed but was developmentally absent. In such situations, it is important for the therapist to depathologize the patient's self-criticism. The patient may be needy and clingy, but she, in all likelihood, acts this way because she feels her boyfriend is elusive or disengaged. She fears losing what she craves and hangs on for dear life. It would not be helpful for the patient if the therapist was to align herself with the boyfriend's experience, by interpreting that the more she clings, the more he feels suffocated and tries to disengage. We recommend that the therapist align herself with the patient's struggle for health by depathologizing her self-criticisms and promoting confidence in her perceptions, as in an articulation such as, "You don't seem to trust your experience that you're not getting the emotional connection you need from him. You blame yourself for being too needy, but you're not getting what you need." Perhaps her needs are excessive (for this boyfriend) because her deprivation has been great. Her need for connection will not diminish because the therapist sides with the boyfriend's experience of suffocation. Her needs will diminish when she feels understood and reassured that she is not intolerable.

Reframing is a technique that is utilized by a variety of psychotherapy systems, especially in cognitive therapies. We are not advocating reframing as a way to change negative thoughts into positive ones. Patients disparage their own affective experience, not out of some mistaken need to catastrophize but out of fear of, or repetitive experiences of, invalidation by significant others in their life.

From our perspective, by depathologizing the patient's subjective affect states and affirming the patient's striving for health, we hope to promote respect for the patient's own subjective affective experience. By validating the patient's affective experience, we promote self-delineation and affect integration. As a guideline, we believe it is affirming and supportive to uncover the kernel of health hidden behind the patient's self-disparaging pathologizing.

Finally, we want to emphasize an important personal quality that tends to be overlooked when we enter into the practice of psychotherapy, that is, the personal courage that is required of the therapist. Psychotherapy, as a meaning-making process, does not follow universal laws. If we jump out a window, we know with absolute certainty that the law of gravity will prevail and we will fall to the ground. When we jump into a psychotherapy relationship, we have no idea where we will land. It takes, not blind faith, but confidence in the method to make such leaps into the unknown.

It happens, on occasion, especially with more fragile patients, that we find ourselves concerned for the patient's safety and well-being. Because psychotherapy is so uncertain an enterprise, we can never know for sure that patients who seem extremely depressed, potentially suicidal, or homicidal will not attempt to hurt themselves or others, or that patients who are under a great deal of emotional stress won't decompensate, requiring immediate hospitalization.

With patients like these, therapists sometimes suffer crises of confidence. We doubt ourselves: Am I helping this person? Am I doing all that I could? Am I not doing something I should be doing? Patients who frequently interface with our subjectivities in this way get labeled "difficult." We believe that what is meant by "the difficult patient" is the one with whom we suffer just such crises of confidence. When therapists subjectively experience stress and feel unsure of what to do or what should be done, there is a tendency to resort to what we can do. To manage our own anxiety or uncertainty we refer the patient for medication, recommend group therapy, or institute some other external intervention. Any of these interventions might be useful for a given patient at a given point in treatment. But we also resort to them, not just to help the patient manage his distress, but to manage our own. It never hurts to ask ourselves, Whose anxiety will be reduced if the patient takes medication—the patient's or our own?

We believe that it takes great courage for therapists to face such crises of confidence by maintaining their trust in the method. Often when we feel the greatest internal pressure to do something external for the patient, the patient has the greatest need for us to maintain our confidence in him and the therapeutic process. Therefore, our final guiding recommendation is to trust the method. Maintain your commitment to the process of unfolding and illuminating the patient's organization of experience and to responding with attunement to his affective experience.

SUMMARY

This chapter has distinguished between principles of technique and guidelines for practice. In contrast to technical recommendations, which have a one-size-fits-all quality to them, guidelines for practice emphasize the need to promote the unfolding and illumination of the patient's subjective experience. Practice is context dependent and addresses the furthering of the process of treatment rather than the specifics of intervention.

6

The Articulation of Subjective Experience*

Critics of intersubjectivity theory mistakenly assume that the therapeutic action is primarily found in the provision of empathy. Thus, they conclude, somewhat dismissively, that treatment based on intersubjectivity theory is superficial therapy because it is merely another version of the discredited corrective emotional experience. Because intersubjectivity theory does recognize the selfobject dimension of experience and the therapeutic benefits of new experience, critics tend to assume that therapy takes place strictly on the surface.

That intersubjectivity theory is indeed a depth psychology is evidenced by two of its central tenets. First, integral to the

---

*Portions of this chapter were published previously in a chapter titled "The Selfobject Function of Interpretation," which appeared in *Pluralism in Self Psychology: Progress in Self Psychology*, 1999, ed. A. Goldberg, vol. 15, pp. 31–49. Copyright © 1999 by *Progress in Self Psychology* and used with permission.

intersubjective perspective is the genetic point of view in which the principles that organize experience are understood to form in the early relationship with caregivers. Second, the intersubjective perspective recognizes that these organizations of experience exert their influence while remaining largely unconscious. The richness and depth of the intersubjective approach to treatment then derives from the way in which these developmentally formed unconscious organizing principles are identified, illuminated, and articulated. This chapter examines from the perspective of intersubjectivity theory how therapist and patient make sense of the patient's organization of experience.

Traditionally, psychoanalytic theoreticians have sought the therapeutic action of psychoanalysis in various activities of the analyst. The Freudian school has located the therapeutic action in interpretation, primarily of the transference (Strachey 1934), conceptualized primarily as cognitive processes whereby the analyst transmits new knowledge or insight to the patient. Relational theorists have emphasized that the therapeutic action resides in the new ways of relating that analyst and patient construct together out of their relationship. For self psychology, the therapeutic action is generally believed to derive from the provision of selfobject functions that mobilize thwarted developmental longings. From the perspective of intersubjectivity theory, the therapeutic action resides in the unfolding, illumination, and transformation of organizations of experience. One way in which new organizations of experience are formed is through the new experience of attuned responsiveness that infuses the therapeutic relationship. However, organizations of experience are also transformed through the identification, elaboration, and articulation of subjective experience that grows out of patient and therapist making sense together.

Interpretation is a term burdened with history. It derives from the classical literature where the focus was on making the unconscious conscious through attaching word cathexes to preconscious thoughts (Freud 1915b). Freud (1900) used *interpreta-*

tion (*deutung*) to describe his procedures for discerning the unconscious meanings of dreams and parapraxes. As Freud (1913b) explained, "The interpretation of dreams has as its object the removal of the disguise to which the dreamer's thoughts have been subjected" (p. 210). *Interpretation* here is being used in the sense of finding a solution to the puzzling mental phenomenon (Freud 1913a). In the sense that it is generally used, *interpretation* refers to the analyst's communication of the solution to the patient. The emphasis is placed squarely on the analyst's promoting cognitive insight by conveying new knowledge to the patient about the contents of the patient's unconscious desires or his defenses against knowing. Within this tradition, Arlow (1987) regards "the principal function of the psychoanalyst to be the giving of interpretations" (p. 69). From this perspective, the transmission of the analyst's cognitive insights into the mental functioning of the patient, through the verbal procedure of interpretation, is the principal therapeutic action of ego psychology, even if the insight forms in the mind of the analyst as an outgrowth of her relationship with the patient. There seems to be agreement that for the cognitive component to have therapeutic impact, it must resonate emotionally for the patient (Neubauer 1980).

From the perspective of self psychology, Kohut (1984) articulated a transitional position, retaining, at least in theory, the role of the analyst as objective observer, while simultaneously emphasizing the primary importance of understanding gained through an empathic bond. We have discussed previously the confusion in Kohut's writings between the use of empathy as both an observational stance and as a description of the relationship that facilitates therapeutic action (Stolorow et al. 1987). Kohut (1984) recognized that a therapeutic intervention consists of two interdependent steps: the analyst's empathic understanding of the patient, and communication of this understanding to the patient through explanation.

The two poles of the debate on the therapeutic action of

psychoanalysis are represented on the one hand by ego psychology, which emphasizes the transmission of new cognitive understanding, and on the other hand by self psychology, which stresses that the therapeutic action is to be found in the new selfobject experiences that come from feeling understood. Atwood and Stolorow (1984) have suggested that both are important and indivisible: "Every transference interpretation that successfully illuminates for the patient his unconscious past simultaneously crystallizes an illusive present—the novelty of the therapist as an understanding presence. Perceptions of self and other are perforce transformed and reshaped to allow for the new experience" (p. 60). In other words, whenever new cognitive knowledge is accepted by the patient as a meaningful formulation of his inner experience, the patient also has a new experience of feeling deeply understood. Therefore, interpretations work on two levels: the level of cognitive understanding, where new knowledge is assimilated, and the developmental level, where needed selfobject functions are experienced through the therapist's attuned responsiveness. The tendency to dichotomize the therapeutic action into a cognitive component and an affective component is seemingly resolved by this stance that accurate transference interpretations convey both (Terman 1989). Nevertheless, the emphasis still seems to be that new cognitive knowledge provided through interpretation has therapeutic effect largely because it is packaged with the selfobject experience of feeling emotionally understood.

In contrast to Kohut's (1977, 1984) view of the curative process, which invoked optimal frustration and transmuting internalization, Bacal (1990) has suggested that the curative process involves a corrective selfobject experience. The notion here is that psychopathology results from archaic developmental longings being disrupted by a failing selfobject relationship with the caregivers. By restoring a needed selfobject tie, thwarted developmental longings will be remobilized in the safety of the attuned selfobject relationship. Hence, "the internalization of the cohesion-fostering selfobject tie constitutes the essence of what is the therapeutic, or 'corrective' experience in analysis" (Bacal and Newman 1990, p. 258).

Traditionally, interpretation derived from a one-person stance in which the analyst is the authority on the truth of the patient's inner experience (Fosshage 1995b). As such, the term *interpretation*, as used in modern relational thinking, is anachronistic; it is a derivative of the myth of the isolated mind (Stolorow and Atwood 1992). Postmodern thinking emphasizes the co-construction of personal meaning. Intersubjectivity theory views psychoanalytic interpretation as "an act of illuminating *personal* meaning" (Stolorow 1994b, p. 43). Personal meaning is illuminated through the process of making sense together. Since our verbal interventions are directed toward putting into words the personal meanings of subjective experience, we propose that, rather than perpetuate the historical associations packaged with the term *interpretation*, we refer instead to the therapist's "articulation" of her understanding of the patient's subjective experience. Articulation specifically addresses the verbal component of putting into words the therapist's understanding of the patient's subjective experience as acquired through the empathic-introspective mode of inquiry.

We would now like to further the discussion of the locus of the therapeutic action in intersubjectivity theory by pulling together the three themes in the debate: enhanced cognitive understanding, the experience of feeling understood, and selfobject functioning. We propose that illuminating personal meanings (new cognitive understanding) through making sense together (the experience of being understood) of the totality of one's life experience has the selfobject function of promoting self-understanding, self-delineation, self-continuity, and self-cohesion. New self-understanding contributes to the construction of new organizations of experience and hence to structural transformation.

Patients respond to the therapist's verbal communications in varied and complex ways. To us, the words chosen by the therapist, in and of themselves, have significance. As human beings we have unique capacities for language and for construing meaning. It is precisely the potential selfobject function of the therapist's verbal communication that we address in this chapter.

In examining what we refer to as the selfobject function of articulation, we favor Donna Orange's formulation of selfobject experience occurring within the context of selfobject relatedness. According to Orange (1995), "Selfobject relatedness is the person's experience, at any age, of a significant human other or attachment figure as support for the establishment, development, and maintenance of continuous, cohesive, and positive self-experience" (p. 177). The subjective experience of the therapist and her interpretive activities provide vitally needed capacities that are missing from the patient's psychological makeup. Subjective experience and the associated meaning made of it by the patient form the basis for the, largely unconscious, organizing principles of the patient. These organizing configurations, and affects associated with them, become the focus of the therapist's sustained empathic inquiry. We propose that verbal articulation of such complex affectively charged configurations are subjectively experienced as providing selfobject functions, specifically through promoting the experience of self-understanding. New self-understanding promotes the sense of historical self-continuity, that one's current organization of experience is meaningfully connected to past experience. In this case, the value of the therapist's articulation derives from the patient's ability to use it to further self-understanding.

As we have discussed earlier, since Freud, analysts have questioned whether words alone produce therapeutic effects. Ego psychologists accept that for new cognitive meanings to be assimilated, the verbal interpretation needs to connect with some affective charge. We would like to refine this notion by proposing that verbal articulations will convey cognitive and affective understanding only within the context of primary selfobject relatedness

(Orange 1995). Verbal articulations are an important part of the process that allows for the conscious recognition and reevaluation of archaic organizations of experience and the emergence of new organizing principles. By putting the patient's subjective experience into words, the therapist promotes self-cohesion and the integration of affect into experience.

Humans are meaning makers, and as Orange (1995) has pointed out, "The urge to make sense is distinctively human. . . . Healthy humans have a developing and lifelong propensity to reflect, to organize experience variously, and especially to wonder and to converse about meanings. . . . Psychoanalysis is a special conversation about meaning; it is an attempt of analyst and patient to make sense together of the patient's emotional life" (pp. 6–7). As humans we have a unique capacity for symbolic representation. At approximately 18 months of age the child develops the use of complex language, and with the acquisition of language, memory, communication, and organization of experience are irrevocably altered. Not only is linear, secondary processing acquired, but through the maturation of the frontal cortex and associational pathways, primary process representation becomes accessible (Lichtenberg et al. 1996).

Levin (1991) discusses at length many possible ways of understanding the effectiveness of psychoanalysis (particularly transference interpretations) in terms of the emerging knowledge about functional neuroscience. According to Levin, metaphorical language, used spontaneously by a therapist, may serve as a bridge among multiple levels of neurological functioning. For example, an articulation framed as a metaphor may link modalities of touch, hearing, and sight; it can bridge past and present experiences simultaneously; it might connect affect with a narration of experience; and it could allow for associations among different developmental levels of cognitive processing (such as preverbal sensorimotor experiences, and, later, more advanced levels of symbolic representation). The ambiguity of the metaphor and its implicit comparison between that which is similar and yet not identical allows for simultaneous multiple processing in the brain by which new associations and therefore new understandings can emerge.

Children suffering from alexithymia present another instance of the developmental imperative of putting words to feelings. By verbally labeling emotional experience, children can be helped to identify and think about their feelings, thereby promoting the organization and integration of affect. According to Reckling and Buirski (1996), "Without the capacity to think about feelings, children will not develop the ability to identify and verbally express affect and will likely continue to express affect somatically. The caregivers' inadequate articulation of their child's affect states interferes with the child's development of a capacity to desomatize and identify affects" (p. 85).

Our position is not that verbal articulations of the patient's archaic organizing principles are the primary or even necessary component of therapeutic action. We have certainly been impressed with Lachmann and Beebe's (1996) demonstration of the importance of nonverbal interaction on therapeutic growth. What we are trying to emphasize is that putting into words the patient's developmental dynamics has the function of promoting self-understanding—the understanding of one's organization of experience in the context of one's personal development. Such self-understanding promotes a sense of self-delineation, self-continuity, and self-cohesion. Understanding how one's experience has become organized and the developmental context and constraints in which this organization took shape gives coherence to one's life. For example, through verbal articulation, an adult male patient developed the awareness that his anger, which served as a shield to ward off hurtful disregard by his parents and formed a protective armor against a threatening world, while vital to his survival as a child, now functions to keep potential good objects at a distance. This understanding now provides the patient with a template against which to assess the dangers of new relationships, as well as a signpost to his self-protective behavior.

He understands that when he finds himself enraged, behind his anger lurks an archaic conviction, derived from his invariant organization of experience, of his vulnerability to the presently perceived threat of retraumatization.

Building on our formulation that verbal articulations given in the context of a primary selfobject relationship provide important selfobject functions, we now turn to the question of the accuracy or exactness of interpretations. It is in just this arena that the different perspectives of historical truth and narrative truth collide.

Freud pursued historical truth. Using the archaeological metaphor, he sought to excavate the buried unconscious layers and unearth veridical memories of past experience. The important tool in excavating the past was interpretation or genetic reconstruction. According to Freud (1937),

> The path that starts from the analyst's construction ought to end in the patient's recollection; but it does not always lead so far. Quite often we do not succeed in bringing the patient to recollect what has been repressed. Instead of that, if the analysis is carried out correctly, we produce in him an assured conviction of the truth of the construction which achieves the same therapeutic result as a recaptured memory. [pp. 265–266]

For Freud, the nineteenth century positivist, "an assured conviction of the truth" referred to his belief in the objectivity of truth, as opposed to the postmodern view of the relativity of the truth of personal meanings. In this vein, then, Freud stressed the therapeutic importance of the accuracy of the construction, even while acknowledging that the therapist arrives at the accurate construction through successive approximations.

As much as Freud stressed the therapeutic importance of accurate interpretations or constructions, he minimized the effect of inaccurate ones. As he clearly stated (1937),

> No damage is done if, for once in a way, we make a mistake and offer the patient a wrong construction as the probable historical truth. . . . A single mistake of the sort can do no harm. What in fact occurs in such an event is rather that the patient remains as though he were untouched by what has been said and reacts to it with neither a "Yes" nor a "No". . . . If nothing further develops we may conclude that we have made a mistake and we shall admit as much to the patient at some suitable opportunity without sacrificing any of our authority. Such an opportunity will arise when some new material has come to light which allows us to make a better construction and so to correct our error. In this way the false construction drops out, as if it had never been made. . . . The danger of our leading a patient astray by suggestion, by persuading him to accept things which we ourselves believe but which he ought not to, has certainly been enormously exaggerated. [pp. 261–262]

Glover (1955) in his famous paper, "The Therapeutic Effect of Inexact Interpretation," published first in 1931, six years before the Freud paper quoted above, takes the opposite position. Glover's view is that an incorrect or inexact interpretation is utilized by the patient as a "displacement-substitute" (p. 356). Such substitutes act like suggestions; they may "bring about improvement in the symptomatic sense at the cost of refractoriness to deeper analysis" (p. 356).

Modern relational thinking discards the notion of historical truth in favor of a hermeneutics/constructivist approach (Mitchell 1993). As Mitchell summarizes it, "The patient's experiences, associations, and memories can be integrated or organized in innumerable ways. The organizational scheme arrived at is a dual creation, shaped partly by the patient's material but also inevitably shaped by the analyst's patterns of thought, or theory. The 'meaning' of clinical material does not exist until it is named—it is not uncovered but created" (p. 58).

From this perspective, it is meaningless to apply the criterion of accuracy or exactness to an articulation or construction. The therapist's articulation of the patient's subjective experience represents the therapist's experience of the patient's subjectivity, filtered through the therapist's subjectivity, which includes the therapist's theoretical system. It is an outgrowth of the context in which it forms in the mind of the therapist.

Thus, an articulation is not an expression of some objective truth about the patient's experience. It is the way in which the therapist has organized her understanding of the patient at this moment, in this place, in this immediate context. This particular understanding of the patient's organization of experience will necessarily be affected by changes in the context of the therapeutic relationship. Verbal articulations, within the hermeneutic/constructivist perspective, are not successive approximations of the truth about the patient's past but are constructions about the patient's current subjective organization of experience. The meaningfulness of the articulation to the patient depends on the selfobject functions provided by the formulation. We judge the clinical usefulness of an articulation or construction, not by its proximity to some criterion of truth, but by whether or not the patient finds the articulation personally meaningful. A personally meaningful articulation is one that leads the patient to new ways of organizing his experience, that is, new self-understanding that is growth enhancing.

We have all probably encountered patients for whom belief in God is a profoundly organizing experience. Questions about the existence of God are irrelevant to the therapeutic enterprise. Belief in God helps organize these patients' experience of themselves in the world. Other belief systems have similar effects. Articulations, being constructed out of the experiences of both patient and therapist, are another form of belief system. The patient accepts the therapist's articulation of his subjective experience because the patient finds it to be personally meaningful and because it helps reorganize the patient's experience, or the patient may reject the articulation because it is experienced as nonorganizing or at worst disorganizing. Such understandings or ways of organizing experience are not fixed but are subject to being superseded as newer understandings or organizations of experience are constructed.

Even though we are dispensing with the notion of true or accurate verbal articulations, we nevertheless believe that some articulations promote transformation of experience, while others might be organizing, but not transformative. Some misuses of interpretation or reconstruction can ultimately be hurtful to the patient's development. Interpretations or constructions that move beyond a focus on illuminating the patient's subjective experience, relational configurations, and affect (but aim instead to reconstruct memories of actual events presumed to have taken place in the patient's past and reside in the patient's unconscious) are potentially very destructive. Such an interpretation as "Your dream is the dream of someone who has been sexually abused by their father" is the type of destructive statement that purports to reconstruct some piece of real experience out of the cloth of subjective experience. One cannot derive objective reality from subjective experience. This is the flaw in the archaeological analogy. Freud believed that by sifting through the strata of the unconscious, one could unearth real artifacts of a patient's buried past. Take for example Freud's (1918) analysis of the Wolf Man's dream (Buirski and Haglund 1998). Freud reconstructed that his patient, at the age of 18 months, had literally observed his parents having intercourse *a tergo*, three times, at five o'clock in the afternoon. That the objective truth of such a specific scenario could ever be known is highly doubtful. Objective reality can only be known through applying the scientific method of empirical observation, not from psychoanalytic exploration of personal meanings.

On a television news magazine program some time ago, a patient in past-lives therapy and his therapist were interviewed. The therapist reported that the patient, who had come for treatment because of his fear of water, had, under hypnosis, been regressed to a prior life. Under hypnosis it was uncovered that in the seventeenth century the patient had drowned in a shipwreck. The patient reported that recovering the memory of this prior life experience had been extremely helpful and he experienced relief from his fear of water.

Following the line of thought we have been developing, the recovery of the prior life experience offered the patient a new way of understanding himself and organizing his experience. We suspect that this new formulation functioned as an antidote, which we will discuss in greater detail in Chapter 7. As an antidote, this kind of interpretation, while organizing on one level, fosters defensive rigidification rather than promoting growth and self-development. It is organizing but not transforming.

Many of the ideas put forth in this chapter represent themes dramatically interwoven in the false memory syndrome controversy (see Harris 1996). While a complete discussion of the controversy is not possible in the context of this book, the relativity of "truth" in the co-constructed understanding developed in psychoanalytic treatment between patient and therapist must be considered. From the intersubjective perspective, the personal meaning of memories, fantasies, and experiences is the focus of analytic inquiry, and such meaning is not assumed to correspond to observable events, past or present. However, it seems imperative that patient and therapist explicitly discuss the subjective nature of their constructions. Harris (1996) formulates a position with which we concur: "We need to assert the importance of provisional knowing, of inquiry, and of creating climates of respect and support. . . . This attention to the potential for distorted listening does not rule out the importance of validating the patient's experience where possible; but when the analyst moves beyond or beneath the experience of the patient, the grounds for doing so must be open for shared inquiry and meaning making" (pp. 183–184).

Verbal articulations always occur within an intersubjective

field, and the patient's subjective experience of hearing them can be as complex as the therapist's motives for giving them. They may be experienced as blaming or gratifying, loving or destructive, genuine or manipulative—depending on the particular intersubjective context. But for verbal articulations to generate meaningful cognitive and emotional understanding, they must be given within the context of a primary selfobject relationship. Verbal articulations promote the important selfobject functions of self-understanding, self-delineation, self-cohesion, and self-continuity, as well as affect-integration and affect-tolerance. We hope to illustrate these points through the clinical material that follows.

CLINICAL MATERIAL

Hannah is a 36-year-old woman with a history of hospitalizations for suicidality who came for treatment to a clinic associated with a training program. Her current symptoms include head banging and cutting on herself. To illustrate the selfobject function of verbal articulations we have chosen to follow three themes over the course of the initial two consultation sessions. This will also illustrate the way in which thematic continuity is maintained through tracking their appearance across sessions. The cumulative effect of putting the patient's experience into words appears to have helped make her past and her present more comprehensible to her, and therefore, we suggest, contributed to her understanding of herself in a way that enhanced a cohesive and continuous self-experience. While this is not a chapter intended to demonstrate the feasibility of short-term treatment, we have chosen only to use material from the first two consultation sessions in order to illustrate the power of verbal articulations delivered within the context of a quickly forming selfobject relationship.

In the opening remarks of session 1, responding to the therapist's invitation to describe what brought her into treatment, Hannah begins:

Patient: (Describing her experience of hospitalization the previous year) Some issues within myself which are not resolved. I didn't feel on kilter, not who I really am. Does this make sense? I feel hopeless. I get a black feeling inside myself that wells up, very black.

Therapist: Is it related to feelings that led to your hospitalization?

Patient: Yes, I think so . . . I have trouble differentiating what's really happening. . . . I have difficulty expressing myself well and making myself understood.

In this summary of the first exchanges between therapist and patient, three themes have been articulated by the patient that the therapist will track and clarify with her over the two sessions: first, Hannah's experience that she does not "make sense," that she cannot make herself understood; second, her unstable sense of self, that she is "not who I really am"; and third, her description of a black feeling inside her that is connected with such extensive personal disorganization that she has required hospitalization in the past. Of course, these themes have been artificially separated in order to simplify illustration of the subsequent effect of the therapist's articulations.

Hannah goes on to express her subjective experience of a lack of a cohesive self-organization in the absence of mirroring selfobject reflection. She presents a developmental dilemma revealed by repeatedly asking, "Does this make sense?" Through this question, Hannah raises the possibility that if the therapist can understand her, then perhaps she can grasp who she is. Tracking the theme of making sense, the therapist responds to her statement that she has difficulty making herself understood:

Therapist: You're awfully worried about making sense. Have you had the experience of being misunderstood?

[Here the therapist tentatively articulates what might be an underlying organizing principle: "People don't understand me."]

Patient: I find that I have difficulty expressing myself well, to get my meaning across.

[The patient blames herself for not communicating clearly.]

Therapist: You're feeling that it's your problem in communicating, rather than people's problem in listening?

[The therapist articulates the patient's experience.]

Patient: Must be.

Therapist: Must be (with a smile).

[The nonverbal communication conveys that both the therapist and the patient are leaving open to question that the patient's problem is an inability to communicate clearly. Through the use of irony and humor, the therapist tries to depathologize the patient's self-blame.]

At this point, though, Hannah identifies the problem as her failure to communicate clearly; she locates the difficulty in her manner of delivery and expression. However, as the therapist invites her to explore with whom and in what contexts she fails to communicate well, the patient reveals that the problem manifests primarily in close personal relationships, such as with both her present and former husbands and her mother. For example, with her mother and sisters who did not visit her during her hospitalization:

Therapist: You were hurt by that.

[Articulation of affect.]

Patient: I was hurt by that because I've pretty much gone out of my way for everybody, and . . . that's my role in the family.

[Hannah identifies the context in which her organization of experience developed.]

Therapist: Your role is to help everybody else.

[Articulation of a second important organizing principle.]

Patient: Right!

[Said with surprise that reveals the novelty of being understood.]

Patient: I basically was (sighs), when people had problems they would come and dump them on me, and I would help them, or listen to them and . . .

Therapist: But nobody listens to you.

[Picking up the theme of the original organizing principle and articulating it again.]

Patient: Right. . . . At that point when I knew I was not together mentally . . . (She describes how her sister tried to get her to take care of her children and became indignant when the patient expressed unwillingness to take on that responsibility.)

Therapist: She wasn't hearing you.

[Therapist stays focused on the theme of the organizing principle that underlies her subjective experience of the encounter with the sister.]

Patient: Right. Exactly.

Therapist: She wasn't hearing what you needed.

[Articulated again.]

Patient: Right. Right. Exactly. I think I have a problem with my family. They don't hear me. They definitely don't hear me.

[At this point the organizing principle of people not hearing her appears to have been made conscious and is accepted by the patient. She no longer blames herself. We need to be alert to the possibility that her verbalizing of this organization of experience reflects superficial compliance with the therapist's articulations.

However, confirmation of the authentic meaningfulness of her understanding comes from traditional sources, that is, her next association. This spontaneous verbalization answers the question of whether she is merely agreeing out of compliance with the therapist.]

Patient: I have a picture, as a matter of fact, that I drew in art therapy. It was really weird because I'm a little girl, kneeling. And my family . . . it's just their heads, and they're real huge, and they're looking away from me. And none of them have ears.

Therapist: So they're not hearing you and they're not seeing you.

[Here the organizing principle is again articulated. In addition, the therapist is validating the subjective experience of the patient, thus fostering self-delineation through the promotion of trust in her subjective experience.]

From this point in the session, Hannah focuses in depth on her relationship with her current husband and how, in her wish to meet his needs she has lost some respect for herself. As she tried to communicate her experience to her husband, he did not respond. She feels unable to make things change, unable to stop the course that their relationship is taking.

Patient: I feel like I can't talk to him, you know. I mean, you reach a point . . . At least I've reached the point where when I feel like it doesn't matter what I say. . . . There's no point in trying to say anything.

Therapist: He's not going to hear you.

[The therapist articulates Hannah's recognition that it is not her failure to communicate clearly, but her husband's unwillingness to hear her that is the problem.]

Hannah moves now to exploring an area in which she does not feel hopeless: her relationship with her children. She contrasts these relationships to her relationship with her own mother, and again the theme of listening and being heard emerges.

Therapist: And they [her children] can listen to you?

Patient: Yeah. . . . That, too. That, too. I try not to be like my mom was. My mom was definitely, "Listen to me. Listen to me. Be my friend." I try not to be that. I try to listen to the things they have to say.

The session ends with the following exchange.

Therapist: Do you have any thoughts about our meeting today?

Patient: Yeah. It's intense. I don't really talk about this stuff very much.

Therapist: It stirred up a lot of feelings.

[The therapist articulates Hannah's affective experience.]

Patient: Yeah, pretty much. I get jumbled and I jump around . . . pretty much.

[Hannah reverts to self-blaming, the original organizing principle.]

Therapist: I think I've been able to follow you.

[The therapist affirms that Hannah has been communicating clearly and that he is available to provide attunement to her affect states.]

Patient: (Laughs) I appreciate that. It's an accomplishment.

[Hannah concludes with a self-deprecating comment. Nevertheless, there has been a shift in her original organization of experience. The session began with Hannah's conviction that she did not communicate clearly. This evolved into the idea that others do not hear her. Finally, with her therapist, she feels that while she may be difficult to understand, that someone who makes an effort can follow her. She has moved from self-blame to an appreciation of the intersubjective context of her problem.]

The second session begins with the patient's thoughts about the previous week's meeting.

Patient: I thought about the part where we talked about me not being heard. And I think that's pretty much true. Yeah. Very much true. I don't seem to have that problem communicating to people that I'm not in a close relationship with.

[Hannah has been able to hold on to the newly forming organizing principle that she can be understood, depending on the context.]

At this point the patient offers an extensive description of an incident earlier in the week in which she and her husband argued about the behavior of his 23-year-old son and the son's thoughtless use of a car that is her only means of transportation. She relates the incident and her subsequent efforts to get support from her husband.

Patient: You know after a while when you try to talk to somebody and they're not hearing you, you give up. What's the point of even trying?

[Hannah has come a long way from her original position that she is unable to communicate clearly.]

Therapist: You feel it's hopeless to get him to hear you.

[Here, the therapist articulates the affect of hopelessness that underlies the organizing principle.]

Patient: Yeah, because, it's like, I'm in a no-win situation. . . . And he just doesn't listen to me at all.

From this point in session 2 the patient produces material that reveals her unwillingness to continue trying to make herself understood. Her first husband was physically abusive to her, and she associates her current attempts to assert herself with her second husband and stepson with the past violence. In further associations, she relates feelings of being alone and unsupported and in physical danger when dealing with her stepson.

Patient: I can never stand up for myself. It's like that's my lot in life. Do you know what I'm saying? And this has been my whole life. And I don't want to be like that. It's hell to live in your own home, and not be free. . . .

Therapist: So, the safest course is not to be seen, not to be heard.

Patient: That's pretty much it. Which really sucks, because I feel like (crying and sighing deeply) . . . For a while I had been in a coma, for ten years or so. You know, I mean, my *self.* Because I started finally thinking of myself as a person instead of, "I need to do this for this person, this for this person, I need to take care of my mother, I need to do this for my husband, and I need to be there for my kids." And I finally started thinking, "Well, I don't do anything for myself." And I started just taking a little time for myself. I felt like I was waking up, the inner me, who I am, not who anybody else needs me to be. I don't know how to hang onto it (crying).

Therapist: It seems like in the face of [husband and stepson's] criticism, it's hard to hold on to who you are.

[The therapist articulates a new organizing principle, that safety comes from hiding what feels authentic to her. This marks the beginning of a conscious awareness of the conflict around self-delineation. To maintain her tie to the important object, she has to subvert her true feelings. We can see here that in a relatively short period of time, Hannah has moved from believing that she does not communicate clearly, to the understanding that the people she has chosen to surround herself with do not want to hear her. She has become aware that it feels unsafe to express herself. The locus of concern has shifted from outside, that is, her husband does not hear her, to an emergent quality of their relationship. Hannah fears provoking him and jeopardizing her tie to him.]

In the above interchange, the patient shifts from the initial theme of not being understood (the absence of attuned responsiveness) to the theme of not knowing who she is (the failure to develop self-delineation). The therapist has consistently put into words her immediate experience of not being heard and in doing so, has apparently identified one pervasive dynamic of her intimate relationships, a core organizing principle—that people close to her do not listen to her or hear her. By putting words to this organizing principle, the therapist has both provided an *experience* in which she does feel heard and understood, and simultaneously has provided her the *understanding* that while she has not felt heard or understood by important people in her life, it is not the fault of any deficiency in her ability to communicate. From this new position, she is willing to move into a slightly different kind of making sense, the area of thwarted self-delineation. Hannah has renounced her authentic sense of herself in order to maintain her tie to her husband, her mother, and other important people in her life.

Patient: I don't even know what to be. I don't know how to be.

Therapist: You want to please him.

Patient: Yeah. I don't know. I'm too aggressive; I'm not aggressive enough. I'm subservient.

Therapist: It sounds like you feel that he doesn't approve of you however you are. You never get it right.

[The therapist, not too successfully, attempts to articulate her experience.]

Patient: Maybe that's it.

[As we have seen, when the therapist succeeds in being attuned, this patient responds very enthusiastically. This response suggests more her compliance than her experience of being understood.]

Therapist: You're always feeling disapproved of.

Patient: I guess not when I'm what he wants me to be. But I never know exactly. . . . It's like, sometimes you get it. But that's not me. Does that make sense?

Therapist: So he approves of you when you're the way he wants you to be . . .

Patient: Right. Which is never consistent.

Therapist: It's not always clear to you what that is.

Patient: Right. That's right. Right.

[The therapist has been experienced as attuned.]

The patient moves with the analyst more deeply into her internal conflict around self-delineation and describes how she begins to lose her sense of herself in the face of conflict with her husband, especially conflict in which she feels she is not being heard.

Patient: My husband can tell me, "I know that it's not just you," but he's not saying anything to his son, so it's all just me. Does that make sense? He may say, "I know that," but for him to only address me . . .

[This statement, questioning her capacity to make sense, is indicative of a fragmentation reaction; under the pressure of intense affect generated by her husband's contradictory actions, she is suffering a disruption to her sense of self-delineation.]

Therapist: It's like saying that *you're* the problem. And you don't feel strong enough to know inside that it's not you.

[Here, the therapist is both validating Hannah's subjective experience and affirming her struggle for self-delineation.]

Patient: Right. I don't. For a while there I thought it wasn't me. And now I don't know . . . and I'm, uh . . .

Therapist: You get confused.

Hannah feels uncertain, again, as to the validity of her perceptions. In her associations, she returns to the experience she referred to in the initial exchange of the first session, the black feeling that wells up within her. In session 1 she identified this feeling: "It's just a really awful, awful feeling. It's awful to almost the point of feeling vile. Does that make sense?"

When she picks up this theme late in session 2 she relates:

Patient: I just have to hurt myself to feel better. . . . And I don't like that . . .

Therapist: But that's something you do.

Patient: Yeah. It's like there's nothing . . . It's just a very alone feeling. It's not like loneliness; it's just totally alone.

Therapist: Isn't that the black feeling you talked about last week?

Patient: That's part of it. That's not entirely it. It's like a self-destructive thing. . . . It's like, if I can make myself hurt enough, then I can quit feeling like that inside.

Therapist: Can you say something about how hurting yourself or injuring yourself makes the hurt inside go away?

Patient: (Lengthy pause) I don't know if it overshadows it, or just makes it dissipate.

[Hannah explains that if there is enough pain, she begins to feel "fuzzy" and can gain equilibrium.]

Therapist: "Fuzzy" makes you forget how hurt you've been by your husband?

[The therapist articulates his understanding of her experience.]

Patient: Exactly. That's it. That's it. (And a little later) If I can make myself hurt enough, then I can quit feeling vile inside.

Hannah connects this pattern of physically harming herself to remove herself from painful feelings of hurt and estrangement with her previous material about not being sure of who she is. She asserts needs of her own that she should rightfully be able to present to her husband. This continues the theme of conflict around self-delineation.

Patient: It's like, OK, once you're a victim, you have this tattoo that says "victim" here (points to her forehead), and like, only weirdos can see it. . . . It's like a magnet.

Therapist: It sounds like you feel that you somehow invite these attacks on you, but I think that must be because you've been attacked so much. And you've come to think it must be you.

[The therapist reformulates Hannah's explanation that she is masochistically inviting attacks. He articulates an alternative perspective that addresses another organization of experience—that she blames herself for the mistreatment she has experienced.]

Patient: Well, yeah. (Pause.) I don't have any other explanation.

[This is how her experience has come to be organized. It is hoped that in further treatment, she will develop new ways to organize these experiences.]

Therapist: You've never had a different kind of relationship.

Patient: In some ways all of my relationships end up, well maybe not, like, yelled at, and treated like I'm, you know, made to feel like I'm stupid and worthless, but . . . Giving more than I want to give. Feeling forced into giving more than I want to give.

Therapist: They haven't been reciprocal relationships where you got as much as you gave.

[The therapist articulates Hannah's longing for a different kind of relationship that, because of the way her experience has been organized, she has no expectation of achieving.]

Patient: No. That's like my M.O. (laughs). Yeah, it's like, it's almost like I seek that out, and *I don't* . . . I don't intentionally. I don't. But I've noticed that I get into relationships with people I don't like (laughs). That's weird, I think. I think that if I met my husband now, and I saw how he is with me now, there's no way that I would get married to him.

[First, Hannah takes pains to reject the formulation that she is masochistic. Further exploration might reveal that her masochism was interpreted to her in prior therapies; or perhaps, being intelligent and well read, she has come across this type of formulation in her readings. Second, she has become, in two sessions, more conscious of her deeper feelings. In the first session she described her relationship with her husband as "The best relationship I have ever had." She now considers that this is not good enough. She is making tentative steps to develop new organizing principles such as, "I deserve better" or "I can have more."]

Hannah develops this theme until, at the close of the session, she reveals an intense interest in writing and a wish to share her writing publicly at a small reading in a coffeehouse.

Patient: I don't feel like I can go (to the reading) without him. I don't feel like I can . . . I don't even feel like I can approach him about that.

Therapist: But writing is something you feel good about.

[The therapist affirms her subjective experience.]

Patient: Yeah. That's *me* when I do that.

[Here we see movement toward increasing self-delineation.]

Therapist: And you want to be able to go and read.

Patient: Right. I would love that. I would love to do a reading.

Hannah and her therapist have illuminated the personal meaning of much of what she revealed in the initial moments of the first meeting. By carefully putting words to Hannah's pervasive experience in close relationships that she has not been heard, she has both felt heard and understands that others, such as her therapist, although perhaps not her mother or husband, can hear her. From that calmed and more secure position, Hannah's feelings of identity confusion and self-fragmentation became available to be talked about. By attending closely to Hannah's evolving subjective experience when in conflict with her husband, the therapist articulated the way in which she loses herself, subjugates her sense of identity, in her attempts to stay related to her husband. This articulation and the understanding conveyed by it then allowed the patient to begin a tentative exploration of the third theme, her emptiness and self-abusive behavior as symbolized by the "black hole." As the therapist closely tracked Hannah's associations, carefully putting into words the feelings and experiences she expressed, she found her way to a part of herself that felt real and positive—her ability to express herself in her writing and her wish to have her writing heard, her openness to trusting the hearing power of an audience. Clearly more working through of these themes would be expected to occur throughout the course of treatment. However, the work accomplished in these two sessions has given Hannah the language tools to pursue further understanding of these themes.

DISCUSSION

In the case material, Hannah appeared to revise her original conviction that she communicated unclearly. The therapist depathologized, reformulated, and contextualized this organization of experience. With her therapist's support and affirmation, she moved away from a view of her communication problem as solely residing in her, to an understanding that her problem arose in the intersubjective context of her close personal relationships. Once she grasped the pervasiveness of this organization, she presented several manifestations of enhanced self-understanding. For example, she asserted that she had legitimate needs in her marriage and that she believed that she had a right to present them to her husband and to have them acknowledged. This assertion appears to illustrate a more solid, cohesive, and delineated self-organization. Additionally, by the close of the second session she revealed that she would like to be "heard" by reading some of her writing to others in an organized setting. She fantasized doing this independently, without her husband, and explored the emotional and relational implications of such a move. These fantasies demonstrate a shift toward increased self-delineation. She understood that her concerns about her communications are historically rooted in the experience of not feeling heard. This connection between her childhood experience and the present supports a developing sense of self-continuity. She ended the second session in an optimistic state, one that suggested the possibility that her improved self-understanding might free her to explore new ways of experiencing herself.

Although the clinical material covers only two sessions, we believe that it illustrates the concept that verbal articulations promote the coming to consciousness of the organizing principles and the accompanying affect states that have shaped the patient's subjective experience. Together therapist and patient made sense of the patient's organization of childhood experience and the way these organizations of experience have shaped her present relationships. Through making sense together, the patient has acquired new self-understanding that promotes the transformation of subjective experience and the formation of new organizing principles.

SUMMARY

Among the selfobject functions provided by a therapist's attuned verbal articulations is that of self-understanding. Earlier discussions of the locus of therapeutic action of the therapist's verbal articulations implied that the benefit for the patient was either in new or enhanced cognitive understanding or in a selfobject experience of feeling understood. We propose that making sense together provides not only both of the previously mentioned experiences for the patient, but that, additionally, such articulations provide the potential for new self-understanding. For the patient, when the elusive past and the troublesome present become comprehensible, through language, in the context of a primary selfobject relationship, the possibility for new organizations of experience arises.

7

The Antidote Dimension of the Therapy Relationship*

In Chapter 4, we discussed the two dimensions of the transference relationship. In the first, the selfobject dimension, the patient longs for a new relationship with the therapist in which developmentally needed but missing selfobject experiences are provided. For these patients, their original relationships with caregivers involved a double failure. First, their developmental needs for attuned responsiveness were not consistently met, producing a painful experience of injury. Second, this experience of injury in response to caregiver misattunements failed to elicit the needed attuned responses from these same caregivers that might have ameliorated and repaired the original injury. Caregivers who fail to provide attuned responsiveness in the first case are unlikely to

---

*Peter Buirski and Michael Monroe published portions of this chapter previously in *Psychoanalytic Psychology*, 2000, 17:78–87, as "Intersubjective Observations on Transference Love."

be emotionally available subsequently to repair the damage that they inflicted.

The second or repetitive dimension of the transference is characterized by the patient's fear that this new relationship with the therapist, like the relationship with the original caregivers, will prove to be disappointing, destructive, and ultimately retraumatizing. The fear of retraumatization in the transference often lies behind what has typically been understood as resistance. By resistance, traditional psychoanalysts usually mean that the patient acts in a way to obstruct or thwart the therapist's efforts to bring knowledge of unacceptable unconscious wishes to consciousness. The implication is that the patient is negatively motivated to avoid the good that therapy can do him. However, from the intersubjective perspective, resistance, or attempts to thwart the therapist's efforts, may be seen as a healthy striving for self-protection. By avoiding a relationship that has the potential to retraumatize, the patient is acting to preserve his self-organization in the face of the dangerous threats posed by the therapist.

Regarding the longing for the provision of missing but needed selfobject functions, Orange and colleagues (1997) have contributed an important clarification:

> The term *selfobject transference* is being used to refer to two types of relational experiences that have distinctly different origins and meanings. In one, the patient longs for the bond with the analyst to supply missing developmental experiences—what Kohut originally meant by selfobject transferences. In the other, the patient seeks responses from the analyst that would counteract invariant organizing principles that are manifestations of what we (Stolorow et al. 1987) call the repetitive dimension of the transference. In the former, the patient longs for something missing; in the latter, the patient seeks an antidote to something crushingly present. [p. 65]

Selfobject experiences promote transformation of the personality organization by providing developmentally needed but missing experiences. Antidote experiences, on the other hand, cover over the painful and disorganizing affects that accompany organizations of experience that are "crushingly present." Rather than suffering from the consequences of having failed to develop some capacity (a deficit model of personality formation) these patients are striving to offset some organization of experience, such as the unconscious conviction that one is disgusting and repulsive, that is all too present in their mental life. The function of the antidote is to ward off such painful affects as shame or self-loathing by seeking out offsetting or countervailing experiences while at the same time preserving the existing organization of experience. Because antidote experiences function to temporarily offset or counteract painful affect states rather than transform them, the need for them never diminishes. The repetitive striving for antidote experiences can take on the appearance of an addiction. One cannot do without them for long and one never gets enough of them.

The term *antidote* in traditional usage refers to a cure that works by counteracting the effects of a poison. As employed in intersubjectivity theory, the usage of the term needs some clarification. In the organization of experience, when antidote experiences are operating, underlying crushing affect states are not cured but covered over. Like painting over rust, the underlying affliction continues to eat away underneath the healthy looking surface. A medical analogy, such as the continuous need for insulin to control diabetes, might fit better. The insulin does not cure the disease process. Rather, it offsets the adverse effects of the disease process, but only as long as it continues to be administered. The need for continuous application is what gives the antidote the quality of an addictive substance. With this clarification in mind, we will continue to refer to the offsetting function as the antidote.

Atwood and Stolorow (1997) suggest that the selfobject

dimension of the transference functions as the central experience of some patients, while the antidote dimension of the transference may be in the forefront of the experience of other patients. While one or the other may characterize the central concerns of different patients, it is not uncommon for both concerns to be operating, at different moments of the treatment, in the same patient. We will now present clinical material from two patients, Theodore and Jennifer, to illustrate how both the selfobject dimension of the transference and the antidote dimension function to transform or preserve the patient's organization of experience. We will show how the antidote functions to ward off the debilitating effects of painful, disorganizing affect states while at the same time preserving or perpetuating the existing organization of experience.

CLINICAL MATERIAL

Theodore is a 23-year-old man who spent most of his childhood in foster homes. He has been working in a convenience store as he tries to put himself through college on a part-time basis. He sought treatment at the college counseling center because of a history of irritability, depression, and inability to sustain relationships with women. His therapist, a female graduate student, grasped the extreme emotional deprivation of Theodore's early life. She initially understood him to be suffering from arrests in the development of self-cohesion with insufficient capacity for affect integration and regulation. This is a deficit model that emphasizes what has been missing or absent in Theodore's development. Her therapeutic stance focused on the selfobject dimension of the transference, providing mirroring and affirming his fragile self-organization—in other words, providing in the new therapy relationship what had been missing in Theodore's development.

During the first few months of treatment, Theodore adopted

a stance of aloof detachment from engagement with his therapist. He gave the impression that he did not need anything or anyone, yet he maintained a record of perfect attendance at sessions. As the three-week college interterm recess approached, Theodore began to talk about termination. His therapist raised the possibility that his thoughts about stopping treatment might be connected to the impending separation. While Theodore initially dismissed this formulation, he soon began to show cracks in his affective armor. As the break approached, he became increasingly agitated and emotional. He revealed that he felt very attached to his therapist and needed to see her. His neediness became increasingly desperate. He asked if they might continue meeting during the break. His therapist informed him that this would not be possible as the clinic was closed during the break period. Theodore became enraged and verbally abusive, insisting that she was a fake, unprofessional, and unethical. He railed that she pretended to care but she was just treating him to fulfill a training requirement. If she cared about him she would meet with him, perhaps at some other location, instead of dumping him. She was just like all his foster families who palmed him off when he no longer suited their needs.

His therapist tried to explore the meaning of Theodore's conviction that she did not care for him. Initially it seemed plausible that his rage toward his therapist represented a displacement onto her of his rage at his foster parents. This traditional transference interpretation would have explained Theodore's displaced anger toward his therapist as a reaction to historical abandonment. Further exploration, however, revealed that the meaning Theodore made of his therapist's stance was that she did not care because he was not worth caring for. Apparently, Theodore had organized his experience around the belief that there was something deeply, fundamentally, unlovable about him, that he was disgusting and repulsive, and that the therapist, like his foster parents, was repelled and disgusted by him. We can appreciate how as a child, Theodore's experience of multiple rejections led him to conclude that he must be to blame. It was not that his foster parents were inadequate or flawed, but that he was defective and repulsive.

This situation was quite complex. On the one hand, Theodore's selfobject longings for validation of his subjectivity were being thwarted and his rage could be understood as being reactive to his sense of narcissistic injury at not being wanted. From this perspective, the therapist's actions had served to retraumatize Theodore. However, along with frustrated selfobject longings, Theodore also felt he was exposing, to his therapist and his own self-awareness, his searing sense of shame underlying his organizing principles that he was repulsive, disgusting, and unlovable. By not being available to meet with him, Theodore's therapist brought to the surface these painful affects associated with his core organizing principles. Thus, Theodore's rage was not just reactive to the retraumatization through abandonment. The rage was also reactive to his having to confront his warded-off painful core organizing principles and the disorganizing affects that accompany them. By heaping blame and scorn on his therapist, Theodore was trying to deflect attention away from his feeling of shame and worthlessness and onto his therapist's failings. As long as the therapist could be devalued, Theodore did not have to experience what an awful person he believed he truly was. This is a very different explanation than the familiar notion of projection. It was not that Theodore was projecting his own feelings of worthlessness onto his therapist, but that the actions of his therapist were hurting him by forcing him to confront his own painful affect states. He blamed his therapist for the hurt and pain he was feeling, but these affects were revivals of earlier warded-off affect states. It is important to note that these painful affects were not displaced from the past onto the present, but were revived by the therapist's actions in the present.

Responding only to the selfobject dimension, Theodore's therapist offered to hold phone sessions with him during the break. In doing so, his therapist believed that she was responding to a selfobject need by providing a new experience of caring and concerned attentiveness to his needs. However, as the break continued, Theodore became increasingly needy and demanding of phone contacts. He began leaving messages asking the therapist to call him. The more she responded to these calls, the more they increased in frequency and intensity. When treatment resumed after the break and Theodore's demand for escalating demonstrations of caring did not abate, his therapist became increasingly aware of her discomfort. She realized she was becoming enmeshed in an enactment. Once the therapist was able to appreciate and explore the extent to which Theodore's need for her limitless responsiveness was a longing not just for developmentally missing selfobject functions, but was also for an antidote to offset his painful feelings of shame and worthlessness, she was able to begin articulating the principles around which his experience had become organized. The therapist tried to make sense of this by saying things like, "When I am not available to you it makes you feel like you are not worth caring for."

Theodore had great difficulty hearing and assimilating this articulation. His organization of experience, that he was fundamentally worthless and unlovable, allowed for no other explanation for his therapist's withholding behavior. He believed that if his therapist really cared for him she would demonstrate it in the ways he wanted, and the therapist's failure to show she cared could only mean that Theodore was not worthy of being cared for. It was not that Theodore had a distorted view of his therapist's actions, but that Theodore's world of experience didn't recognize any other demonstrations of caring. Like the person who is unknowingly becoming hard of hearing, if he cannot make out the movie dialogue it must be that the sound system is defective. Such is the pervasiveness of the organization of experience that it allows for no alternative explanations.

Theodore's therapist repeatedly explained that she understood how difficult it was for Theodore to grasp that she cared for him even though she would not demonstrate it in the way he wished. She spelled out her understanding of his organization of experience, that he had not been cared for in his childhood, and that she was not abandoning him but was staying connected to him. Over several months, as his therapist was able to accept Theodore's hurt and anger without rejection or retaliation, Theodore began to establish a feeling of trust in the care of his therapist.

Because of his history of being shunted to various foster homes, it made sense that Theodore was suffering primarily from arrests in development. However, exploration of the meaning of his subjective experience revealed that rather than strictly searching for something missing in his development, that is, needed selfobject experience, Theodore was also striving to offset what was crushingly present: his affects of shame, worthlessness, and self-loathing. That new reparative experience was not sufficient was made evident by Theodore's seeming addiction to the therapist's responsiveness.

The case of Jennifer offers a somewhat different perspective on the striving for antidote experience. Rather than trying to engage the therapist in an enactment cycle in which the therapist felt called upon to offer concrete demonstrations of his caring, as was the case with Theodore, Jennifer developed a romantic fantasy that functioned as an antidote for her. It was only when this fantasy went unrequited that her underlying disorganizing affects were exposed, leading to reactive rage reactions.

"I want to make love with you. There's a difference between sex and making love. Sex is a dime a dozen, right? Making love is like . . . is kind of like a symbolic, uh, culmination of everything. And it makes two people closer. Brings 'em closer together. That's what I would think because I never had that. I've had sex, but, you know, whoopee doo."

What, we might wonder, would arouse these sentiments in Jennifer, a 53-year-old woman, for her 35-year-old male therapist? Might she be rationalizing feelings of love to disguise her lust?

Might she be displacing onto her therapist feelings she had as a child for her father? Might she be attempting to seduce or overpower her therapist so as to defeat his attempts to treat her?

These hypotheses are examples of the kind of explanations Freud, in his 1915 paper "Observations on Transference-Love," offered to account for the seemingly inappropriate, perhaps irrational, emotions that Jennifer was expressing. Freud believed that such "falling in love" was a manifestation of the patient's transference and has nothing to do with the person of the therapist. He cautioned that therapists not be unduly flattered by being the objects of such emotions (as Breuer was by Anna O.'s profession of love), for it is not the therapist's charms that evoke such emotions. Rather, for Freud, as we discussed in Chapter 4, transference love was motivated by displacement and/or the repetition compulsion. It represents a "false connection" or a distortion of reality. Having little to do with the person of the therapist, Freud predicted that the patient would certainly fall equally in love with the next therapist, and the next.

As we discussed in Chapter 4, intersubjectivity theory offers a very different conception of the nature of transference in the therapeutic relationship. From the perspective of intersubjectivity theory, "Transference in its essence refers neither to regression, displacement, projection, nor distortion, but rather to the assimilation of the analytic relationship into the thematic structures of the patient's personal subjective world. Thus conceived, transference is an expression of the universal psychological striving to organize experience and create meanings" (Stolorow et al. 1987, pp. 45–46). This should not be misunderstood as implying that transference is solely an intrapsychic process generated within the mind of the patient. On the contrary, both patient and therapist contribute to the construction of the patient's subjective experience of the therapist and the relationship with the therapist.

In Jennifer's case, her love for her therapist does not derive from her unconscious longings for a real or fantasied love object from childhood being displaced onto her therapist. Rather, it is a complex construction that developed in the intersubjective field created by the coming together of two subjectivities. The intersubjective field includes Jennifer's life experience and her organization of that subjective experience in relationship with her therapist and his organization of experience. (As will become evident, the intersubjective field also included the therapist's supervisor and his impact on the subjective experience of both Jennifer and her therapist.) Nor, we contend, is her love merely an irrational distortion of the present relationship in terms of the past. It is important to recognize that Jennifer has not fallen in love in a vacuum. She had spent many hours over the last year alone in a room with a man whom she reported experiencing as attractive, caring, and able to understand much of her experience. It is crucial to acknowledge Jennifer's subjective experience of being cared for by her therapist. Her therapist experienced genuine feelings of concern and care for Jennifer and it is unlikely that, given her sensitivity to others, she missed the subtle (or not so subtle) expressions of these feelings. It seems likely that Jennifer utilized these very real feelings as building blocks upon which to base her romantic attraction.

Going even further, it is important to recognize that there were specific attributes about the therapist that Jennifer had identified as the reasons that she had fallen in love with him. She had told him repeatedly how much she appreciated his acceptance and attunement. Also, she had talked about such personal characteristics as his sense of humor and his beard. Within the intersubjective field of the patient–therapist relationship, Jennifer was not a woman in love with the past but was using her love in the present to find her way through her past.

During the first eight months of the treatment, Jennifer asked that the frequency of sessions be increased from once a week, to twice a week, and then three times a week. As the frequency of sessions increased so, too, did her experience of, and capacity to verbalize, her love for her therapist. She seemed to become increasingly preoccupied with her therapist. Alone at night in her apartment, she constructed elaborate fantasies of their loving relationship. Whereas she used to drink a lot of wine in the evenings, now, on occasion, she renounced alcohol in order to immerse herself more purely in the loving feelings. She could spend entire evenings lost in rapturous fantasy of their union.

Jennifer's fantasies could be roughly sorted into two categories: those that expressed the love she felt for her therapist, which was unlike any feeling she had ever had for another person, and those in which she imagined that her therapist loved her in return. In an example of the first type of fantasy, Jennifer imagined that her therapist had cancer and she devoted herself to ministering to his every need. In the second type of fantasy, she imagined her therapist was involved with another woman. The other woman died (of unelaborated causes) and Jennifer's therapist was now free to follow his heart and be with her.

While we are well aware that these two fantasies are rich in personal meaning for Jennifer and can be profitably viewed from multiple perspectives, we will focus on the extent to which they parallel the selfobject and repetitive dimensions of the transference that Stolorow and colleagues (1987) have identified.

The first fantasy, in which Jennifer provided loving ministrations to her ill therapist, reflected the selfobject dimension of her relationship to her therapist. She was in love with his idealized qualities and wished to devote herself to him. In the therapy relationship, her experience of his attention to her distress, his concern for her well-being, his attunement to her fluctuating affect states and his ability to contain them, his validation of her subjective experience, and his constancy had fostered more coherent organization, positive coloration, and temporal stability of her self-experience. He has been unlike anyone else in her life and her feelings for him were unlike anything she had felt for another.

Like the first type of fantasy, the second also reflected a selfobject dimension of the transference. In the second, Jennifer fantasized the mirroring she received from her loving therapist. However, we would like to draw attention to one important way in which the second fantasy differed from the first. While the first fantasy centered around Jennifer's subjectively experienced affect states, the second fantasy, that her therapist reciprocated her love, was centered on what she wished the affective experience of the other might be. This fantasy reflected an attribution of reciprocal feelings of love, which had their seeds in her experience of his care and concern for her but did not match her therapist's subjectively experienced affect state.

What other function might be expressed or served by this fantasy? We believe that by attributing reciprocal feelings of love to her therapist, Jennifer had constructed an antidote to the painful affects underlying her invariant organizing principles. More specifically, her fantasy of reciprocated love functioned to offset or undo the crushing affects of shame and self-loathing associated with her archaically formed organizing principles that she was inherently defective and unlovable.

As the two types of fantasy described above illustrate, contained in Jennifer's transference love for her therapist was the selfobject dimension, in which missing developmental experiences were provided, and the repetitive dimension of experience in which the antidote function was contained. Her love for her therapist operated in the selfobject dimension where Jennifer could have a new growth-enhancing experience. At the same time, her fantasy of her therapist's reciprocated love functioned as an antidote to the crushing affects associated with her invariant organizing principles. To avoid having this fantasy disconfirmed, Jennifer mostly kept it to herself, enveloping herself in it privately. When she did reveal its presence on occasion, this aspect of the transference love had a ritualized, obsessional quality, much like an addiction.

The antidote function of the fantasy that her love was reciprocated served to cover over her painful affects of shame and self-loathing. However, unlike the selfobject functions provided by the new experience with the therapist, which served to organize and integrate her self-experience, the antidote function operated to obscure and defend against crushing affect, without bringing about any new illumination or transformation. Therefore, for the antidote to be effective, it had to be repeatedly applied. Antidote functions do not promote change to the invariant organization of experience. Instead, like painting over rust, the antidote hides or obscures the underlying corrosive affect states. It functions to maintain the existing organization of experience.

Jennifer's need to maintain the antidote function of her transference love can be clearly seen when its existence was most threatened or it failed to operate. Jennifer was an experienced patient. In addition to having been hospitalized in her twenties for depression, she had had numerous therapies, although none of her prior outpatient treatments lasted long or were experienced as especially helpful. Nevertheless, she knew about the ethical boundaries that guard the patient–therapist relationship. Part of the threat to the maintenance of the antidote function was Jennifer's awareness that her sessions were being videotaped and shown to her therapist's supervisor. She would periodically turn to the one-way vision screen and address the supervisor, reassuring him that her therapist was behaving appropriately. Jennifer initially feared that the supervisor would view expressions of her love for the therapist as grounds for terminating her treatment. So she whispered her feelings or turned away from the camera. After reassurance by her therapist and the passage of time without interference from the supervisor, Jennifer became more comfortable expressing her love. But she remained convinced that reciprocal expressions of love by her therapist would be viewed as inappropriate and might jeopardize their connection. Thus, while she reassured the supervisor and her therapist that she understood her therapist would not act out his reciprocal love for her, she simultaneously maintained the fantasy that her therapist loved her in return—he dared not show it, but he nevertheless felt it. Here the supervisor served as a kind of chaperone whose presence prevented the therapist from reciprocating her love. In this way, the antidote function of her transference love was retained in the absence of any direct confirmation of love by her therapist.

On one occasion, Jennifer presented her therapist with a gift of a key chain that she hoped would remind him of her whenever he used it. Her therapist, who had shown great courage in accepting her verbal professions of love in the past, became very uncomfortable with the meanings Jennifer attributed to the gift. His discomfort was apparent to Jennifer as he struggled to find a way to explore the meanings of the gift without making Jennifer feel rejected. Jennifer sensed that he was uncomfortable, and by incorporating her observation into her organization of experience, concluded that he found her unlovable, and became enraged. She had never before displayed such rage, either to her therapist or, as she later reported, to anyone else.

The traditional self-psychological formulation has been to understand such rage as occurring in reaction to narcissistic injury (Kohut 1972). Narcissistic injury might result from the absence of needed mirroring or disillusionment with idealized others. However, to characterize Jennifer's rage reaction solely as the product of narcissistic injury does not capture the complexity of the experience. Throughout her life, Jennifer had responded to narcissistic injury with depression and resignation. What appeared to have instigated Jennifer's rage reaction was that, by rejecting her gift, Jennifer's therapist had threatened the antidote function of her fantasy of reciprocated love. Her therapist had, in effect, stripped the paint off the protective coating, exposing the underlying corrosive affects of shame and self-loathing that had been disguised by her fantasy of reciprocated love. In this formulation then, narcissistic rage may result not only from the failure to provide needed selfobject functions, but also from exposing the painful affects covered over by the work of the antidote function.

The antidote function is comparable to the familiar notion of defense. However, from the perspective of ego psychology, defense is understood to protect the individual from knowledge of unacceptable instinctual impulse. The antidote function, as it is conceptualized here, also serves a self-protective function. But instead of protection from unacceptable instinctual impulse, the antidote functions to protect the individual from painful, disorganizing affects. In the case of Jennifer, the fantasy of reciprocated love functioned to protect her from experiencing the searing shame and self-loathing that underlay her organizing principles of fundamental unlovableness and worthlessness.

It is curious that Jennifer's therapist, who had courageously accepted her many expressions of love, became uncomfortable with the gift of the key chain. Apparently, the meaning of the key chain to Jennifer, that the therapist would think about her when he used it, threatened the therapist's sense of himself as an appropriate and ethical practitioner. He felt that if he accepted the key chain he would be validating her fantasy that he reciprocated her love and thereby encourage her to misconstrue the nature of the relationship. Jennifer's therapist was also concerned that his supervisor would be critical of him for accepting the gift, which played into other of his archaic organizing principles. From this perspective, the patient's experience of her therapist as serving antidote functions felt comforting to her, but the therapist's experience of himself as an effective, appropriate, and ethical practitioner felt threatened. In the key chain example, the therapist's rejection of the gift served to reduce his personal discomfort at the expense of exposing the patient to hurtful affect states.

Since the selfobject function had become intertwined with the antidote function, the therapist faced a dilemma in which either course of action was fraught with complications. If he did not accept the key chain, he risked undermining the selfobject function of the transference relationship; if he did accept it, he participated or colluded in maintaining the antidote function.

How might the therapist have addressed the antidote dimension of experience differently? Orange and colleagues (1997) suggest that mirroring of antidote functions, like defensive grandiosity, only leads to addiction to the analyst's responsiveness. They recommend that the approach to antidotes to crushing affect states underlying invariant organizing principles is "neither to mirror nor to puncture it, but to wait for openings in it—that is, for opportunities to make contact with the painful affect walled off on the other side of the vertical split. Such efforts invariably evoke intense shame in the transference" (pp. 82–83). To this recommendation we would add the importance of articulating the function served by the antidote in warding off painful affects associated with invariant organizations of experience.

With both Theodore and Jennifer, their therapists found that once the walled off affects emerged into the transference relationship, they came with great intensity. Both, in their own way, indicated that they had never felt so much pain before. Over time, the therapists offered articulations describing the original contexts in which the affects emerged. Simultaneously, they connected these archaic affect states with the patients' current disappointments with their therapists. Theodore and Jennifer gradually recognized that this new pain was also an old, but heretofore warded off, pain. The impact of these articulations illustrates the selfobject functions provided by putting the patient's experience into words (discussed in Chapter 6).

During the weeks following the key chain incident, the treatment seemed to move back and forth between the selfobject and antidote dimensions of experience. Jennifer would expand on how wonderful it felt to love her therapist, with occasional inferences about being loved by him in return. At one point, Jennifer articulated a fantasy that her therapist was influencing her radio to play certain love songs as a demonstration of his love for her. This was alarming to both therapist and supervisor who feared a pathological regression was in process. They were tempted to confront Jennifer with a dose of their reality but knew that, while this would serve to reduce their anxiety, it would likely feel very injurious to her.

In the end, the therapist and supervisor adopted two approaches. First, they managed their anxiety by reviewing the healthy behavioral changes that Jennifer was making in her life. These included changing her midnight to 8:00 a.m. work shift to 4:00 p.m. to midnight so that she would have more opportunity to interact with people, which she had been avoiding; distancing herself from a friend who has been verbally and emotionally abusive to her; making a new friendship with a more supportive, affirming woman; and moving from her old apartment, where she had many painful experiences, to a nicer location not associated with past hurts. Second, when openings presented themselves, the therapist offered a series of articulations, the aim of which was to promote self-delineation and self-cohesion by communicating his understanding of her organization of experience.

The sequence of articulations began with her therapist's expressing his concern that Jennifer believed he was the only person in the world who could love her, and only his love could save her. He explained that her conviction that no other person would find her worthy made her feel addicted to her therapist and the fantasy of his reciprocated love. Furthermore, sequestered behind this belief were her core organizing principles of worthlessness and unlovableness and the accompanying crushing affects of shame and self-loathing. Within a few weeks, Jennifer reported several new experiences indicating greater self-cohesion. She renewed contact with a former friend who liked her but from whom she had withdrawn. Also, she began to reexamine her reasons for giving up her training as a dental assistant. (Apparently several years earlier, Jennifer had completed a course of study to become a dental assistant. However, she believed that the woman who served as her mentor did not like her. She was suspicious and confused when this woman offered her a job and she withdrew from this new possibility.)

This series of articulations was directed at the antidote

function of the fantasy of reciprocated love. However, care had to be taken not to undercut the selfobject dimension of the transference that continued to be so growth enhancing for Jennifer. By moving back and forth between providing needed selfobject functions and articulating antidote functions, the treatment promoted new self-transforming experience, greater self-cohesion, and the formation of new principles to organize her new experience.

As the key chain example illustrated, selfobject and antidote dimensions of experience occur within an intersubjective field and engage the invariant organizing principles of both patient and therapist. There are treatment contexts formed with certain patients, often those labeled as difficult, where the therapist's organization of experience is also threatened. Perhaps foremost among these are the threats to the therapist's organization of experience that are aroused by their patients' longing for the provision of antidote experiences. In the face of attacks on the therapist's self-esteem, professionalism, and ethical functioning, therapists often feel inclined to provide reality testing, structure, limits, and medication for the patient. These interventions are usually justified as being in the patient's best interests, providing the patient with something needed but missing, when instead they often function to reduce the therapist's personal sense of disorganization and fragmentation and restore and repair the therapist's threatened sense of self-cohesion. These options then serve antidote functions for the therapist.

This highlights an interesting area for further exploration: the countertransference experience of providing selfobject functions in contrast to antidote functions. It is our impression that the experience of serving antidote functions may be much more disruptive to the therapist's self-organization than the experience of providing selfobject functions. With damaged or deprived patients whose need for selfobject relatedness from early caregivers went unmet, the consistent experience of selfobject relatedness with the therapist has growth enhancing and transforming effect. Over the course of therapy, as self-cohesion and affect integration and regulation increase, the patient's capacity to tolerate the therapist's occasional misattunements improves. Unlike what might be predicted by a typical reinforcement paradigm (rewarding the patient's selfobject-seeking behavior would be expected to increase the frequency of such behaviors), the therapist's provision of needed selfobject functions actually leads to a reduction in the patient's urgent need for such functions. As the patient develops greater self-cohesion through the selfobject relationship with the therapist, the patient is able to tolerate misattunements without risk of fragmentation. Thus, when the therapist provides needed selfobject functions, the patient's need for the further provision of these selfobject functions begins to diminish over time.

Just the opposite occurs with the need for antidote functions. In those patients where an antidote function covers over disorganizing affects associated with core organizing principles, the urgent need for antidote experience does not diminish; rather, it intensifies and escalates. With such patients, like Theodore's need for phone contacts and Jennifer's belief that her therapist reciprocated her love, therapists often feel that they are being pulled into enactments in which they must provide more and greater evidence of care or love for the patient who never seems to get enough. The therapist's experience is that there is no end or limit to the patient's need because the patient has become increasingly "addicted" to the function the antidote has served in providing protection from intolerable affect.

Therapists who become enmeshed in providing antidote experience for their patients may begin to entertain thoughts of referring the patients out or increasing their medication. They experience themselves as withholding, rejecting, angry, and agitated. Awareness of these affect states occurring in relationship to the patient can serve as useful countertransference indicators that one is engaging in a repetitive antidote relationship and not a transforming selfobject relationship.

Our understanding of the function of striving for antidote experiences provides an additional dynamic formulation for making sense of some of the most perplexing and challenging behaviors we encounter in treatment. Theorists frequently invoke dynamic explanations like self-destructive and self-punitive motives or masochistic striving to account for patients' behaviors that bring about hurtful outcomes. For example, Theodore's needy and demanding behavior seemed self-defeating because it provoked the very situation he dreaded; he behaved in demanding and insistent ways that tended to drive his therapist and others away rather than bring them close. However, we must not confuse the motive that instigated the behavior with the effect or outcome the behavior produced. A striving for antidote experience motivated Theodore. He desperately needed his therapist to demonstrate her care for him so that his conviction of his fundamental repulsive unlovableness was offset and sequestered out of awareness. The effect of his desperation was that he behaved in ways that produce an undesired outcome, but his motive was not to provoke injury or rejection. His motive was to obscure the affects associated with his core organizing principles through securing antidote experiences. Similarly, Jennifer's delusion-like fantasy that her therapist reciprocated her love grew out of her wish to offset and counteract her self-loathing by securing antidote experiences. That the fantasy had the unwanted effect of destabilizing her therapist and jeopardizing his engagement with her was an unfortunate and undesired outcome.

SUMMARY

The functions of selfobject and antidote dimensions of the transference experience for the patient may operate in the same patient, with first one then the other being in the forefront of the transference experience. We have stressed the therapeutic importance of distinguishing between selfobject functions and antidote functions in furthering the illumination and transformation of subjective experience. Both selfobject and antidote dimensions of experience occur within an intersubjective field that engages the invariant organizing principles of both the patient and the therapist.

8

Expanding the Field: Intersubjectivity Theory and Supervision

The supervisory relationship is an intersubjective field. When supervisor and supervisee(s) meet for the purpose of teaching and learning about treatment informed by intersubjectivity theory, the occasion is one of "making sense" of a patient through the interfacing subjectivities of all concerned. Given our theoretical assumption that *all* experience (including what has been called "intrapsychic") is contextual, supervision presents an opportunity both to facilitate learning treatment practices based on the ideas and principles articulated in this book, and, inevitably, an in vivo experience of mutual influence and making sense together.

The literature on psychoanalytic supervision has tended to focus on working with countertransference reactions and on examining the process of supervision (Dewald 1987, Ekstein and Wallerstein 1959, Fleming and Benedek 1966, Lane 1992, Wallerstein 1981). These works provide the foundation for an in-depth study of psychoanalytic supervision. (See also Jacobs et al. 1995,

Levy and Kindler 1995, and Rock 1997 for contemporary thought on psychoanalytic supervision.) In this chapter, however, we offer, not a comprehensive model of supervision, but a wide-ranging exploration of the process and content of supervision based on intersubjectivity theory. Primarily, we illustrate ways in which intersubjectivity theory applies to the art and practice of supervision.

The sensibilities outlined in Chapter 2 are fundamental to supervision based on intersubjectivity theory. To recast some of those ideas in terms of the supervisory process, we explore the unique context and domain of inquiry in supervision. Because intersubjectivity theory is a "process theory offering broad methodological and epistemological principles for investigating and comprehending the intersubjective contexts in which psychological phenomena . . . arise"(Orange et al. 1997, p. 68), we suggest that the goals of supervision include guiding the supervisee's ability to facilitate the unfolding, illumination, and transformation of the patient's subjectivity. To promote such a process, the supervisee must develop an appreciation for the contextual nature of psychotherapy, specifically for the irreducible mutual influence of the subjectivities of the therapist and patient. A supervisee presumably enters a supervisory relationship expecting to learn the "how" and "what" of doing psychotherapy. Instead, she is offered a theory that requires her to understand each patient in his own terms and in his own context, rather than from within fixed frames of reference, such as specific developmental stages or defensive maneuvers. The supervisee is asked to engage in a therapeutic dialogue in which a patient reveals his personal experience, including the contributing influence of the subjectivity of the therapist/supervisee.

From our experience with graduate and postgraduate students, we consistently find that, upon entering supervision, supervisees feel anxious and without direction. As we noted in Chapter 2, therapists (and supervisees) are frequently motivated by a wish to help and fix. Supervisees often feel they are not "doing anything" (i.e., not doing real therapy) if they consistently focus on attuning to the patient's subjective experience. So here is an instance where intersubjectivity theory and the practice of supervision overlap. The supervisee's insecurity and anxiety, her wish to help or to fix, constitute, in part, her subjectivity, and it will bear on the patient's experience in treatment. As supervisors, we recognize the destabilizing and anxiety-provoking experience of trying to listen and understand while gradually becoming aware that one is inextricably part of what is heard and understood. As supervisors, our sensitivity (or lack thereof) to these aspects of the supervisee's subjectivity inevitably becomes part of the supervisory context. Creating an atmosphere that recognizes and allows for these affects to enter the supervisory dialogue is fundamental to the ultimate reorganization of the supervisee's sense of herself as a psychotherapist. The transformation is from a person who sees herself as helper or fixer to one who understands, articulates, and illuminates the patient's subjective experience.

Just as core organizations of experience emerge from early childhood contexts in which affects are attuned to and mutually regulated (or misattuned to and walled off), attunement to and management of affect in supervision are significant factors in the supervisee's developing professional identity. And, of course, the supervisor's experience of herself *as supervisor* is emerging from this same context of "differently organized, interacting subjective worlds" (Stolorow et al. 1987, p. ix). The supervisor's affective experience of working with this supervisee on this particular case enters their coconstructed field. This continual mutual interplay of subjectivities and affective influence is the ground of all experience. From whatever vantage point and through whatever lens, we invariably are faced with the "unbearable embeddedness of being" (Stolorow and Atwood 1992, p. 22), and the supervisory context is no more or less "embedded" than any other. The primary difference is that the intersubjective field has been enlarged to contain three participants.

Because mutual influence is the matrix of all experience, we recognize that for supervisor and supervisee (or expert and novice, teacher and student, mentor and mentee), their identities are constituted within the dyad. Ultimately, the personal meaning for each person involved in the supervisory process is an expression of the system. This view is radically different from one that restricts the supervisory responsibility to teaching the elements of theory and monitoring a supervisee's progress in implementing theoretical concepts. Everything and anything about the supervisor contributes to what a supervisee takes from supervision, and everything and anything about the supervisee influences the supervisor. A supervisor working intersubjectively recognizes the irreducible nature of this interplay while maintaining the focus on training for the supervisee. Like the psychotherapy relationship, the supervisory relationship is mutual but not symmetrical. The two are focused on the training needs of the supervisee and the therapeutic needs of the patient. While both supervisor and supervisee may learn and grow from the relationship, it is primarily an educational mission.

We supervise a number of students in a clinical training program where entering students have a limited choice of supervisors. These beginning therapists also arrive inclined to a range of theoretical preferences as the curriculum offers clinical specialties including family systems, cognitive-behavioral, child and adolescent, radical behavioral, and psychodynamic. Frequently, a faculty member with a psychoanalytic orientation must supervise a student disposed toward a very different orientation.

> In one such instance, Greg, changing careers in midlife from a technology-oriented field, entered supervision as a requirement of his first year curriculum. The supervisor's emphasis on attuning to the subjectivity of the patient and "following" the patient dismayed him. Greg, who valued his previous training in science, technology, and positivism, yearned to reason with his patient and to dispute the irrationality of her

thinking. Greg's view of the world and of himself in the world was framed by objectivity and reason. He found most troubling his supervisor's conviction that what really happened in his patient's daily life was not objectively knowable or verifiable, that all that Greg and his supervisor could know were the subjective meanings, beliefs, and feelings the patient formed as a result of her experiences. Greg had difficulty understanding the supervisor's persistent focus on the patient's subjective experience and the personal meanings she made of it. In particular, Greg, who was somewhat literal minded, was perplexed by the notion that the patient could be assimilating him into her organization of experience. It was hard for him to appreciate that the powerful themes of her prior relationships could be contributing to her experience of him.

The patient complained bitterly that her husband stayed out late without offering a reason, but she feared pressing him for explanations. Greg wished to strategize with his patient about how to talk with her husband; he described the patient as codependent and enmeshed; he reasoned that the logical course was to address the husband directly about his behavior, overriding the patient's "unreasonable" fears. Greg spoke up in supervision about what he felt the right course was and about his frustrations with the supervision. Simultaneously, the supervisor felt devalued and pressured to change the supervisee's perspective. Casting about for some way to overcome the impasse, the supervisor eventually was able to attune to the subjective experience of the supervisee—Greg's feeling that his therapeutic and ethical responsibility to this patient was to confront her passivity. The supervisee was moved by the supervisor's appreciation of his dilemma and her recognition of an organizing principle of his professional identity. Although the supervisee remained committed to a nonpsychoanalytic orientation to treatment, the supervisory pair used this parallel moment in supervision to illuminate the soothing effect of attuned recognition of one's subjective experience.

As we have said before, one's theory is an aspect of one's subjectivity and, therefore, contributes to the intersubjective fields of supervision and treatment. One of the strengths of intersubjectivity theory is the extent to which it can be turned on itself, furthering the unfolding and illuminating of the personal meanings constructed by patient, therapist, and supervisor.

As the work with Greg illustrated, one of the most important aspects of practicing intersubjectively that we hope to communicate in supervision is an understanding and appreciation of "process." Time pressures or goal-directedness do not promote unfolding and illuminating. Making sense together, as opposed to fixing or problem solving, occurs over time. Some treatments cover extensive time frames, in part because we are not trying to uncover some objective truth about our patient but because we are collaborating in the unfolding, illumination, and reorganization of subjective meanings. These meanings are often out of awareness or disguised and were invariably formed within unique relational fields. Coming to understand these meanings requires patience and a willingness to follow where the patient leads. Such a process implies that transformation occurs not in an "aha" moment of insight, but through a gradual restructuring of one's organization of experience.

Another important responsibility of a supervisor is that of affect regulation. No one learns effectively in a state of disruptive anxiety. For many people, revealing their work to a supervisor induces a sense of vulnerability, dread, or shame (Fosshage 1997b). To facilitate professional growth for the supervisee and to support effective treatment for the patient, a supervisor needs to attune to the affective state of the supervisee. Of course, once the supervisor notices that a supervisee is having some emotional response to the work or to the supervision, the question is raised as to how best to respond. Supervision differs from the treatment context in a number of ways. For instance, a supervisor may be required to evaluate the supervisee in some formal way or, as illustrated above, the two may have agreed to work together without much choice in the matter. However, strong emotional reactions have great bearing on the work of psychotherapy and on the possibility for change in each of us. So the challenge becomes how to make use of the emotional experience of a supervisee in ways that maintain the supervisory frame and, simultaneously, help a supervisee mature as a therapist.

> One supervisee, a woman in her mid-twenties, consistently expressed feelings of inadequacy and bewilderment in the treatment of her patient, a woman close to her own age. The case was the supervisee's first adult in individual treatment, and the patient frequently asked for advice with significant life-changing issues. She did so with little obvious emotion. For example, early in treatment, the patient separated from her husband and considered divorcing him. She wanted direction from the student therapist on whether she should, in fact, divorce her husband. The therapist, in turn, felt considerable responsibility for the outcome of the patient's dilemma and expressed in supervision the urgent need to know what to do with and for the patient. As this complex system of patient, supervisee, and supervisor organized and evolved over three years, attention to affect—noticing it, naming it, and regulating it—became the salient transforming experience for both supervisee and patient. As the supervisor recognized the disruptive effect on the supervisee of her belief that in order to be a good therapist she must solve the problem for the patient (an organizing principle of her developing professional identity), the supervisor acknowledged the supervisee's anxiety regarding wanting to help. Recognizing and articulating that the supervisee talked rapidly and said a great deal in session drew the supervisee's attention to her anxiety and allowed her to understand the

> pressure she felt to perform well for the supervisor by "helping" the patient. Supervisor and supervisee created an ongoing dialogue about her anxiety, and, in doing so, the supervisee had the experience that naming and wondering about her own fears decreased the pressure to perform and to "do something" for the patient (see Schlesinger 1995 for a discussion of similar ideas). The supervisory pair also talked periodically about the paradoxical phenomena that one provides great help to a patient by listening and containing rather than advising and directing. In this parallel process (Doehrman 1976) both the supervisee and the patient grew calmer, listened more, and matured during the three-year treatment.

Specific attitudes derive from the recognition that all subjective experience is contextual. The context of the supervisor differs from that of the supervisee, which differs from that of the patient. Appreciating the possible different meanings for each requires that the supervisor embrace her own formulation of the patient's problems tentatively (see Orange 1995 for a discussion on falliblism and perspectivalism in treatment). The supervisor finds herself in a paradoxical position. On the one hand, she knows that her formulations, however well informed, represent a construction limited by her own history, personal organizing principles, and her theoretical preference. Therefore, she may miss important information about the patient, overvalue other aspects, or fall into any number of other misunderstandings of the patient based on the unique interplay of the supervisor's once-removed experience of the patient's subjectivity, her own subjectivity, and that of the supervisee.

On the other hand, the supervisor has knowledge and understanding to impart to a supervisee. In this sense, the supervisory dyad, like the psychotherapy relationship, is characterized by mutuality but asymmetry. The asymmetry of the supervisory context concerns the disproportionate power, knowledge, and expertise of the participants. The supervisor, by virtue of the extent of her clinical training and her breadth of experience, is better informed about the psychotherapy process. Psychotherapy as a practice can be taught and the supervisory relationship is one of the major classrooms. While there is no one right way to do psychotherapy, some ways are better than others in promoting a successful psychotherapy process. It is "irresponsible relativism" (Mitchell 1997, p. 211) that treats every psychoanalytic interpretation or explanatory construct as if it were as good as any other. In part, the expertise and experience of the supervisor guide a supervisee toward that which is closest to the heart of the patient's experience. "Psychoanalytic theories vary greatly in their capacity to enhance empathic access to the patient's subjective world and . . . psychoanalytic theories often address fundamentally different realms of experience" (Stolorow et al. 1994b, p. 45).

What is thought to be meaningful in a patient's experience is determined in large measure by one's theory. Intersubjectivity theory emphasizes articulations that reflect the subjective state of the patient and place them in a context. Simply put, such a process is hermeneutic. That is, the meaning a patient makes of his subjective world emerges in terms of the context in which it formed. Simultaneously, the subjective meaning created by an individual influences the context. Supervisors guiding student therapists toward an intersubjective understanding of their patients help them form articulations that can be "evaluated in light of distinctively hermeneutic criteria. These criteria include the logical coherence of the argument, the comprehensiveness of the explanation, the consistency of the interpretations with accepted psychological knowledge and the aesthetic beauty . . . in disclosing previously hidden patterns of order in the material being investigated" (Atwood and Stolorow 1984, pp. 5–6).

Through imparting knowledge about contextualism, recognizing affective expression, and helping to identify and articulate organizations of experience, the supervisor is positioned as an authority figure in relation to the therapist/supervisee. Inevitably, the personal meaning for the supervisee of such a relationship to an authority figure finds expression in her subjective experience of supervision. Similarly, the supervisor's sense of being an authority contributes to her subjectivity, and, of course, their mutually influencing subjectivities (of the personal meaning of "authority") are part of the matrix of this particular supervisory system.

> The issues of the supervisor's authority and expertise arose in supervision with a student therapist in her late twenties who was treating a single man about 40 years old. The patient's sense of how to be in relationships was organized around the principle that sustained connection and emotional safety lay in tending to the needs of the other person. As supervisor and supervisee recognized the variety of ways this organization of experience revealed itself in the treatment, they noticed a way he routinely began the session. After an initial greeting in the waiting area, the two walked down a hallway into the office, often exchanging a few pleasantries en route. Once in the office, before sitting down, the patient invariably asked the therapist how she was. The supervisor saw this as a manifestation of the patient's organizing principle, that he must take care of others before he could legitimately express himself. She suggested that the supervisee identify and explore with the patient the subjective meanings of this interaction pattern. The supervisee balked. While she agreed that the interaction pattern might reveal exactly what the supervisor thought it did, she nevertheless felt uncomfortable analyzing this polite gesture. Her sense was that the recommended course of action would make the patient feel exposed and criticized, leading to increased self-consciousness and defensive posturing.

This difference of opinion highlights one of those choice points that often confronts supervisors. Should the supervisor wield her authority by insisting that the supervisee try her proposed intervention, or should the supervisor defer to the subjective experience of the supervisee? It is likely that both positions had merit. The organizing principle behind the patient's social pleasantries was evident to both supervisor and supervisee, but the supervisee, ultimately the one in personal relation to the patient, had an understanding that the patient would experience the intervention as hurtful and demeaning. The supervisee felt that, at this point in the therapy relationship, to identify the organizing principle in the transference would be injurious and counterproductive.

Of course, the possibility existed that the supervisee's reticence had to do with some unconscious organizing principle of her own, like the belief that confrontation is unladylike, rather than with some accurately sensed vulnerability in the patient. In this situation, the supervisor chose to defer to the supervisee's assessment of what the patient could comfortably tolerate and took the opportunity to affirm the supervisee's developing sense of confidence in her own judgment. In this interaction, through encouraging the therapist/supervisee to articulate her subjective experience, validating it, and affirming the therapist's developing clinical intuition, the supervisor was making herself available as a selfobject to the developing therapist and serving as a role model for promoting a therapeutic relationship.

Another aspect of the potential impact of the supervisor's authority on the context of supervision has to do with multiple roles of the supervisor. In graduate and postgraduate training programs, supervisors are routinely expected to evaluate the progress of their supervisees. While the dual functions of teaching and evaluating work well in the classroom, in psychotherapy supervision such mixing of roles and functions creates the possibility that a supervisee may not reveal her concerns or difficulties for fear of receiving a negative evaluation that might adversely affect her academic progress. These factors influence the experience of the supervisee in idiosyncratic ways, unique to the particular intersubjective field. Just as our perspective calls for the therapist to be alert to her influence on the intersubjective field she creates with the patient, supervisors need also to be cognizant of the considerable impact they make on the psychotherapy field.

Intersubjectivity theory asserts that one's subjective experience is formed in a context of interfacing subjectivities. One implication of this fundamental idea is that a supervisor's characteristic response to mistakes or failures contributes significantly to how the supervisee comes to organize her experience. If the supervisor misjudges the supervisee's capacity for constructive feedback, the supervisee's willingness to reveal her work and ultimately to grow as a therapist will be thwarted. Similarly, if the supervisee fears spillover from supervision to other areas of evaluation, it is not likely that in-depth learning will take place. Clearly, it is the supervisor's responsibility to be sensitive to how the supervisee experiences the supervision, particularly to her willingness to show her work.

> This point was brought home when, as a beginning supervisor, one of us was starting work with a beginning therapist. The therapist agreed to tape-record his first session. He came to his supervision session, tape in hand, but when he went to play it, it turned out that nothing had been recorded. The supervisor offered the suggestion that perhaps the supervisee's ambivalence about exposure played some part in the absence of sound on the tape. The supervisee assimilated this interpretation and returned for the next supervision session confident that the therapy session had been successfully recorded. He put the tape in the player but pressed the record button instead of the play button and began to record over the therapy session.

The supervisor was probably correct in interpreting the supervisee's fear of exposure; however, the supervisor was oblivious to the part he played in contributing to the supervisee's fear and he certainly misjudged the level of the supervisee/therapist's anxiety. The interpretation was unhelpful because, despite the truth it conveyed about the supervisee's fear of exposure, it did not address the person of the supervisor who participated in promoting or coconstructing this anxiety-producing context. It would have been preferable, we believe, for the supervisor, once he recognized the supervisee's fear and shame, to acknowledge the pressure placed on the supervisee by the interpretation. Without such an acknowledgment, a supervisee (or patient) is left feeling the double humiliation of, first the exposure of the interpretation, and second, the isolation of being considered the only one to blame. Such interactions reveal a one-person view of disruptive affects, the antithesis of what intersubjectivity theory asserts.

In our previous discussion, we have illuminated aspects of the influence of the supervisor on the supervisee; we now turn to that of the patient on the supervisee. Of course, the influences are not unilateral. They flow in both directions. Expanding the frame of intersubjectivity to include supervision compounds the complexity of understanding the experience of a patient. How the patient influences the therapist/supervisee is inevitably connected with the supervisor's response to the supervisee. Intersubjective fields are "indissoluble psychological systems" (Atwood and Stolorow 1984, p. 64) formed by patient and therapist (and now, supervisor), and adequate treatment or supervision requires awareness of their unremitting mutual influence. Therefore, learning to practice intersubjectively requires appreciating the impact of the patient on the therapist/supervisee and upon the supervisor.

Previous writing on how to manage countertransference in supervision dealt primarily with identifying the point at which exploration of the supervisee's reactions should move from the supervisory context to that of psychotherapy. That is, how deeply should the supervisee's countertransference be explored in supervision? There has also been some discussion in the literature as to whether the supervisor should address the therapist's countertransference therapeutically or educationally and whether the approach should vary with the experience level of the therapist (Cook and Buirski 1990). The problem with these questions is that they focus on the isolated mind of patient or therapist and neglect the intersubjective field. From the intersubjective perspective, these are not answerable questions and posing them this way obscures the complex interplay of forces at work in shaping the intersubjective field. Sense cannot be made of the patient, the therapist, or the supervisor as isolated minds. The answer to these and so many other questions about supervision or treatment is, "It depends." An answer unique to each intersubjective field will emerge as a property of that context.

Historically, much of the literature on supervision has been concerned with understanding and managing the impact of the therapist's countertransference on the treatment. Freud (1912) identified two different sources of countertransference: first, as a reaction in the therapist to the patient's transference; and second, as an outgrowth of the therapist's own unconscious conflicts. In both cases, countertransference was viewed as a unique property of the therapist that served as a contaminant of the treatment process.

Heimann (1950) introduced the idea that "the analyst's countertransference is an instrument of research into the patient's unconscious" (p. 81). This contributed to a new line of thought that viewed countertransference as a source of illumination about the patient and the therapeutic process. While this view treats countertransference not as a contaminant but as an illuminant, making available a new source of data about the patient and the treatment process, it is still, nevertheless, a perspective grounded in Cartesian isolated mind notions. The therapist's experience of the patient is understood as instigated by the patient and tells us only about the patient.

The notion of countertransference as a contaminant suggests pathological distortion on the part of the therapist in hearing and understanding the patient's material. The idea of "pathological distortion" implies that some fixed, objectively knowable version of the patient and his history exists and that the therapist's personal past, conflicts, and character interfere with her ability to understand the patient or to work effectively with him. Because intersubjectivity theory considers the therapist's response to a patient as an emergent property of the dyadic system (that is, forming from elements of both subjectivities), countertransference cannot be isolated and "treated" apart from the intersubjective field. The same may be said of transference, the "real" relationship, or the working alliance. (See Orange 1995 for a discussion of *cotransference,* the term she uses in preference to transference-countertransference.)

From the intersubjective perspective, which views the supervisor as an indissoluble component of the treatment field, countertransference cannot be divorced from the complicated three-person context. While other perspectives have treated the therapist's countertransference, whether as contaminant or illuminant of the therapeutic process, as a separate and distinct characteristic of the therapist, we have become convinced that the therapist's subjective experience of the patient is a construct of the field and not of any one player. The implication of this perspective is that countertransference is neither contaminant nor illuminant, but another piece of experience that emerges from the intersubjective field, and which cannot be understood except through an examination of the various elements of the context.

The role of the therapist's experience of the patient is recognized in intersubjectivity theory as profoundly important to the course of treatment. Therefore, a supervisor, hoping to expand the supervisee's sensitivity to the intersubjective field, must address the supervisee's experience of, and contribution to, the field

(Fosshage 1995a). Nevertheless, as important as it is to draw attention to the therapist/supervisee's part in how a treatment develops, doing so veers supervision in the direction of a more personal, experiential process. The supervisory setting, itself an indissoluble intersubjective field, must facilitate learning by being "pro-supervisee" (Teicholz 1999b). At a minimum, this requires a non-judgmental atmosphere where the supervisor is sensitive to the affective experience of the supervisee. A brief recall of supervisions in which such an accepting atmosphere was crucial to the subsequent course of treatment includes cases where the supervisee was frightened of the patient, attracted to the patient, awed by the patient, overwhelmed by the patient's traumatic history, or grief-stricken by losses similar to those of the patient. In line with the theory of intersubjectivity, such influences are always at work. Part of teaching the theory demands making room in supervision for what we know transpires in all meeting of subjectivities.

For supervisees, the supervisory setting often becomes a model of the treatment setting. This is true, we believe, of supervision from most theoretical perspectives. Given that theories of technique are grounded in theories of development and psychopathology, what one notices in patients one also tends to see in supervisees, friends, family, and colleagues. One example where our theoretical understanding influences how we respond to others is the case of anger. If anger is thought to be an expression of drive aggression, then we might respond to situations where another person expresses anger with us as evidence of his (one person) excessive, poorly defended innate tendencies. However, if anger is believed to be a response to narcissistic injury (as in intersubjectivity theory), then the recipient of the anger is implicated in precipitating anger. What may differentiate supervision done from the perspective of intersubjectivity theory from that of other theories is that the theory itself may usefully be directed at the supervisory process as a way of illuminating key concepts for the supervisee. Specifically, the assumption that meaning in human subjectivity is context-dependent applies equally to the context of supervision as to treatment. So, in addition to a supervisor's attunement to the supervisee's affective experience, she should also be alert to how her own subjectivity contributes to the supervisory milieu.

Exactly what and how much is appropriate to reveal about one's subjectivity as supervisor (or therapist) brings us into an arena of intense debate in psychoanalytic theory today. Our guideline to therapists is always to give priority to the patient's subjectivity. That is, when one is tempted to disclose one's feelings or to discuss one's reaction to a patient, consider what the probable meaning and impact would be for the patient. Given the patient's vulnerabilities and the context, as fully as it has come to be understood, would such a revelation benefit the patient? Similarly, in supervision, when considering the potential impact of the supervisor's discussion of her subjective experience of the supervision with a supervisee, care must be given to the potential benefit versus possible harm to the supervisee. However, one important difference between supervision and therapy is that a supervisee has undertaken the project of learning the why and how of the practice of psychotherapy. One potentially salient modality for both understanding the experience of interacting subjectivities and learning to talk about them is through the supervisor's articulation and illumination of her subjectivity. In our experience, it is very difficult for novice therapists to begin to talk with patients about the patient–therapist relationship, the transference. When supervisors model such a discussion by talking candidly about the supervision, a supervisee experiences and understands the power of talking directly about what is going on between two people.

A common scenario experienced in supervision of young female supervisees (today, about 75 percent of all graduate clinical psychology students are women) treating men is their disbelief or skepticism about feelings of attraction for the other that may be experienced by either the therapist/supervisee or the patient or both.

> One soft-spoken and gentle supervisee in her late twenties began treating a bright, athletic man of about the same age who presented with problems in his marriage. He spent much time fantasizing about a former girlfriend and frequently asked the therapist for advice as to whether to contact this woman. The supervisee initially found working with this man very difficult. She felt pressured by him to be directive and to provide interventions that were different from the model of treatment of the supervisor. She did not like the patient and found him arrogant and demanding. The supervisor sensed that the patient was probably attracted to the therapist and the therapist to the patient. She speculated to herself that the therapist/supervisee was having difficulty integrating these feelings into her sense of herself as a therapist.
>
> The sessions were recorded on videotape and there were no obvious references or demonstrations by the patient of such feeling toward the therapist. However, the supervisor wondered aloud about attraction between the two. From viewing the videotapes, the supervisor registered an impression that therapist and patient formed an attractive "couple." At first, the therapist/supervisee was embarrassed when the supervisor suggested that part of the difficulty in aligning with this patient had to do with tension based on feelings of attraction. However, as the supervisor continued over time to notice and share her observations about these feelings in an accepting, nonjudgmental manner, they became less alien to the supervisee. The supervisor's disclosure of her fantasy of this "couple" and many subsequent observations about the push and pull between this therapeutic pair gradually allowed the supervisee to tolerate and integrate feelings that she felt were not acceptable in the professional relationship.

> At no time in the brief treatment did therapist and patient explicitly talk about mutual feelings of attraction, but accepting and validating them in the supervisory setting enabled the supervisee to align with the patient rather than remain distant from him. The supervisee's professional organizing principle, that therapists do not feel attracted to their patients, was modified through dialogue with her supervisor. Specifically, her feelings of attraction and discomfort were put into words by the supervisor, who disclosed her subjective sense that the therapeutic dyad made an "attractive couple." Not only did the supervisee find her subjectivity validated, she experienced (and learned) that putting words to feelings is a powerful modality, one that can influence, even transform, the intersubjective field.

It is impossible to overestimate the significance of a contextualist perspective to either training or treatment. In fact, when one begins to appreciate the intricacy and complexity of interfacing subjectivities, it can feel overwhelming. The implications of this view represent a fundamental shift from an objectivist theory of human development and psychopathology to an appreciation of the codetermination of symptoms, dysfunction, and health. If the legitimate area of inquiry in psychoanalytic treatment is that which is subjectively experienced, and if subjectivity is always contextually constituted, then making sense of the context is a fundamental supervisory endeavor. It seems likely that any given relational context can never be fully understood in all its complexity. Trying to grasp it in its entirety would be like trying to stop a moving stream with one's hands. We need to communicate to supervisees that what patients experience and bring to therapy was formed in a context and will be understood and reorganized in a context. Expanding and exploring subjectivity means looking at the context.

To illustrate the fundamental importance of context, we offer some observations of the influence of context in supervision. First, as we talked about earlier in the chapter, whether a supervisor is responsible for evaluating a supervisee can be a significant factor in how the intersubjective field is constructed. This factor can inhibit supervisees from questioning or challenging a supervisor. A second way that context becomes important is the influence of professional considerations on the treatment. Since the standards of informed consent and disclosure require that patients be informed that their treatment is being supervised and of the identity of the supervisor, the supervisor must necessarily become a part of the context.

In Chapter 7 we described a treatment where the patient was aware that sessions were videotaped. Subsequently, the patient occasionally spoke directly to the supervisor by facing and addressing the camera. The patient's awareness that a supervisor would be reviewing the sessions became incorporated into her experience of the treatment. In that case, the supervisor as authority and chaperone over the therapist/supervisee was thought to be the reason the therapist would not declare his love for the patient. Ultimately, this construction allowed the patient to express deep longings for the kind of sensitivity embodied by the therapist without demanding reciprocal vows or acts of love. The significance here is not that, in order for the patient to reorganize and expand her organization of experience, she should be aware that the therapist is in supervision. Rather, the point is that the patient, aware that the therapist showed the videotapes to his supervisor, used that aspect of the context to maintain an antidote to powerful negative feelings that she was unworthy of love. Over time, the patient found that the safety of the treatment context and her therapist's genuine attuned responsiveness allowed her to transform her organization of experience from one who is not worthy of love to one who is available both to give and receive love.

Ultimately, any aspect of a context may be significant for any one of the participants. Again, referring to the case described in Chapter 7, there was a period of several months when the patient's belief that her therapist loved her deeply and was only constrained from declaring his love by the inhibiting presence of the supervisor rose to nearly delusional levels. The patient's construed meaning was disruptive to both supervisor and supervisee. The supervisee worried that he should be correcting the patient's unrealistic idea that he loved her. He feared that staying focused on her subjectivity (her core organizing principle that she was unlovable and the corollary that only the love of this therapist could make her whole) was not helping her. He wondered whether she needed to be faced with what was objective and real in his experience. The supervisee feared that his interventions were harmful rather than growth promoting for this patient. For his part, the supervisor had concerns that the patient might decompensate. At times, they lost heart that the patient could benefit from this form of treatment. Did she need to be medicated or possibly even hospitalized? These shared concerns of both supervisee and supervisor and the affects associated with them were brought into the supervisory relationship and became part of the dialogue of supervision. The collaborative and mutually respectful relationship that had evolved within the supervisory dyad provided a context in which their affects became regulated, their subjective concerns examined, and sense made of their experiences. They reviewed the patient's progress and her overall improved functioning in her social and work life, and decided to trust and persist in the method.

The context of supervision often provides a type of vicarious treatment for both supervisees and supervisors. Since most therapists have themselves been patients, they naturally have much in common with their own patients. While, theoretically, there are an infinite number of ways in which subjective experience can be organized, in practice, people, by virtue of sharing common biology and cultures, are more nearly similar than they are different. Thus, ways that patients have come to organize their subjective experience bear some resemblance to how therapists have organized theirs. The articulation of patients' subjective experience will inevitably touch on analogous experiences for therapists.

Small-group supervision is an especially powerful modality for the articulation of shared experience. As they listen together to case presentations where the patient's subjectivity is dealt with sensitively and organizations of experience and affect states are articulated, students and teachers alike often make connections to their own life experiences. As they begin to attend to the patient's organizations of experience, to the patient's affective experience, to the context in which symptoms developed and are maintained, and to the patient's striving for health, supervisor and supervisees may resonate with what they hear. They recognize and reorganize their own subjectivities. For supervisees, in particular, when they listen to others' clinical material without the anxiety of presenting their own cases, they often hear acceptance and validation for their own foibles and shortcomings. A similar process is at work when we articulate the affective experience of another. Since we all share similar affect states, even if they are generated by different experiences, when the supervisor puts words to the patient's affective experience, she is also articulating something of the therapist's affective world and her own. One frequent outcome of this vicarious way of beginning to understand and reflect on one's experience has been for supervisees to enter psychotherapy in order to deepen the process for themselves.

Self-reflection may develop from a broad range of circumstances other than supervision. For instance, reading professional literature or novels, consulting informally with peers, or simply listening to our patients can heighten our awareness of our own organizations of experience and contribute to a transformative process. What is significant is the context. That is, any new understanding and reorganization of subjective experience for an individual occurs within a process uniquely situated in time and history, encompassing past, present, and future (Orange et al. 1997). What we draw attention to here and what an intersubjective sensibility requires is awareness of the contextual nature of experience. Contextual understanding is fundamentally nondogmatic. It is, at base, open to exploration of personal meaning in any and all details as relevant to individual subjectivity.

One example of the exquisitely contextually constituted nature of our subjectivity can be heard in the following vignette.

> A supervisee reported on a female patient in her late thirties who had great difficulty connecting with her affective experience. In one typical session she reported on her weekend with little conviction that her activities had much to do with her goals of creating an intimate relationship and having a less frenetic life. She recalled that she was listening to music as she worked late into the night, doing filing and cleaning her office. Both therapist and patient were on the verge of being lulled into a too-familiar moment where any meaning or emotion seemed difficult to grasp. The therapist wondered aloud what music the patient was listening to. With no hesitation, the patient repeated the words to a song about a much-loved child with a birth defect. As the song-story unfolded, the therapist formed an image of the patient's organization of experience, which she articulated for the patient, of a bright, energetic child who wanted nothing more than to please her parents. No efforts on her part produced the kind of acceptance and love that were expressed in the song of the child with the birth defect. The lyrics spoke to the patient's unmet needs for caring, attuned responsiveness and her view of herself as fundamentally flawed. As they came to recognize the meaning of this song, the patient's tears flowed. For the first time, she understood in an emotional way the effect of her parents' efficient, distant, and conditional caregiving. In this case, the therapist's attention to the context—listening to music—proved to be a key to why the patient brought the event to treatment.

SUMMARY

This chapter offered a view of supervision as seen through the lens of intersubjectivity theory. Ultimately, the supervisory relationship is a field consisting of the mutually influencing subjectivities of supervisor, supervisee, and patient. Certain aspects of the field, such as authority, evaluation, and professional identity, have been explored in light of their impact on the system. In our work, we have found it illuminating for both supervisee and supervisor to articulate the influence of these factors of the supervisory context.

9

The Treatment of a Patient from the Intersubjective Perspective

(written in collaboration with H. C. Brunette)

Translating theory into practice is an imprecise task. Anyone who has read about the physics of a golf swing and subsequently tried to hit a golf ball appreciates the difficulty. Not surprisingly, for teachers and supervisors of psychotherapists, our attempts to bridge the gap between ideas and clinical work is subject to the same frustrations. Compounding the problems of imprecision in finding the right words and identifying the salient processes is the inevitable limiting factor we address in this book—our own subjectivities.

In an attempt to capture some of the complexity of translating theory into practice in the context of supervision, we enlisted a doctoral-level graduate student to participate with us. Together, student therapist and authors undertook the treatment and supervision of a new case. Some of the context variables, then, included the four subjectivities of the two supervisors, the student therapist and the patient, as well as the patient's awareness that sessions were being videotaped for professional use (we have taken steps to preserve the patient's anonymity, while attempting to minimize the distortions of the content due to considerations of discretion). In addition, we attempted to observe the unfolding processes in both treatment and supervision and to articulate the intersubjective principles that seemed to emerge. Nevertheless, many aspects of the field remain unarticulated because they reside outside the awareness of the participants. However, the effort allowed us to identify, understand, and integrate many ideas and practices that for us had not previously been illuminated.

In this chapter we present an extensive case example designed to illustrate attunement to the patient's subjective experience and articulation of his organizing principles. We follow the unfolding, illumination, and transformations that occurred during the first nine months of therapy. In addition, we observe the process of supervision itself from the perspective of intersubjectivity theory. The case is addressed from the point of view of a therapist at an early stage of training in order to more clearly identify and clarify case conceptualization, interventions offered during treatment, the intersubjective field created among all four participants, and how these factors might have influenced the treatment.

CLINICAL MATERIAL

Brad is a 40-year-old Caucasian male musician and songwriter seen twice a week at a clinic associated with a training program. He has a fraternal twin brother, and unlike his taller, handsome brother, Brad is of average height, slightly built, and carefully groomed. Initially, he seemed self-conscious about his appearance, often touching his hair or adjusting his shirt collar. Early in treatment he dressed provocatively, wearing tight-fitting jeans and a shirt unbuttoned a few buttons to reveal his chest. He wore fairly strong cologne and continued to do so until recently. Brad appeared anxious and uncomfortable at the start of most sessions, and giggled or shifted in his seat when painful or embarrassing material was discussed. His affect has fluctuated since the beginning of treatment; at times he is tearful, at other times very angry.

Brad came to therapy to address issues related to his difficulty in appropriately managing his anger, his feelings of depression related to the recent loss of an exclusive relationship, and feelings of low self-worth. He reported that he had experienced feelings of depression for "as long as I could remember," and that these feelings had been exacerbated with the apparent end of this yearlong relationship three months earlier.

Initially, Brad sought therapy at the suggestion of his girlfriend, in order to "work on myself." Brad hoped that by resolving his anger he might repair the lost relationship with his girlfriend. He described his problems in relationships with others as being directly related to his "blow-ups," or angry outbursts during which he felt entirely incapable of controlling himself and his behavior. He characterized these experiences as having to do with feelings of jealousy or perceived betrayal by those he cared about, and reported that they often include yelling, crying, begging, and, at times, name-calling and verbal attacks.

Brad reported a childhood history of severe physical and emotional abuse at the hands of his father. He had no recollection of receiving encouragement from either parent. Instead, he felt that his parents expected him to be perfect and to live up to the impossible standards they set for him. He believed that he should be just like his twin brother, an athlete and leader who could do no wrong in the eyes of his parents. Brad was not supported in the pursuit of his own, more aesthetic, interests. On the contrary, Brad was demeaned and ridiculed for attempts at expressing his musical talents.

Brad currently lives at home with his divorced mother and depends on her entirely for financial support. His father has no contact with the family. Brad has not had success in his professional life and, while he and others view him as talented, he has been unable to make a living as a musician and songwriter. Occasionally Brad begins composing a new song, but until recently he has not completed these projects.

From the beginning of treatment, working with Brad presented challenges to his therapist's sense of competence. After only the first session, Brad called the clinic in crisis, experiencing intense suicidal and homicidal ideation related to finding his former girlfriend with another man. Brad came in with his mother for an emergency session, and requested that she sit in on the meeting. He was disheveled, agitated, and extremely distraught, expressing intense feelings of rage and anger, as well as feelings of betrayal and abandonment.

Patient: (Speaking as if to his girlfriend, yelling, crying and banging his fist on the arm of the chair) It's your responsibility to let him know you're in a relationship and in love. . . . She's telling me she loves me all the time, ten times a day, and I'm telling her that too . . . and then she's in bed with somebody else . . . and then the neighbor, the neighbor was after her too. . . . What the hell? What the hell is going on behind my back?

Therapist: It's not showing respect for your relationship with her.

[Here the therapist attempts to articulate Brad's subjective state. It might have been more accurate for the therapist to say, "You felt betrayed."]

Patient: It's not respecting me; it's not respecting how much I cared for her, and I loved her so much.

Therapist: You've said you loved her more than you loved anyone.

Patient: And it's this over and over and I'm suspicious of everything she does at this point.

Therapist: It's hard to trust her.

[Again, the therapist puts words to her understanding of the patient's subjective experience.]

Patient: (Crying again) Yeah, and it's like, why'd you do that? Why'd you break my trust? How could you do that to me and us? Why are you making it so hard on me?

This session brought up many feelings for the student therapist, particularly anxiety about managing a potentially suicidal patient and uncertainty about her ability to navigate the logistics of ensuring his safety. She expressed these fears in supervision, explicitly requesting direction from the supervisors in an effort to contain her emotions. Without providing specific direction, the supervisors emphasized instead the positive way she had stayed very close to the patient's experience, providing attuned responsiveness to him. They noted that Brad appeared to be focused on his feelings of rejection and devastation. He seemed calmed by the presence of someone who would listen to him and validate how painful this experience was for him. At this early point in treatment, patient and student therapist had parallel experiences of affective disruption, followed by affirming and validating responses by significant others. The supervisee was subsequently able to reflect on the powerful effect her listening stance had on the patient. Additionally, supervisors and supervisee recognized the patient's significant needs for validation of his subjective experience and articulation of his underlying organizing principles of inferiority and unworthiness.

Dealing with the issue of Brad's anger was a dominant theme in both treatment and supervision for the first half year. One organizing principle related to his anger became apparent early. Brad had considerable difficulty integrating what he considered the good and bad aspects of himself and others. He characterized his anger as something outside of himself, and vacillated in these early sessions between blaming either himself or his girlfriend for the end of the relationship. He seemed incapable of understanding that both of them could have played a role in the conflicts that arose, and spoke about his need to eradicate all anger from his life.

Patient: The anger I've had, I've had it all my life in certain things, and I've shed most of it. . . . It's kept me from writing music, friendships and relationships, it causes so much damage.
Therapist: You feel it keeps you from a lot of things.
Patient: Um-hmm, it's time to let it go, to clear myself of all of the anger I have in my heart, to find peace.
Therapist: So if you could, you'd like to let it all go, not to have it as a part of your life.
Patient: Um-hmm, it's not worth it, it's not worth it; it causes too much destruction, takes too much out of me.

At a later session, he speaks to this theme again.

Patient: You know, to find peace you have to forgive, not to have any anger towards anybody . . .
Therapist: So you feel like being angry with her wouldn't allow you to be forgiving of her.
Patient: Oh, being angry would destroy me; it's not worth it. I don't feel any anger towards her. Whatever she does, she does it for a reason.
Therapist: Being angry doesn't allow you to be who you want to be. You feel like anger's not a part of that.
Patient: Definitely no, not in a healthy life it's not.

Dealing with the patient's anger presented the opportunity in supervision to discuss its self-protective function. Initially, the student therapist held a view of anger similar to that of the patient—that his anger had destroyed his relationship. Therefore, she felt the need to make Brad aware that anger is an emotion experienced by all people to some degree in hopes that he would be able to manage his anger more appropriately. She also expressed the wish to support him in his experience of the overwhelming and frightening nature of his anger.

The topic of anger dominated supervision during this period in treatment. The supervisee came to appreciate that part of what would change Brad's anger was her understanding of the despair and abandonment he anticipated as his girlfriend withdrew from their relationship. As she understood the connection between Brad's anger and his fears, she could articulate how Brad's anger functioned to both protect himself against being hurt, and, more importantly, to distance himself from the intense emotions associated with his treatment as a child. This understanding enabled her to respond to Brad in a way that was different than others had, to be attuned instead of afraid during his angry outbursts. Brad appeared visibly calmer and would often move from being extremely angry and loud, to crying, and seemed much more vulnerable.

Patient: (Shouting and pounding his fist on the arm of the chair, as if speaking to his ex-girlfriend) Sara! Do you know what a relationship is? Maybe your past relationships sucked; maybe the guys weren't decent and civil to you. . . . Maybe she's willing to say, "That's the way relationships are," but that's NOT what they're about. They're about trust and love and being together and caring and letting the other person into our inner circles, NOT keeping them on the outside. Why are you dating guys like that? They have nothing to offer.

[Here Brad was articulating the kind of acceptance he longed for as a child.]

Therapist: I'm hearing that a lot of the hurt and the anger is really about feeling that you had so much that you wanted to share with her, and the hurt that you're not able to do that.

[The supervisee tries to grasp the patient's experience and articulates the hurt and loss behind his anger.]

Patient: (Calmer) Yeah, and if she would have just seen that. It's so frustrating to me . . . leaving me on the outside.

[The effect of the supervisee's attuned response is that the patient becomes able to modulate his anger.]

Therapist: You really wanted to have that intimacy with her.

[The supervisee addresses Brad's subjectivity, what he consciously hoped to have with his girlfriend.]

Patient: (Visibly calmer) Yeah, I want to know all about her dreams, what she's scared of, all of the wonderful things a boyfriend's supposed to get.

[Again, Brad appears to be expressing the longing for intimacy he needed but did not experience as a child.]

As Brad found that his therapist would not respond in a frightened, rejecting, or judgmental manner to his anger, he seemed relieved. Gradually, Brad began to verbalize the feelings of hurt and betrayal that precipitated his angry reactions.

Patient: That night I got into trouble [when he caught his girlfriend with another man] I was feeling some rage.

[Brad appears to have increased his ability to tolerate his own anger.]

Therapist: It sounds like you were very hurt.

[The therapist articulates the feeling of hurt that instigated his anger.]

Patient: I walked by her window and I saw her cuddling him—it hurt seeing her be so affectionate with him, it just hurt so bad.

[Feeling understood, Brad reconnects with what was hurtful to him.]

As Brad began exploring the hurt behind his anger, he started to resonate with the therapist's (and supervisors') idea that his anger was a reactive and protective response to feeling injured. As the process deepened, the therapist was experienced as more trustworthy and the patient as more vulnerable. In supervision, the student therapist expressed concern that by being attuned to the hurt and injury rather than dealing directly with anger management she would somehow reinforce Brad's anger and ignite further outbursts. She feared that he would feel justified in lashing out and would give his anger free reign. At this early point in the work, the supervisors stressed teaching basic conceptualizations of their theory, such as their understanding of anger as reactive. However, subjective affects and their associated beliefs clearly come into play. In particular, the supervisors addressed the student's fear of unleashing anger and her conviction that she had a responsibility to tame her patient's rage. As the supervisors recognized and articulated the fears of the supervisee and shared their alternative perspective, an atmosphere of collaboration and mutually making sense developed. Gradually, the patient's shame and vulnerability touched the supervisee and she began to feel more attuned to Brad and to better understand his psychodynamics. She came to trust that, as Brad felt stronger and more cohesive, he would improve his capacity to modulate and tolerate his intense affective experiences.

Soon other important organizing principles came to light. These were related to Brad's sense that he was fundamentally a bad person and that he had no value in the eyes of others. Brad discounted any subjective experience of his environment or interactions with others that were incompatible with this way of organizing his experience. He believed that his anger and resulting outbursts were the sole cause of the end of the relationship. This precluded the possibility that his own experiences of hurt and betrayal within the relationship mattered. As the therapist addressed these issues in supervision, she began to understand more clearly the importance of her role as a reparative selfobject, that her validation and understanding of Brad's subjective experience would help to offset his sense that no one had ever understood or valued his experience.

This organizing principle (of himself as not understood or valued) began to emerge much more frequently as Brad became more invested in treatment. He tentatively accepted that his relationship with his ex-girlfriend was unlikely to go back to the way it had been. Brad talked about coming to therapy for himself, to "work on myself" so that he might better understand the ways in which his past experiences had contributed to his current difficulties in functioning.

Brad's outward behavior seemed to change at this time as well. He began to dress more casually and in a less seductive manner than before. This subtle change in Brad's presentation contributed greatly to a shift in the therapist's feelings about him. Whereas she had previously felt somewhat distant from him and wary of his seductive posturing, she now felt much more warmly toward him as he appeared more vulnerable and open. The improving connection between them seemed to create a more genuine atmosphere in which they could explore the painful aspects of his experience.

As stated previously, Brad's early childhood experiences contributed strongly to shaping his negative feelings about himself, and he began to address these issues in treatment.

Patient: I was always overshadowed by my twin brother. People knew I was good at what I did but they didn't see any value in it, so I started not to see any value in myself after ten years of this stuff.

Therapist: So it sounds like it's been difficult to find people who've been able to acknowledge and value you.

Patient: Yeah.

Therapist: It didn't happen in your family.

Patient: No, oh no, oh no, it was probably some control. They wanted to keep me in the role of the bad brother.

Therapist: Tell me about that.

Patient: Well, I don't know, I probably felt guilty about having things that other people didn't have—I felt guilty so I made sure I didn't have anything. I mean I've had deep guilt about that, and I've made myself so down and out it's not even funny anymore.

Therapist: So you haven't felt like you've been worthy or deserving of . . .

Patient: Yeah, and with my music, I played gigs for free—I gave it away. I mean if they cared about me they'd pay for it.

Therapist: You felt like you had to give it away.

Patient: Yeah.

Therapist: Tell me about that.

Patient: To have some friends or to feel valued.

Therapist: So it was hard to feel valued for yourself.

Patient: Yeah, it was hard for me to say, "This is what I do, I'm worth it."

Therapist: I'm wondering if you have some idea where that came from.

Patient: Well, I didn't have a very good self-image growing up. I was overshadowed by my twin brother and my dad always made me feel bad for what I did. I still don't have a very good self-image.

Therapist: So it's hard even now to see the worth in yourself.

[Implicit in the therapist's stance and interventions is the notion that he has worth and she values him.]

Patient: Yeah, and that's a hard thing to turn around, and I've always felt weird when people acknowledge it.

Therapist: It feels strange when people acknowledge your worth.

Patient: Yeah, I know I need to get used to it a little bit. My self-esteem has always been really bad. I think of myself as this skinny, horrible looking guy, and I settled for less than I deserved, I think.

Therapist: It was hard to feel like you deserved more.

Patient: Yeah.

As Brad began to perceive that the therapist would validate his subjective experiences and affirm his worth, his comfort in revealing painful aspects of his childhood increased. In this way, the selfobject relationship formed between Brad and the therapist created a zone of safety in which these distressing issues could be explored. Brad began to feel comfortable exposing the vulnerable side of himself. The more the therapist's subjectivity included understanding and appreciating Brad's feelings of worthlessness, the better able she was to articulate her understanding to Brad. Feeling more accepted, Brad felt less need to impress the therapist. He became calmer and increasingly invested in exploring his internal world. The therapist's feelings toward Brad softened. Their mutually influencing subjectivities created a context for altering the patient's organization of himself as misunderstood and not valued and the therapist's sense of herself as not competent and worried about reinforcing his anger.

In supervision, the focus became the patient's organizing principle that he was inherently worthless. The following formulation emerged regarding Brad's recent relationship and the reason it had been so difficult for him to relinquish it. For Brad, getting *some* affection from this girlfriend, even though she was unfaithful, fueled his wish for love and acceptance. As little as she gave him, for him "a little was a lot" and losing her propelled him into an affective experience of unmet longing for acceptance and the subsequent pain of rejection. Brad had had very few experiences of feeling loved or valued by others, especially from his family, and receiving just a little of this love and affection from someone seemed to feel like a lot. Therefore, losing what she gave him was unbearable. This idea matched Brad's subjective experience of the loss of the relationship, which he considered "absolute devastation."

In her enthusiasm, the supervisee decided to articulate the organizing principle that "a little is a lot" to Brad in the hope that doing so would capture his compulsive need to pursue the relationship with his ex-girlfriend. She realized quickly that this articulation did not match his experience but instead moved him into a different direction. Brad began to doubt the painful subjective reality of his previous relationship—a reality that the two had worked hard to help him acknowledge.

Patient: I just wanted to be able to do my own thing.

Therapist: Um-hmm, you just wanted to be accepted for who you are.

Patient: Yeah, yeah, and I just couldn't do it. People would be like, "Put your songs out; you're so good," and I'd be like, "You guys don't understand; it's just not that easy. There's stuff going on inside of me that I can't do it."

[Here the patient appears to be close to a sense of what has held him back.]

Therapist: I'm wondering if you ever felt like you've had someone who's been able to accept and appreciate that.

Patient: Liza [a girlfriend from several years ago], probably she accepted me.

Therapist: So it's been hard to find people.

Patient: Yeah, yeah, I don't think I'm going to find that in too many people.

Therapist: I'm wondering if that was part of why it was so difficult to let go of Sara [his most recent girlfriend with whom he had a very volatile relationship].

Patient: That she was kind of accepting of that? I don't know, I don't know.

Therapist: I'm wondering if that feeling of a little bit of acceptance made it hard to let go.

Patient: Yeah, she did believe in me, she did appreciate what I did, and she did believe in me. I mean, I don't know, it's just kind of hard to let go of her.

Therapist: I'm wondering if that's part of it, if there have been very few people who've been accepting.

Patient: Well, Sara was very accepting; she was very understanding. She was willing to stick with me forever. I screwed up, I scared her, and she pulled away. And she wanted to make a lifelong commitment.

In this portion of the session, it becomes apparent that the therapist's agenda, to introduce this idea that "a little is a lot" overrode the principle of attending to what is in the forefront of the patient's subjective experience. In her enthusiasm to communicate her understanding of an aspect of the patient's organization of experience, she forced the opportunity to introduce the idea to him. Undoubtedly, part of her determination was influenced by the conviction on the part of the supervisors that the phrase "a little is a lot" stood for many aspects of the patient's experience—it took very little to provoke his father's hostility; a small level of affect becomes very disruptive; some support and attention from others is enough to inspire a lot of idealization and gratitude. The therapist responded to some felt pressure from the supervisors who generated the organizing principle "a little is a lot" as a way of articulating and illuminating the patient's willingness to accept what his ex-girlfriend offered and his persistence in trying to reestablish a relationship with her. As elegant as the idea seemed to the supervisory group, introduced at this point in their work it seemed to have the effect of pushing Brad away from his own subjectivity ("There's stuff going on inside of me that I just can't do it") and toward his idealizing stance toward Sara.

Rather than illuminating for the patient how meager the resources have been to support his development, he incorporated the therapist's observation into an alternate organization—that he was fully responsible for the breakup of a relationship in which his girlfriend was providing "a lot" for him. Reviewing this session highlighted for the supervisory group how powerfully one's core organizing principles function to keep our world familiar and predictable, even at the expense of our self-esteem. This speaks to the notion that a primary motivation is to maintain the organization of experience. Only when a context is altered significantly and consistently over time (referring to those aspects of the world as subjectively experienced as salient) does a new organization of experience emerge. At the point that the organizing principle, "a little is a lot," was introduced, it failed to offer Brad a new way of understanding himself—as someone who had been given very little to support his personal talents and who had consequently learned to make do with almost no validation and affirmation of his experience from important others. Rather, Brad heard the therapist's articulation as more of the same—that the end of the relationship was entirely his fault, and that he should not have felt hurt or betrayed by this woman. In this way, he once again doubted his own experience. This illustrates how powerful is the need to maintain the organization of experience that even contradictory new experience can be misshaped to fit into the old jigsaw puzzle.

Fortunately, as the supervisory group anticipated, this theme came up again in the treatment, and the therapist was able to attune to Brad's feelings of hurt within the context of his previous relationship. Eventually, he himself began to talk about the enduring absence of love and affection in his life. He came to own the idea that for him, "a little bit is a lot."

Patient: Yeah, I got a little bit from Liza and it was really hard to let go of her, and I got a little bit from Sara and that's it. That's all it's ever been, you know.

Therapist: That's part of why it's so difficult. Even though hurtful things have happened, it's hard to let go of because of that little bit.

Patient: It's like if your life was good and growing up was healthy and you got all of those things, then you could do this without falling apart.

Therapist: And you didn't have it.

Patient: I didn't have it growing up. I didn't have it growing up.

Therapist: So, a little bit is a lot at this point.

Patient: And that little bit, I guess that's why I'm going through this, to cling to that little bit.

Therapist: Because you haven't had it before.

Patient: Yeah, yeah, I feel like I lost a lot.

Brad began to explore deeper issues related to his feelings of worthlessness and his reactive and protective anger. At the same time, he continued to appear very depressed. He reported feeling fatigued, unmotivated, and extremely irritable. He cried during most sessions and frequently alternated between tears and anger within the hour. He brought up the idea of depression and that he had always had a sense of something being wrong with him.

Patient: Sometimes I wonder if I have a chemical imbalance because I can change so quickly, so fast. I mean, I was like that growing up. I'd change so quickly.

Therapist: Tell me more about that.

Patient: I'd just get irritable—one minute I'd be fine and the next I'd be so angry.

Therapist: So this has felt like something that's gone on since you were a child.

Patient: Yeah, I was talking to my brother and he said, "Mom wanted to get you help but Dad wouldn't allow it." I mean, they thought there was something wrong with me, but I didn't get help.

In the next session, Brad again brought in the idea that his labile mood has been present since childhood.

Patient: I get angry and irritable; it's not normal. I want to get more balanced. I mean, so I take a pill every day, that's how it'll be. I mean, I wasn't real thrilled when I brought up to you, you know—depression [he whispers the word and giggles].

Therapist: You weren't really thrilled when we started talking about that.

[The therapist has a tendency to avoid saying difficult or charged words, like "depression," saying "that" instead. This became a topic of discussion in supervision.]

Patient: I was like, you know, I don't want to use it as an excuse. I mean, I've always had problems, and I still have issues.

Therapist: In terms of bringing it up, maybe you were wondering what I would think about that or how I would respond.

[Here the therapist directs Brad's attention to the transference, his experience of her. The absence of transferential material had been noted in supervision. The therapist had been concerned that calling attention to Brad's experience of her might precipitate powerful and uncomfortable sexual or romantic feelings in Brad that she would have to manage.]

Patient: Well, people with depression you know, I don't know . . . I just didn't want to acknowledge that I was weak in that way, you know, because I'm very strong willed, I think, but I didn't want to admit this is something I can't battle. I mean, I always thought you should be strong enough to battle it.

Therapist: So admitting that even in here meant showing a side of yourself you haven't shown to many other people.

Patient: Yeah, I mean Liza brought it up at first and I was like, "No way," but I mean, that's what I have and it's a serious illness.

Therapist: It's had a serious impact on you in every area of your life.

In this session, Brad revealed both his shame about appearing "weak" and his concern that the therapist might see him as making excuses for his behavior. Brad eventually talked about wanting to try antidepressant medication, and after consultation with the supervisors, the therapist recommended to Brad that they meet jointly (training clinic procedure) with the training clinic's consulting psychiatrist. In supervision, the discussion centered on the importance of attuning at this time to Brad's longing to be cared for. In light of his childhood experience that no one had been available to help him, Brad's desire to be evaluated for medication presented an opportunity to respond affirmingly to his wish to be helped. The therapist had successfully created an environment where Brad could feel safe even though he felt vulnerable. This enabled Brad to risk bringing up with the therapist the possibility of medication.

Until the question of medication came up, Brad had not acknowledged the person of his therapist. When Brad asked about medications, he appeared concerned that in bringing up his depression, the therapist would see him as weak or ineffectual. He was concerned that she might view him with disdain for being weak and making excuses. It became important to Brad that his therapist appreciate how hard he was working to make changes in his life.

Brad's selfobject need for validation emerged in response to the therapist's attunement to his lifelong mood problems. She heard his confusion about the extremes of his moods, the bewilderment at his parents' inattention to his needs, and the wish for help with his overwhelming problems of anger and depression. A correlate of these lifelong unmet selfobject needs was an organization of experience that no one would understand him. Others attributed his poor level of functioning to his being lazy or unmotivated rather than to his solitary struggle with unmanageable affects. He was worried that the therapist would disapprovingly view him as lazy. Brad's tentative exploration of medications as a possible way of dealing with his affective overload marked an important transition in the treatment. He revealed his lifelong struggle with affective dysregulation, his parents' chronic misattunement to his difficulties, and his growing perception of the therapist as someone who could cocreate an opportunity for new experience.

About four months into the treatment Brad regularly began to bring aspects of the therapeutic relationship into session. Initially he apologized for coming twice a week, expressing concern that the therapist must get tired of hearing him talk about the same things. Shortly afterward he stated, "I feel like I'm on my own besides you." Simultaneously, Brad became concerned about an upcoming break in treatment, which then became a focus during sessions.

Patient: How long is the break again?

Therapist: Two weeks.

Patient: That sucks.

Therapist: Let's talk more about that. Recently, you've been telling me things that you said you had never told anyone else. I imagine this break brings up a lot of feelings for you.

Patient: This holiday will suck.

Therapist: I realize this might be difficult and I would like for us to talk more about it.

Patient: Well, thanks for seeing me two times a week. How long are you going to be here?

Therapist: Another one and a half years, a while.

Patient: Oh, because you know, pouring everything out just so you can get a good picture because I need to get well. I know on the outside people think I'm fine, but on the inside I'm not very well. I'm, like, maybe I'm going to lose you on this.

Therapist: I'll be here for a while. I'm not going anywhere.

The patient asked for specific information and the therapist responded straightforwardly with the details, passing up the opportunity to explore the possible meanings behind his question. This interaction illustrates that many moments in treatment present choice points for a therapist, with no clear right or wrong intervention. Here the therapist's subjective sense was that, facing an upcoming break, exploration of the personal meanings behind the question might increase the intensity of his affects. She opted instead to provide some regulatory function for the patient.

At a later session:

Patient: Well, I mean, I come in here and say the right things, don't I?

Therapist: It sounds like you're anxious about making sure we're doing, or that you're doing, what you need to do.

[This intervention may not have gotten the patient's concerns quite right. The patient seems to be seeking his therapist's approval for his efforts in therapy, but the therapist has avoided the transference implications of the question.]

Patient: This is really the most important thing. Sorry.

Therapist: So you feel like you need to apologize for that.

[Here the therapist does pick up on the transference, but it might have been stronger if she said, "You need to apologize *to me* for that."]

Patient: I don't want to put a lot of pressure on anybody, or you, but I've had the depression all my life and these issues and I've never had anybody to talk to, or people were just dismissive. I mean these are legitimate, painful things, and crippling things to me.

Patient and therapist together created a field in which the patient felt safe to reveal more and more of his experience. He has come to depend on her for nonjudgmental affirmation of his subjectivity. No doubt Brad tends to be dependent. After all, he has lived his entire adult life in his mother's home and has never earned enough, or shown any inclination, to live on his own. He brought these organizing patterns with him. However, Brad's therapist sought to listen from his perspective and to respond in ways that acknowledged his view. So, in this unique dyadic system there are pushes from the past and pulls toward new possibilities in the future. The supervisory group, following the lead of the patient, began to notice and discuss ways in which Brad indicated what he thought and felt about the therapist. For several months what was in the foreground was Brad's enthusiasm for coming to sessions and his somewhat seductive manner of dress. As the break approached, Brad became more explicit about how much he depended on his therapist.

One of the important themes throughout the nine months of treatment has been Brad's view of love, affection, and physical intimacy in a relationship. His involvement with women ranged between two extremes. Sometimes he sought out exotic dancers or prostitutes, but he has been very tentative about revealing much of his involvement with them. On the other hand, he elaborated his ideal of romantic love that explicitly did not include intercourse or any genital contact.

Vague references to Brad's sexuality had come up from the very beginning of his treatment. In the first session, he talked about previous therapy related to "sexual problems" and "pain down there." This topic came up intermittently throughout therapy. Brad appeared very uncomfortable when discussing his sexuality and often giggled or avoided eye contact.

In supervision, the group wondered how to facilitate Brad's exploration of his sexuality. In the process, elements of the therapist's subjectivity appeared to influence how she attuned to Brad's experience. She was aware that, as a beginning therapist and a woman, she was very reluctant to introduce or pursue the topic of sexuality with Brad. She let pass Brad's allusions to his sexual problems with his most recent relationship. For example, when Brad reported that he and his ex-girlfriend had "gotten off on the wrong foot sexually" and that he "did not require sex in our relationship," she did no further inquiry.

In a session about five months after the start of treatment, Brad talked for the first time about an incident that occurred when he was 26 years old. He had intercourse with a prostitute, and for the next seven years had suffered from intense genital pain for which no medical cause could be determined. He also talked about the fact that sex was rarely discussed in his family, and the family standard was apparently that children lived in the parents' home until getting married. Brad felt guilty and dirty about engaging in sexual behavior and believed that he had developed the pain as a punishment for his behavior. When Brad started to discuss his sexual patterns, the therapist felt uncomfortable but did not want the patient to sense her discomfort. In an effort to minimize her own anxiety, she responded obliquely, referring to his feelings of insecurity and his need for affection and caring from others rather than explicitly discussing Brad's sexual concerns.

Patient: I mean, if someone is nice to me they can have me (giggles). If anyone is nice to me, they can have me. That's just bad. I don't care what they look like. It's just some validation, so I have sex with them.

Therapist: Your need for affection is so great that if someone offered it [meaning sex, but avoiding use of the word], you took the opportunity.

Patient: Yeah.

Therapist: You hadn't gotten that physical contact and affection at all.

Patient: Yeah, and I still do that, and it's bad, it'll get me into trouble.

Therapist: You're still in need of that affection, so if someone offers it, sexual or otherwise, you take it.

Patient: Yeah, if someone is nice to me, I'm with them. I'm not too picky. It's not right.

Therapist: So you feel bad that you need this.

Patient: (Shifting in seat and looking very uncomfortable) Yeah, I just don't think it's right to be that affectionate and needy—I'm needy for affection and love.

Therapist: You really crave that affection you didn't receive, any way that you can get it.

Patient: Yeah, yeah, so I give stuff away and give myself away.

Therapist: Tell me about that—when you give yourself away. Is that still in a sexual way?

[The therapist is able to reintroduce the explicit topic of sexuality.]

Patient: Still in a sexual way. I'm not very smart about what I do. I mean, I've been with a few people lately, and sex isn't enjoyable. It's not something I feel good about, physically or mentally. I mean, I go out with them one time and have sex with them. . . . it just doesn't feel very comfortable to talk about.

Therapist: I understand.

[This intervention avoids discussing Brad's discomfort with talking about sex with the therapist, probably because his therapist continues to be uncomfortable with the topic.]

Patient: It makes me look like this lowlife.

Therapist: Maybe you're worried that by telling me these things I'll think badly of you?

[Here the therapist is able to direct focus to the transference.]

Patient: It makes me look like "Where are my standards?" Like a total sleaze.

Therapist: So maybe you're worried that I'll think of you that way, that I'll see you as those things?

[Again the therapist's discomfort with using explicit

terminology is evidenced by her use of the vague word "things."]

Patient: Yeah, I mean I'm not sure. I know I need to bring it up with you.

Therapist: But it sounds like it's something you've worried about bringing up to me.

Patient: Well, I haven't wanted to.

Therapist: So that maybe after you told me these things I wouldn't like you anymore?

[The therapist is affirming that she does find him likable.]

Patient: (Giggling and clearly uncomfortable) Well, yeah, I guess.

This session illustrated how the therapist's discomfort with the topic of sexuality and the patient's sexual practices played into the patient's feelings of shame. The supervisory group considered this exchange from a number of angles. In terms of the unique intersubjective field of this dyad, we speculated that the therapist's uncertainty influenced the patient in ways we did not yet understand. Reviewing the session, the therapist feared she had conveyed that the subject of sex was off limits, or, worse, that she judged him negatively based on what he did tell her. Her introspection, shared with her supervisors, demonstrated her increased sense of safety with her supervisors and improved confidence in herself as a clinician. She could wonder about the process and her contribution to it without becoming disrupted or defensive.

As supervisors we initially emphasized what we felt went well with the session (Teicholz 1999b). First, despite her anxiety, the therapist stayed with the topic in a general way, tracking Brad's need for affirming experiences. In doing so, she was following a theme that the two had developed over many months, illuminating the pervasive influence of these unmet needs throughout his life. We tentatively formulated that in the process of highlighting the patient's selfobject need for validation, the therapist was building trust in the relationship and supporting the potential that this relationship will not repeat past misattunement and injury. The therapist attuned to Brad's selfobject needs, strengthened the therapeutic relationship, and thereby furthered the possibility that a new organization of experience could form. Brad has seen himself as flawed, defective, and unworthy of care and attention from others. Despite his expectations, his therapist responded sensitively, recognizing the strength of Brad's longing for both physical and emotional connection. In the context of this new relationship, he will have to revise his long-standing organization of experience that he is worthless and unlovable.

A second way in which this therapist dealt effectively with her anxiety in this session was by directly addressing the transference, the patient's incorporation of her into his organization of experience. We find that beginning therapists are hesitant, even resistant, to following up on a patient's allusions to them. The therapist in this instance heard Brad's fear that people would find him a "sleaze" and a "lowlife." She risked shifting the focus of his fears from people "out there" to her. In doing so, she implicitly drew Brad's attention to the fact that she was not responding to him as if he were defective.

Despite the supervisors' emphasis on these positive aspects of the session, the therapist felt strongly that her own difficulty in responding directly and comfortably to Brad's allusions to his sexual behavior inhibited him from revealing important experiences. Her sense was that her stance re-created for him earlier shame for his own sexual needs and desires. In the particular way their subjectivities interfaced, an intersubjective experience was created in which the patient did not feel safe to reveal himself. Instead of depathologizing his sexual impulses, in this instance the therapist questioned him about his discomfort, possibly leaving him confused as to her acceptance of him.

However, the patient's sense of safety had been preserved through the therapist's attuned responsiveness. As the supervisory group sensed, the patient's need to reveal his difficulties prevailed and he continued to talk about his sexuality in a roundabout way. The supervisors had not yet found a way to help the therapist manage her anxiety about the topic. Certainly, the supervisors approached the boundary between what could appropriately be dealt with in supervision and what the therapist needed to deal with privately in her own way. The therapist's discomfort with discussing Brad's sexuality continued, and, at times when Brad referred to his sexuality indirectly, she failed to hear the reference. The potential danger in this disjunction was that the therapist's difficulty might have reinforced Brad's idea that his own sexuality was a shameful and dirty thing, and that he should not have these feelings or act on them.

Patient: I mean I've always been, I've always had a sense of being scared all my life. Scared when I'm out. Maybe that's why I don't go out. I mean, if I go out to a bar to listen to music or watch people dance, whatever, it's frightening beyond belief. I think someone is going to see me walk in there and that's just scary.

Therapist: In those situations, what do you imagine would happen?

Patient: Well, I'm walking in and imagine they think "Well, he's just here to pick up a girl" or something, you know, "He's just here for a one night stand." It petrifies me to where I don't go out.

Therapist: So, an idea that people are thinking something negative about you?

Patient: I think, or they're looking at me. I don't know what they're thinking when they look at me.

Therapist: That they're critiquing your appearance?

Patient: I think, I guess, because when I go out I stand in a dark corner somewhere, I want to go where nobody can see me or what I do.

Therapist: Maybe if you stand out, you'll be criticized or judged.

Patient: I think.

Here Brad tried to bring up shameful feelings about his sexual desires. He alluded to his fears that others will perceive that he thinks of women in a sexual way. This exacerbated his shame about having sexual thoughts. He wanted to go where nobody would see him and no one would know that he has these feelings. Instead of exploring this with Brad, the therapist sidestepped the importance of his statements about "picking up women" or "having a one night stand" and chose instead to respond to the "negative" thoughts others would have about him. The therapist's choice did follow a theme well established in the work—Brad's pervasive experience that no one could accept what feels personally meaningful to him. However, it avoided Brad's more specific dreaded revelations. The therapist might have depathologized and implicitly affirmed Brad's sexual desires by articulating, "You seem to feel it is shameful to want to have sex."

The group spent several supervisory sessions dealing with both the patient's and the therapist's anxiety. The supervisors felt that in order for Brad to deal with his sexuality openly in treatment, it would be necessary for the therapist to be able to speak candidly about sexual matters. The therapist understood that below the surface of Brad's anger with his recent girlfriend were feelings of humiliation and inadequacy connected to her apparent sexual involvement with another man. In addition, Brad's traumatic shame response to his own earlier sexual behavior promoted avoidance of sexual situations. However, Brad was still not aware of the personal meanings of his sexual desires, which were covered over by shame and, at times, a moralizing and superior attitude. To further Brad's exploration into the subjective meaning of his sexuality, the therapist, together with her supervisors, would have to find a way to quiet her fears that she would be doing something inappropriate, either clinically or personally, by explicitly talking about Brad's sexual patterns.

The supervisors faced a similar dilemma. The therapist needed to take a risk, trying something with her patient that was difficult for her. The supervisors, agreed, however, that supervision was not the place for her to explore fully her own subjectivity regarding the frank and nonjudgmental talk about sexuality considered vital to the treatment. Over the course of a couple of months, the supervisors continued to point out the theme of Brad's sexual practices and fears and sought to depathologize what they heard, and the supervisors practiced articulating possible responses to Brad's material. In doing so, they hoped to support her increased competence as a therapist without pushing her beyond her level of comfort nor shaming her into intervening in the way they preferred (their subjective choice based on their individual treatments, training, and experiences.) Much like treatment, the mutual influence of the interfacing subjectivities in supervision constructed a context where the therapist risked responses based on what the supervisory group concluded was Brad's self-loathing regarding his sexual desires.

The next time Brad began to talk about his fears of being judged or criticized by others, the therapist attuned to these experiences and listened for the veiled sexual themes suggested by what he said. She hoped to depathologize his fantasies and to talk with him about the feelings of shame associated with them.

Patient: I don't know what they're thinking about me. Usually I think it's something bad towards me. It keeps me away from people.

Therapist: You've talked about them thinking you're funny looking or making judgments about you. I wonder about some of the other bad things you imagine.

Patient: I don't know. When I go out and listen to music and stuff (looks very uncomfortable) I think people would think, "Oh, he's just here for a one night stand" or whatever.

Therapist: So, any thought that you'd have about talking with a woman or being with a woman are somehow very bad.

Patient: I don't know. I think women assume you have ulterior motives. I mean, don't flatter yourself—I'm just being friendly. I'm not going home with you or something. I'm just being friendly; it doesn't mean that much.

[Obviously the patient has become quite defensive.]

Therapist: You're very worried that someone would think you meant it in a sexual way. You see that as a bad thing.

Patient: It doesn't mean I'm hitting on them just because I'm talking to them.

Therapist: So you would see that as a bad thing that you had a sexual interest in them, that's something you would feel badly about.

[Here the therapist does what she had not previously felt comfortable to do. Rather than follow the theme of his feeling criticized and bad, she picks up on the importance of his sexual interest as a factor in these feelings.]

Patient: Well, I think they flatter themselves. I mean, just because a guy is friendly, it doesn't mean it's a come-on.

[Based on his own shame at his sexual interests and the traumatic reaction he has experienced in the past when he has been sexual, Brad becomes somewhat defensively grandiose. He persistently focuses on what he imagines others think, avoiding his own feelings. The therapist consistently returns to the issue of his sexual interest instead of his sense of being misunderstood. It is possible that Brad's grandiosity and defensiveness have become antidotes to his organization of experience relative to his sexuality.]

Therapist: It sounds like you would see it as bad or shameful if they did see it as a come-on. That natural sexual attraction for you feels like a very negative or shameful thing.

Patient: No, (looking uncomfortable) but, I don't know, I think they're quick to categorize.

[The patient continues to struggle with his long-standing way of organizing his sexual interest and feelings. The therapist's use of the word *natural* is an attempt to depathologize Brad's sexual desires.]

Therapist: Tell me about that.

Patient: Like, if you're here listening to music, you're here for a one night stand.

Therapist: You're worried that others would look at you and say, "That's what he's here for."

Patient: It's not healthy.

Therapist: So, having a sexual relationship is not healthy?

Patient: Yeah, yeah, I guess in a relationship it's all right, but the girls I've been with place a high priority on it and I don't.

Therapist: Having sex in a relationship is okay but a one night stand is not.

Patient: No, no, not for me. I'm not interested. Because of conflict before, I'm not interested.

Therapist: You've had bad experiences with one night stands before.

[Here the therapist closely tracks what the patient has said and moves slightly into what he has left unspoken.]

Patient: Oh yeah. I get sick afterwards.

Therapist: So for you sex really carries a lot of shame.

[An alternative might be to follow up on "getting sick" but both patient and therapist have tolerated significant expansion of their subjectivities. Probably, the therapist's decision reflects good judgment in containing their mutual anxiety—a decision formed at the interface of their subjectivities.]

Patient: Yeah, yeah.

Here the therapist, in her effort to depathologize his behavior, suggested that Brad's needs are legitimate. She chose not to point to the dangers, the conflicts, the "perversion," or the inconsistencies in what he has told her before about his sexual fantasies and experiences. But she moved beyond affirming his experience of being judged and misunderstood as she had previously done, choosing instead to speak directly about his feeling about his sexuality.

An important practice guideline discernible in the session was a preference for responses to be as specific as possible. Once the therapist overcame her difficulty with discussing Brad's sexual feelings, the patient made a similar shift. In the following session the therapist was able to focus on both the sexual aspects of the patient's discussion as well as the deep shame and guilt he felt. Within this context the patient began to talk about how these feelings of shame have impacted his sexual relationships and the subsequent rejection he has felt as a result of his sexual difficulties.

Patient: Well, Sara did. She placed a lot of importance on it [intercourse]. I didn't do it well with Sara so she just made up all kinds of excuses with me. She was very cold and distant to me.

Therapist: You feel like the sexual aspects of that relationship really created problems.

[The therapist reflects some aspects of the patient's subjective experience, but again she sidesteps an explicit discussion of Brad's feelings that, "I didn't do it well."]

Patient: Oh yeah, she would just . . . she thought it felt awkward and wrong and I'm just not that comfortable with it so I only fooled around with her a few times.

Therapist: It felt like she didn't find you attractive?

Patient: No. She never said it. She never told me that. She didn't want to be physical with me so obviously I don't feel very good about myself.

Therapist: So her discomfort with the sexual relationship made that even more painful.

Patient: Well I felt pretty unwanted. I felt totally unwanted.

Brad began to talk about areas of his life in which he felt "shut down," and related this feeling to both his difficulties in being successful as a musician and songwriter, as well as to his sexual problems. He described feeling shut down for his entire adult life, and began to connect it to his childhood experiences of consistent criticism by his family, his sense that he was not accepted for what he wanted to be or to do. Brad talked about all of the people in his life who had expectations of him, that often he felt completely inadequate in the face of these expectations, and unable to achieve them.

Brad's organizing principle—that he is inadequate, a failure, in the face of other's expectations—created a sense of paralysis on his part and a deep sense of shame that he could never live up to others' expectations. Brad had been punished for asserting his own needs and was expected to be perfect, and to follow in the footsteps of his "perfect" twin brother. His own needs and desires were ignored or punished, and he developed a sense that he had no value.

Patient: Yeah, I got it from my dad and I was getting it from my mom, too. I feel like I wasn't good enough, so when I did play, I felt like I had to be really sharp.

Therapist: It has to be perfect.

Patient: And I can't do that, so I shut down. Maybe that's why I don't get out. I feel like I have to put on thirty pounds of muscle, redo my teeth, and change the color of my hair, and then maybe I'll feel like going out. Isn't that pathetic?

Therapist: It sounds like it's been a very painful experience.

Patient: Yeah, because I feel embarrassed when I go out.

Therapist: You feel like you have to change yourself.

Patient: Yeah. I can't meet those standards.

Therapist: Perfection is impossible for anybody.

[This intervention was no doubt aimed at being reassuring; however, the supervisors suspect that it would have been more effective to continue articulating his feelings of inadequacy and worthlessness.]

Patient: Yeah, so I just shut down.

Later, in another session, Brad spoke about his feelings of inadequacy again.

Patient: I didn't get any of that value [feelings of competence]; I mean, none of that from my parents. I was just supposed to know the rules, to know better. I mean I was just a kid.

Therapist: It feels like a ridiculous expectation.

Patient: Yeah! I mean, I was just always supposed to be the best, like my brother. It's like a self-defeating attitude because you can't be the best. I just wanted to be me. And that really came out in my music. I mean, I can't always be the best so I would destroy everything, and I was destroying myself.

Therapist: It felt very personal; it felt like destroying yourself.

Patient: Yeah, yeah. I mean failure—it's not acceptable. It's been a matter of life and death for me, and it shouldn't be.

Therapist: Tell me about that feeling.

Patient: I wasn't allowed to fail at anything. I mean to have a lot of successes you have a lot of failures too, but I couldn't.

Therapist: You were punished for it.

Patient: Yeah. I just take it as life and death.

Therapist: So, failure is equal to death.

[Brad reveals the depth of what failing means to him.]

Patient: Yeah, and I really beat myself up because I don't have any worth or value or any of that.

Brad continued to explore these feelings of inadequacy and poor self-worth in the context of his professional life, and seemed to feel overwhelmed at the prospect of performing in public for fear of failing in the eyes of others.

Patient: Yeah, I'm sitting there at the piano and all of these thoughts keep entering my mind: "You're not good enough at this." I'm comparing myself to all of these people.

Therapist: So you're imagining people saying you're not good enough, not up to standard.

Patient: Yeah, yeah. A lot of people have high expectations of me. I mean they think I'm better than I actually am. I feel like with a song, if I don't do it right they'll say, "I was wrong about Brad."

Therapist: And that's a scary feeling for you to have.

Patient: Yeah. I don't care for it when people have these superexpectations of me. I don't want to hear that.

Therapist: It feels like too much pressure.

Patient: It feels like a lot of pressure; it feels like a lot of pressure.

Therapist: It makes it scary for you to think about living up to these expectations.

Patient: I just don't want anybody to have any expectations of me.

Having failed in comparison to his successful twin brother, Brad seemed powerless in the face of expectations—of sexual prowess, making music, and other nonspecific expectations attributed to almost everyone. The supervisory group discussed this issue of expectations, particularly as it related to the therapist's expectations of Brad. The supervisors proposed that in many ways Brad did not want the therapist to have expectations of him, probably out of fear that he would fail in some way, that she would be critical and consider him a failure much as had the important people early in his life. He was at a crossroads, balanced between the fear of retraumatization and the need for a relationship where he could experience himself in a new way. The supervisors felt that through this new relationship with his therapist Brad might have the experience of being valued and, seeing himself as someone of value mirrored by another, begin to develop more of a sense of his own value. Ideally, Brad would eventually be able to be more assertive and less concerned about what others would think of him.

Brad alternated between periods of vulnerability and insight into his bad feelings about himself and grandiose proclamations of his musical abilities. Initially, these oppositions in his behavior confused the therapist, who did not understand how someone who felt so bad about himself would then talk expansively about his unparalleled musical talents. The supervisory group addressed the patient's moving between the two extremes. The therapist began to understand that Brad's grandiosity served as an antidote to his feelings of self-loathing and allowed him initially to present himself in treatment as a very talented and capable individual. The discussion related primarily to choosing appropriate interventions during session. One option would have been to challenge his beliefs because he had not achieved success in his professional life—to focus on the reality of his professional failure. However, the supervisors recommended, instead, that in response to his defensive grandiosity, mirroring his positive accomplishments and qualities would be more effective in working through the shame underlying this defensiveness. Through experiencing the therapist's acknowledgment of his worth in general and his musical talents in particular, it was hoped that Brad would become more comfortable expressing his feelings of shame and inadequacy about not working independently and supporting himself.

As treatment progressed, with continued affirmation and validation, Brad was able to reveal a more vulnerable side of himself. He began to talk about the negative feelings he had about his ability to be a successful musician.

Therapist: So it's hard for you to take compliments.

Patient: Yeah, because I just don't feel good about myself.

Therapist: It really doesn't feel genuine.

Patient: Yeah, I think because my mom, over the years, when I'd say that someone said this or that about me, she'd say, "Oh, they're just saying that to be nice." I guess she was kidding, but over the years that sank in.

Therapist: You really started to feel that was true.

Patient: Yeah.

Therapist: That they weren't really genuine. You didn't really believe it, so it's hard to believe it now.

Patient: Yeah, yeah, yeah. It was partly that, and I was never really sure. So, I'm really insecure.

Therapist: You feel like you couldn't believe those compliments.

Patient: Yeah, I guess because my mom said that.

Therapist: I can see where it was difficult to believe those compliments were genuine when you were getting a message like that.

Patient: Yeah, that's a message I got from my mom for a long time.

Therapist: That makes it difficult to value what you're doing and to value yourself.

Patient: You think so? Yeah, it did for me. And then I had to stop taking myself seriously. I mean, I thought I was ugly, and my playing isn't good, and I wasn't getting gigs, so I thought it must be true.

Therapist: You believed it was true, that you weren't good enough.

Patient: Yeah.

In this way, by the therapist's staying attuned to Brad's subjective experience of his mother's criticisms, Brad became able to express how hurtful these interactions with his mother really were. Brad was able to acknowledge the pervasive destructive impact his mother's statements had on his feelings about himself. As he continued to explore these feelings in session, Brad started to make connections between his bad feelings about himself and his "shutting down" as related to his musical and sexual performance.

Gradually, a new formulation of Brad's organizing principles began to emerge in the supervisory group. How might they make sense of Brad's experience of "shutting down," his inability to complete things, both professionally and sexually. Brad, they suspected, had learned to define himself in opposition to these expectations others had of him. The only way he could feel good about himself was by renouncing what others expected. It seemed that Brad felt a complete loss of personal agency when he capitulated to the expectations of others. This was drawn from several discussions Brad brought up throughout treatment.

Patient: My mom said that my dad and I were just the worst combination ever—he's strong willed and I'm strong willed. I was very defiant. I fought back and I wasn't going to take it.

Therapist: It sounds like some of your defiance was asserting yourself and what your needs were.

[The therapist recontextualizes his defiance, not as oppositionalism, but as healthy self-assertion.]

Patient: Yeah, I mean I just fought back. We always had to be well presented all the time. We were supposed to rely on them for everything. We weren't supposed to leave home until we got married.

[The patient seems to describe a rigid, controlling atmosphere in which little extrafamilial influence was allowed.]

Therapist: So you weren't really given the opportunity to develop yourself individually in the way you wanted to.

Patient: No, not at all. I was supposed to be perfect in every way.

Therapist: The expectations were impossible to live up to.

Patient: Yeah, yeah.

In a later session Brad connected his oppositional tendency with his sexual difficulties, illuminating the pervasiveness of the newly understood organizing principle that for him, self-delineation necessitated opposition to others. Brad revealed that one of his specific sexual difficulties concerned the inability to achieve orgasm with a woman.

Patient: I feel like women take something from me. I'm not going to let them take it from me anymore.

Therapist: So they take something. I'm wondering if you have any thoughts or ideas about what that is.

Patient: I don't know. I feel like I'm being used or just taken from.

Therapist: They are taking advantage of you in some way.

Patient: I don't feel like I'm getting anything from them. I feel like they're taking something from me. So I think I guard myself by not, um . . . (looking uncomfortable).

Therapist: Having an orgasm.

Patient: Yeah, by not coming.

Therapist: So that if you do?

Patient: I'm giving all of myself. They're taking from me, and I didn't want to give myself up anymore. I feel like women have been taking things from me all my life. They stole everything, and I'm not going to let them take me anymore. By not coming, I think that's significant by not allowing them to take something from me.

In this session segment, the therapist used the word *orgasm* when Brad shied away from being explicit about his behavior. In doing so she accomplished two things. First, she let the patient know that now she was available to speak openly about the topic of sexuality and to hear whatever he had to say. He responded by revealing his belief that he experiences a loss of something vital when he has an orgasm. Second, she deepened the process between them. Rather than speaking in euphemisms and generalities, they spoke in terms that have an emotional valence. She listened to him, knew what he was trying to say or avoid saying, and she said the word for him. It seemed that Brad experienced relief and gratitude when the therapist indicated that she could talk with him in this way.

Returning to the theme of Brad's oppositional and withholding stance, it seemed clear that his adaptation to the impossible demands of his family was to construct an identity as the rebellious family member, one who did not fit with the others. Being a "rebel" was an organization of experience formed at the interface of the subjectivities of Brad and his family members. It represented an effort toward self-delineation. This organizing principle illustrates how each of us finds within our early caregiving contexts a way to make sense of our experiential worlds and ourselves. Brad's struggle for self-delineation has been accomplished by opposing the expectations others have had of him. This had occurred in his professional life, and to a great extent in his personal relationships as well. At age 40 his rebelliousness does not provide a constructive basis for connecting with others or achieving occupational fulfillment. However, he is now torn between a need to align with someone who can help him (his therapist) in a reparative relationship and the fear that he will be demeaned and retraumatized. For Brad, rejecting the expectations that he be a successful musician and an independent man who can satisfy his own sexual needs and those of women gave him a sense of who he was. But the satisfaction is hollow.

When this articulation was presented to Brad in session, he seemed to feel it really described his experience, and began to speak forcefully about his feelings on the subject. He described this feeling as having been with him from the time he was very young.

Patient: I know what I'm about and what I want.

Therapist: You know what you want and what people expect of you, and in some ways these are very different things.

Patient: And what people expect is not what I'm going to do anymore.

Therapist: So by doing something completely different you can assert your autonomy and independence.

Patient: Yeah, I think, I think, yeah. I don't want people telling me what to do. Dad was always telling me what to do. I did my own thing. I was always different, day and night, black and white; I didn't wear a coat in the wintertime. I did the exact opposite; I didn't want anybody telling me what to do.

Therapist: That sounds like a way you could assert yourself, by opposing those expectations.

Patient: Yeah, they said I always did the opposite of everyone else. Whatever they said, I did the opposite. And I mean it got me hit.

Overall, the need to be oppositional seemed to be a powerful organizing principle for Brad. He assimilated it and elaborated on it almost immediately after it was articulated. This enabled him to understand his experience in a new way.

CONCLUSION

Brad's treatment is an ongoing process of making sense together between therapist and patient. Each is influenced by the other and changed by the other. As they focus on understanding Brad's experience, the therapist strives to find analogues within herself of memories and emotions that guide her responses. As she has participated in supervision, she has courageously faced many strong feelings as well as inhibitions that have been stirred up by her work with Brad and by the influencing subjectivities of her supervisors. In her own process as supervisee, this therapist has enlarged her view of herself as a novice therapist to one who is more and more competent to share the affective experiences of her patient. She is both calmer and livelier in session, with a parallel marked enlivening in her patient. In the context of a supervisory group that explicitly aspires to support the positive efforts of the supervisee, to help contain and regulate the predictable affective disruption of providing treatment, and to facilitate a change in professional identity, this supervisee's talent and hard work have paid off.

The interplay of subjectivities in a supervisory group consisting of two supervisors, a student therapist, and the patient's material provides more complexity than can reasonably be discussed in this chapter. Our goal in reporting this case in depth was to highlight the application of some of the ideas presented in the preceding chapters. No doubt many readers will notice aspects of the material we did not. In fact, our understanding of the nature of subjectivity means that it could not be otherwise. Each of us has come to make sense of the world and ourselves through a continual process of formation and reformation, of construction, deconstruction, and coconstruction. We hope that, as the thoughts and observations put forth in this book become part of a larger context of the practice of psychotherapy, the dialogue expands.

References

Arlow, J. A. (1987). The dynamics of Interpretation. *Psychoanalytic Quarterly* 56:68–87.

Aron, L. (1996). *A Meeting of Minds.* Hillsdale, NJ: Analytic Press.

Atwood, G. E., and Stolorow, R. D. (1984). *Structures of Subjectivity: Explorations in Psychoanalytic Phenomenology.* Hillsdale, NJ: Analytic Press.

——— (1993). *Faces in a Cloud.* Northvale, NJ: Jason Aronson.

——— (1997). Defects in self: liberating concept or imprisoning metaphor. *Psychoanalytic Dialogues* 7:517–522.

Bacal, H. (1990). The elements of a corrective selfobject experience. *Psychoanalytic Inquiry* 10:347–372.

Bacal, H. A., and Newman, K. M. (1990). *Theories of Object Relations: Bridges to Self Psychology.* New York: Columbia University Press.

Beebe, B., and Lachmann, F. (1996). Three principles of salience in the organization of the patient-analyst interaction. *Psychoanalytic Psychology* 13:1–22.

——— (1998). Co-constructing inner and relational processes:

self- and mutual regulation in infant research and adult treatment. *Psychoanalytic Psychology* 15:480–516.

Brandchaft, B. (1994). To free the spirit from its cell. In *The Intersubjective Perspective*, ed. R. D. Stolorow, G. E. Atwood, and B. Brandchaft, pp. 57–76. Northvale, NJ: Jason Aronson.

Brenner, C. (1982). *The Mind in Conflict.* Madison, CT: International Universities Press.

Buirski, P., and Haglund, P. (1998). The Wolf Man's subjective experience of his treatment with Freud. *Psychoanalytic Psychology* 15:49–62.

——— (1999). The selfobject function of interpretation. In *Pluralism in Self Psychology: Progress in Self Psychology*, vol. 15, ed. A. Goldberg, pp. 31–49. Hillsdale, NJ: Analytic Press.

Buirski, P., and Monroe, M. (2000). Intersubjective observations on transference love. *Psychoanalytic Psychology* 17:78–87.

Cook, H., and Buirski, P. (1990). Countertransference in psychoanalytic supervision: an heuristic model. *Psychoanalysis and Psychotherapy* 8:77–87.

Darwin, C. (1872). *The Expression of the Emotions in Man and Animals.* London: Murray. (Reprinted by University of Chicago Press, 1965.)

Davidson, R., and Fox, N. (1982). Asymmetrical brain activity discriminates between positive versus negative affective stimuli in human infants. *Science* 218:1235–1237.

Dewald, P. A. (1987). *Learning Process in Psychoanalytic Supervision: Complexes and Challenges.* Madison, CT: International Universities Press.

Doehrman, M. (1976). Parallel process in supervision and psychotherapy. *Bulletin of the Menninger Clinic* 40:9–28.

Ekman, P. (1984). Expression and the nature of emotion. In *Approaches to Emotion*, ed. K. Scherer and P. Ekman, pp. 319–343. Hillsdale, NJ: Lawrence Erlbaum.

Ekstein, R., and Wallerstein, R. (1959). *The Teaching and Learning of Psychotherapy.* New York: International Universities Press.

Emde, R. (1983). The prerepresentational self and its affective core. *Psychoanalytic Study of the Child* 38:165–192. New Haven, CT: Yale University Press.

——— (1988a). Development terminable and interminable: I. Innate and motivational factors from infancy. *International Journal of Psycho-Analysis* 69:23–42.

——— (1988b). Development terminable and interminable: II. Psychoanalytic theory and therapeutic considerations. *International Journal of Psycho-Analysis* 69:283–296.

Emde, R., and Sorce, J. (1983). The rewards of infancy: emotional availability and maternal referencing. In *Frontiers of Infant Psychiatry,* ed. J. Call, E. Galenson, and R. Tyson, pp. 17–30. New York: Basic Books.

Fleming, J., and Benedek, T. (1966). *Psychoanalytic Supervision.* New York: Grune & Stratton.

Fosshage, J. L. (1995a). Countertransference as the analyst's experience of the analysand: influence of listening perspectives. *Psychoanalytic Psychology* 12:375–392.

——— (1995b). Interaction in psychoanalysis: a broadening horizon. *Psychoanalytic Dialogues* 5:459–478.

——— (1997a). Psychoanalysis and psychoanalytic psychotherapy: is there a meaningful distinction in the process? *Psychoanalytic Psychology* 14:409–425.

——— (1997b). Toward a model of psychoanalytic supervision from a self-psychological/intersubjective perspective. In *Psychoanalytic Supervision,* ed. M. Rock, Northvale, NJ: Jason Aronson.

——— (1999). A reply to Golland's "Politics of Leveling." *Psychoanalytic Psychology* 16:110–114.

Freud, A. (1936). *The Ego and the Mechanisms of Defense. The Writings of Anna Freud,* vol. 2. New York: International Universities Press, 1966.

Freud, S. (1900). The interpretation of dreams. *Standard Edition* 4/5:1–627.

——— (1910). 'Wild' psycho-analysis. *Standard Edition* 11:219–227.

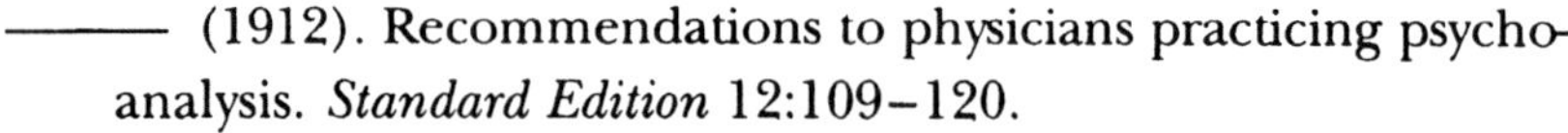

——— (1912). Recommendations to physicians practicing psycho-analysis. *Standard Edition* 12:109–120.

——— (1913a). On beginning the treatment. *Standard Edition* 12:123–144.

——— (1913b). On psycho-analysis. *Standard Edition* 12:207–211.

——— (1915a). Observations on transference-love (further recommendations on the technique of psycho-analysis lll). *Standard Edition* 12:157–171.

——— (1915b). The unconscious. *Standard Edition* 14:159–215.

——— (1918). From the history of an infantile neurosis. *Standard Edition* 17:3–122.

——— (1923). The ego and the id. *Standard Edition* 14:12–66.

——— (1937). Constructions in analysis. *Standard Edition* 23:257–269.

Gendlin, E. (1996). *Focusing-Oriented Psychotherapy: A Manual of the Experiential Method.* New York: Guilford.

Glover, E. (1955). *The Technique of Psycho-Analysis.* New York: International Universities Press.

Greenberg, J. R., and Mitchell, S. A. (1983). *Object Relations in Psychoanalytic Theory.* Cambridge, MA: Harvard University Press.

Greenberg, L., Rice, L., and Elliot, R. (1993). *Facilitating Emotional Change: The Moment-by-Moment Process.* New York: Guilford.

Grigsby, J., and Stevens, D. (2000). *Neurodynamics of Personality.* New York: Guilford.

Harris, A. (1996). False memory? False memory syndrome? The so-called false memory syndrome? *Psychoanalytic Dialogues* 6:155–187.

Heimann, P. (1950). On countertransference. *International Journal of Psycho-Analysis* 31:81–84.

Herrigel, E. (1971). *Zen in the Art of Archery.* New York: Vintage.

Izard, C. E. (1971). *The Face of Emotion.* New York: Appleton-Centrury-Crofts.

——— (1977). *The Human Emotions.* New York: Plenum.

Jacobs, D., David, P., and Meyer, D. (1995). *The Supervisory Encounter: A Guide for Teachers of Psychodynamic Psychotherapy and Psychoanalysis.* New Haven, CT: Yale University Press.

Kardiner, A. (1977). *My Analysis with Freud: Reminiscences.* New York: W. W. Norton.

Kohut, H. (1959). Introspection, empathy, and psychoanalysis. *Journal of the American Psychoanalytic Association* 7:459–483.

——— (1966). Forms and transformations of narcissism. *Journal of the American Psychoanalytic Association* 14:243–272.

——— (1971). *The Analysis of the Self.* New York: International Universities Press.

——— (1972). Thoughts on narcissism and narcissistic rage. *Psychoanalytic Study of the Child* 27:360–400. New Haven, CT: Yale University Press.

——— (1977). *The Restoration of the Self.* New York: International Universities Press.

——— (1982). Introspection, empathy, and the semicircle of mental health. *International Journal of Psycho-Analysis* 63:395–407.

——— (1984). *How Does Analysis Cure?* Chicago: University of Chicago Press.

Kriegman, D. (1998). Interpretation, the unconscious, and analytic authority: toward an evolutionary, biological integration of the empirical-scientific method with the field-defining, empathic stance. In *Empirical Perspectives on the Psychoanalytic Unconscious,* ed. R. F. Bernstein and J. M. Masling, pp. 187–272. Washington, DC: American Psychological Association.

Krystal, H. (1988). *Integration, and Self-Healing: Affect, Trauma, and Alexithymia.* Hillsdale, NJ: Analytic Press.

Lachmann, F. M., and Beebe, B. (1996). The contribution of self- and mutual regulation to therapeutic action: a case illustration. In *Basic Ideas Reconsidered: Progress in Self Psychology,* vol.

12, ed. A. Goldberg, pp. 123–140. Hillsdale, NJ: Analytic Press.

Lane, R. C., ed. (1992). Psychoanalytic approaches to supervision. *Current Issues in Psychoanalytic Practice.* Monographs of the Society for Psychoanalytic Training, no. 2.

Levin, F. M. (1991). *Mapping the Mind.* Hillsdale, NJ: Analytic Press.

Levy, J., and Kindler, A. R., eds. (1995). Psychoanalytic supervision. *Psychoanalytic Inquiry* 15.

Lichtenberg, J. (1989). *Psychoanalysis and Motivation.* Hillsdale, NJ: Analytic Press.

Lichtenberg, J., Lachmann, F., and Fosshage, J. (1992). *Self and Motivational Systems.* Hillsdale, NJ: Analytic Press.

——— (1996). *The Clinical Exchange.* Hillsdale, NJ: Analytic Press.

McWilliams, N. (1999). *Psychoanalytic Case Formulation.* New York: Guilford.

Mitchell, S. A. (1988). *Relational Concepts in Psychoanalysis: An Integration.* Cambridge, MA: Harvard University Press.

——— (1993). *Hope and Dread in Psychoanalysis.* New York: Basic Books.

———, ed. (1996). Symposium on "false memory" controversy. *Psychoanalytic Dialogues* 6(2).

——— (1997). *Influence and Autonomy in Psychoanalysis.* Hillsdale, NJ: Analytic Press.

Neubauer, P. B. (1980). The role of insight in psychoanalysis. In *Psychoanalytic Explorations of Technique: Discourse on the Theory of Therapy,* ed. H. P. Blum, pp. 29–40. New York: International Universities Press.

Orange, D. M. (1995). *Emotional Understanding.* New York: Guilford.

Orange, D. M., Atwood, G. E., and Stolorow, R. D. (1997). *Working Intersubjectively: Contextualism in Psychoanalytic Practice.* Hillsdale, NJ: Analytic Press.

Plutchik, R. (1962). *The Emotions: Facts, Theories, and a New Model.* New York: Random House.

——— (1980). *Emotion: A Psychoevolutionary Synthesis.* New York: Harper & Row.

Reckling, A. E., and Buirski, P. (1996). Child abuse, self-development, and affect regulation. *Psychoanalytic Psychology* 13:81–99.

Rock, M., ed. (1997). *Psychodynamic Supervision.* Northvale, NJ: Jason Aronson.

Ryan, M., and Buirski, P. (in press). Prejudice as a function of self-organization. *Psychoanalytic Psychology.*

Schlesinger, H. (1995). Supervision for fun and profit: or how to tell if the fun is profitable. *Psychoanalytic Inquiry* 15:190–210.

Schore, A. (1994). *Affect Regulation and the Origin of the Self.* Hillsdale, NJ: Lawrence Erlbaum.

Shane, M., Shane, E., and Gales, M. (1997). *Intimate Attachments: Toward a New Self Psychology.* New York: Guilford.

Stern, D. (1985). *The Interpersonal World of the Infant.* New York: Basic Books.

Stolorow, R. D. (1992). Closing the gap between theory and practice with better psychoanalytic theory. *Psychotherapy* 29:159–166.

——— (1994a). Converting psychotherapy to psychoanalysis. In *The Intersubjective Perspective,* ed. R. D. Stolorow, G. E. Atwood, and B. Brandchaft, pp. 145–154. Northvale, NJ: Jason Aronson.

——— (1994b). The nature and therapeutic action of psychoanalytic interpretation. In *The Intersubjective Perspective,* ed. R. D. Stolorow, G. E. Atwood, and B. Brandchaft, pp. 43–55. Northvale, NJ: Jason Aronson.

——— (1998). Clarifying the intersubjective perspective: A reply to George Frank. *Psychoanalytic Psychology* 15:424–427.

Stolorow, R. D., and Atwood, G. E. (1992). *Contexts of Being.* Hillsdale, NJ: Analytic Press.

Stolorow, R. D., Atwood, G. E., and Brandchaft, B., eds. (1994). *The Intersubjective Perspective.* Northvale, NJ: Jason Aronson.

Stolorow, R., Atwood, G., and Orange, D. (1999). Kohut and contextualism: toward a post-Cartesian psychoanalytic process. *Psychoanalytic Psychology* 16:380–388.

Stolorow, R. D., Brandchaft, B., and Atwood, G. E. (1987). *Psychoanalytic Treatment: An Intersubjective Approach.* Hillsdale, NJ: Analytic Press.

Stolorow, R. D. and Lachmann, F. M. (1984/1985). Transference: the future of an illusion. *The Annual of Psychoanalysis* 12/13:19–37. Madison, CT: International Universities Press.

Stolorow, D., and Stolorow, R. D. (1987). Affects and selfobjects. In *Psychoanalytic Treatment: An Intersubjective Approach,* ed. R. D. Stolorow, B. Brandchaft, and G. E. Atwood, Hillsdale, NJ: Analytic Press.

Strachey, J. (1934). The nature of the therapeutic action of psychoanalysis. *International Journal of Psycho-Analysis* 15:117–126.

Sullivan, H. (1964). *The Fusion of Psychiatry and Social Science.* New York: W. W. Norton.

Teicholz, J. G. (1999a). *Kohut, Loewald, and the Postmoderns.* Hillsdale, NJ: Analytic Press.

——— (1999b). A radical self psychological model of supervision. Paper presented at the meeting of the Department of Psychiatry, Harvard Medical School, Massachusetts General Hospital, October 20, Boston, MA, and at the scientific meeting of the Massachusetts Association for Psychoanalytic Psychology (MAPP), November 1, 1989.

Terman, D. (1989). Therapeutic change: perspectives of self psychology. *Psychoanalytic Inquiry* 9:88–100.

Tomkins, S. (1962). *Affect Imagery Consciousness: Vol. 1: The Positive Affects.* New York: Springer.

——— (1963). *Affect Imagery Consciousness: Vol. II: The Negative Affects.* New York: Springer.

Tronick, E. (1989). Emotions and emotional communication in infants. *American Psychologist* 44:112–119.

Wallerstein, R., ed. (1981). *Becoming a Psychoanalyst.* New York: International Universities Press.

Winnicott, D. W. (1965). *The Maturational Process and the Facilitating Environment.* New York: International Universities Press.

Index

ABOUT THE AUTHORS

Peter Buirski, Ph.D., is Dean of the Graduate School of Professional Psychology at the University of Denver, as well as Clinical Professor of Psychiatry at the University of Colorado Health Sciences Center. He trained as a psychoanalyst at the Postgraduate Center for Mental Health in New York City, is affiliated with the Colorado Center for Psychoanalytic Studies and the Denver Psychoanalytic Institute and Society. Editor of two books, *Frontiers of Dynamic Psychotherapy* and *Comparing Schools of Analytic Therapy*, Dr. Buirski has published widely on primate and human behavior. He holds the Diplomate in Clinical Psychology and in Psychoanalysis from the American Board of Professional Psychology, and maintains a private practice in Denver.

Pamela Haglund received her Psy.D. from the Graduate School of Professional Psychology at the University of Denver, where she now serves as Adjunct Assistant Professor and Clinical Supervisor. She completed postdoctoral training in psychoanalytic psychotherapy at the Denver Institute for Psychoanalysis. Dr. Haglund has taught self psychology and intersubjectivity theory there and at the Colorado Center for Psychoanalytic Studies. Author of several articles on contemporary psychoanalytic theory and treatment, she is in private practice in Denver.